Adventures of a Small Game Hunter in Jamaica

By Max Overton

Writers Exchange E-Publishing

http://www.writers-exchange.com

Adventures of a Small Game Hunter in Jamaica
Copyright 2016 Max Overton
Writers Exchange E-Publishing
PO Box 372
ATHERTON QLD 4883

Cover Art by: Julie Napier
Butterfly photographs by Julie Napier from specimens in the author's collection

Published by Writers Exchange E-Publishing
http://www.writers-exchange.com

ISBN **ebook**: 978-1-925574-17-3
Print: 978-1-925574-00-5 (WEE Assigned)

Review of Adventures of a Small Game Hunter in Jamaica, by Max Overton

Max **Overton** has published an amazing gem of natural history. His descriptions of butterflies and their behaviours - from the rapid, assertive flight of Blue Kites, to *Calisto*'s association with the deep shade of a forest, to the two *Historis* species' attraction to fermenting fruit--all revealed him to be a keen observer and a reliable young "expert" far beyond his pre-teen years. His collections of an '88' and an '89' butterfly (i.e., Cramer's 88 butterfly, *Diaethria clymena*) certainly merit re-evaluation, particularly in light of the fact that this species has been reported to stray as far north as South Florida. It also reminds us that we should always be vigilant to look for natural 'blow over' events. As an amusing aside, in its natural mainland range from Mexico to South America, the larvae of the '88' feed on *Trema micrantha*, a plant commonly called "Jamaican nettletree".

Although the author's primary love clearly was butterflies, his descriptions of birds and lizards also highlight his ability to reliably describe wildlife. This leads to another hidden treasure in this book: his description of a Jamaican Iguana (*Cyclura collei*) in Hellshire Hills is the only reported sighting during the period of the late 1940s through the 1960s when this endemic species was feared to be extinct. Overton's observation gives us a link from 1940, when the last iguanas were collected in the wild for a (failed) captive-breeding effort to the subsequent discovery of an iguana carcass in Hellshire by a pig hunter in 1970 and the discovery of a live Jamaican Iguana in 1990. It reminds this reviewer of how important it is to keep up with her field notes as one never knows what mundane, daily event could prove important or interesting for someone in the future.

Unfortunately, many of the gardens and woodlands along the gullies described by the author no longer exist: in Kingston, much has been paved-over and converted to apartments and commercial buildings. However, as more residents recognise that they would like (and need!) 'green space' in their lives, Max Overton's records of the diversity of butterflies in the early 1960s gives us a baseline to which we can aspire for improving green space in the Kingston urban landscape.

This reviewer hopes that the infectious enthusiasm woven throughout the book will inspire young (and old!) Jamaicans to explore and enjoy their natural world. Today's 'small game watchers' have the best technology in their hands - with smartphones and digital cameras, everyone can record gems of natural history.

Prepared by:
Dr. Susan Koenig
Windsor Research Centre
Trelawny, Jamaica

Preface

A bearded man with dreadlocks stepped out in front of me shaking his fist as I swerved my bicycle to avoid him.

"White man blood and fire!" he called after me as I pedalled away.

This memory popped unbidden into my mind the other day, more than fifty years after the event, and brought with it a flood of other memories from my youth. I went to my stored butterfly collection and opened up the two boxes that house all I have left of my butterflying days in the Caribbean.

Memories fade and warp with time but looking at my small collection of Jamaican butterflies, caught between the years of 1959 and 1961, when I had the extreme good fortune to live in Jamaica, that beautiful Caribbean island, I remembered many other things I thought I had forgotten. I realised then, as I examined my faded and tattered specimens that have followed me from house to house and country to country, that each one had the potential to tell a story. As I considered my collection, many of those stories came back to me, some in great detail, and some with no more than a place, a date, and the old muscle memory of the swing of a butterfly net.

I am an only child and both my parents are dead, so I am the only person now living with memories of the Overton family in Jamaica, and unless I write them down, they will vanish with me. I don't believe that my memories have any great historical significance, but they may be of interest to my sons and grandchildren (six grandchildren and step-grandchildren at the time of writing). These stories are more for them than the general public, though other people may be interested in what an eleven to thirteen year old boy could do in a vanished time and a gentler land. I know I would not let my own children get up to half of what I got up to, wandering alone in a foreign country.

These are stories of butterfly collecting and a few other escapades of a young boy--nothing startling, but all basically true. I have had to refresh my memory in places from old snapshots, tattered maps, and the information pinned beneath my specimens. For the most part, dialogue has had to be invented, and serves to lubricate descriptions of places and events. I, and others, may not have said exactly the words reported here, but we said something very like them, at those times. The chapters don't necessarily follow on, one from another, but can instead be viewed as a series of snapshots, each connected to a particular butterfly or memory.

I have added pictures of some of these butterflies at the end of the book. I make no apologies for the condition of the specimens. They are the product of a small boy's enthusiasm, and I lacked proper setting boards and entomological pins. If they look skewed and tattered, that is my own fault, but their inclusion, I hope, will give my stories more meaning. I think I have made the correct identifications, but there is often some doubt with groups of butterflies that look alike.

I have taken a small dipper to a large well, and drawn up no more than sips of memory. I spent about twenty-seven months in Jamaica and was busy most of the time doing boyish things. I went to school, played with friends, interacted with my family, but I lived for my butterfly collecting, and a lot of my sips reflect my passion. I cannot hope to relate everything that happened to me but I hope these words will offer a taste of what life was like for a small game hunter in Jamaica.

Oh, one other thing...memory is a strange beast and a sometimes elusive one. It is not above presenting itself as something quite different from the facts. False memory comes into play, where one is sure something happened when it is, in fact, quite impossible. I have one instance of this in my stories of Jamaica, of catching a butterfly I am assured by experts could not exist on the island--yet I remember catching it. I say a bit more about this in the relevant place. So too, with the characters that populate my stories. I remember the individuals well, and I would swear that I portray them correctly within each story, but one of my friend's memories of events differs from mine. What am I to make of that? Is his memory or mine faulty? All I can reasonably do is tell the story as I remember it, but if he wants to tell the story elsewhere in a different manner, I won't complain.

So, in the meantime, enjoy the recollections of a Small Game Hunter in Jamaica.

Arrival

I was snatched out of boarding school with no more than five minutes warning. I'm sure my parents must have told me this would happen, but I honestly don't remember. We lived in Düsseldorf, Germany at the time, and I went to boarding school in England--Thorpe House Preparatory School for Boys in the little Buckinghamshire town of Gerrards Cross. I went home for the Christmas holidays and my birthday, and returned to school in mid-January. I had issues with Thorpe House and my parents, not least of which was the feeling of abandonment by my mother when she first took me there and left me, a six year old softie, to sink or swim in a cruel environment. I hated school--or at least that school--so I think I did not really believe my parents were about to liberate me from its confines. I may have told someone I was leaving--I had a few friends there--but if I did I don't remember.

I think it was a Friday morning--the last Friday in the month--and I was sitting in class struggling to absorb a lesson on the geography of the Midlands, when the school matron entered the class and went over to the teacher Mr Wood. She whispered something and he looked at me.

"Overton. Put your books away and go with Matron."

"Sir?"

"Now, Overton. Your taxi's waiting."

I went, casting an apologetic look backward at the puzzled faces of my school friends. I never saw them again, but I can remember some of their names--Mugford, Young, Newton, the Jude brothers. I still have an informal class photo that has us all in it and I sometimes wonder what became of them. I was a dreamy child and I had possibly not told them I was leaving for good.

On that day, the taxi took me to the railway station in Gerrards Cross where my luggage and I were loaded aboard a train and sent off to London. You might think that travelling alone as an eleven year old was a risky venture, but times were different back then. It did not trouble me as I had been commuting between England and Germany by air alone since I was eight. I just followed instructions, held out my ticket, and waited for an adult to tell me where to go. My mother met me at Marylebone Station and we boarded another train for the trip to Southampton.

"Where are we going, Mum?" I asked.

"Max, we told you all this. We're going to Jamaica. Your father retired from the army and has a job as manager of an insurance company."

"Oh." I thought about this for a while, then, "Where's G. Peek?"

G. Peek was our female tortoiseshell cat. Her full name was Gregoria Peek, named for one of my mother's favourite actors, Gregory Peck, except that she was female and her usual cry was a quiet 'Peek' rather than a miaow. She was a champion hunter, though she never killed anything, taking great pains to deliver her prey alive and kicking at our feet. I remember her turning up with the usual assortment of rodents and small birds, but also with a young pheasant, a mole, and a baby hare.

"We found a good home for her."

I was sad for a while, but soon cheered up as I stared at the countryside rolling past whenever the smoke and steam from the train cleared enough to let us see it. My father was waiting for us in Southampton and had booked us passage on a cruise ship, sailing the next day. My grandmother Rose had come across from her home in Devon to see us off, and we went out to dinner that evening, to a local restaurant.

I can only remember one thing about the meal, and it must reflect the turmoil of my young mind though I was unaware of any conflict at the time. I found I was unable to swallow any food without sipping from a glass of water, and unable to drink anything in more than small sips. Later, I found myself unable to swallow pills and had to chew them instead. I have largely overcome my need for water during a meal but I still eat and drink very slowly; and fifty years on I still have to chew medication. I have learned to cope with the foul tastes of sugar-coated pills and have even come to enjoy the bitterness of some.

We set sail on the S.S. Antilles, a French Line cruise ship, amid great excitement, but the initial part of the voyage was dreadful for me. As we headed south into the Bay of Biscay I remember sampling a delicious water chestnut and ice cream dessert at dinner one night, being quite taken with the sweetness and the crunch. Just after that we hit rough weather and what was locked firmly together in my adolescent mind was the taste and texture of water chestnut and prolonged vomiting. It was years before I could mentally dissociate the two.

We weathered the storm and put into the port of Vigo in northern Spain. I spent the day there and wandered the markets with my parents where I bought a letter opener in the form of a rapier with a delightful basket hilt. It had 'Toledo steel' stamped on its blade. I had it for years before it finally fell apart. The next day we headed south-west across the Atlantic and fair weather encompassed us for the rest of the voyage.

I've always thought life on a cruise ship is boring for a youngster. I was too old for the organised fun of the 'littlies' and too young to join my parents in the lounges and bars. My mother could be persuaded to play table tennis sometimes, but usually I spent my days wandering through the decks or leaning on the rail imagining all sorts of things or just losing myself in a mindless contemplation of limitless skies and moving water. As we sailed further south and the weather grew warmer, I saw flying fish skittering across the surface away from the predatory ship and dolphins plunging in our bow wave. Very cliched, I know, but those cliches had to come from somewhere, and those visions were new to me. I saw fragments of weed floating in the water and learned that we were near the famed Sargasso Sea. I had visions of us encountering vast mats of weed and perhaps even getting mired in it like the Ancient Mariner. Alas, we never saw more than a few clumps so I missed out on that source of excitement.

As the ship was a French one, first landfall in the New World was the French island of Martinique in the Lesser Antilles. We steamed around the southern end of the island and put into the port of Fort-de-France, where we stayed for a few days. It was exciting to be on dry land after our long crossing of the Atlantic. The first day we spent in the capital city and I remember the glorious feeling as I realised I was on a tropical island with all these strange sights and sounds and smells. The people looked so different and I stared at the colourful clothes of the people in the markets, and listened in fascination to the mixture of French and Creole spoken by the people crowding the streets. The vegetation was completely different from anything I'd seen, and my first glimpses of tropical butterflies and strange birds made my heart race. I saw lizards on the trees and a snake coiled up in a basket and wanted to touch it, but my parents ushered me away. On the second day we took a day trip north along the west coast to the town of St Pierre.

St Pierre was once a large city, but on May 8, 1902, the volcano that looms over the town, Mont Pelee, erupted violently and destroyed the city and all its inhabitants but one, two or three, depending on which account you hear. The destruction was caused by a pyroclastic flow--a superheated cloud of ash and gas that flows down the slopes at speeds of hundreds of kilometres an hour. I have always preferred the French term for this phenomenon--*nuee ardente*--which means 'glowing cloud', a very apt description of the red-hot pumice and ash as it billows down the mountainside at night.

It was not as if the people of St Pierre had no warning. For weeks, the mountain had been shaking and emitting ash amid huge explosions, but few people fled. The mayor of the city refused to budge, telling everyone the mountain was safe, and died along with his fellow citizens when it finally erupted.

We visited the museum in St Pierre, where old photographs lined the walls showing the city before and after the eruption. A full account was there, and eye-witness statements and I learned that the sole survivor (by that account) was a condemned prisoner locked away in an underground cell. When he was dug from his cell, the authorities freed him, believing Divine Providence must have had a hand in his survival. Later, I found out there were other survivors, but not many, and I thought the sole survivor tale was far more romantic.

The mountain itself was shrouded in cloud the day we were there, but it still looked ominous and I wondered why anyone would build a city that close to an active volcano. The bay was beautiful and the slopes of the hills covered in dense vegetation, with productive farms and orchards, but surely the place was too dangerous for anyone to live comfortably.

From Martinique we sailed north to another French island--Guadaloupe. Here I formed the impression that French colonists must like volcanoes as there was another one looming over the western city of Basse Terre, this one called La Grande Soufrière. This is an active volcano, like Mont Pelee, and had erupted only three years before we visited. It had been a small eruption, with pyroclastic flows, but nobody had been killed. In the ways of small boys, I remember being a little disappointed.

Interestingly, there is another volcano called La Soufrière on the island of St Vincent, and yet another called Soufrière Hills on the island of Montserrat. I thought the people who named them must have been lacking in imagination until I was told 'soufrière' means 'sulphur', which is found issuing forth from every volcano. I suppose Soufrière becomes a reasonable name for a volcano then.

We only stayed a few days in Guadeloupe, and for some reason I can remember very little apart from the volcano and street markets. Stalls filled with fresh fruit and vegetables, live chickens cackling and goats bleating, and around it all the babble of unknown tongues. It was there that I first sampled a green coconut. I had had the dried coconut bought from shops or won at fairs in England, but I watched a lithe young man hack away the outer layers of a green coconut fresh from the palms, lop off the top, fashioning a scoop from a piece of the husk. He handed me the coconut with an expectant look on his face and I took a sip of the 'water'. A sweet and strange taste filled my mouth; I sipped again and grinned, draining the rest of it. The man showed me how to scoop the clear gelatinous flesh from within the young nut. This sensation was even stranger, but I had to admit that green coconuts were a cool and delicious treat.

Before long we were steaming north and west, threading out way through the green and blue hues of the seas and islands of the Antilles, finally coming into the great protected San Juan Harbour on the island of Puerto Rico. The battlements of Fort San Felipe del Morro loomed above us to the east. My father, as befitted a retired colonel, told us the military history of the place as we eased past it. I even listened to some of it, though many things distracted me.

"We're in San Juan for a couple of days," he said. "We can go and have a good look round."

There was a long broad road leading to the fort, the Calle del Morro, bisecting a huge grassy area, but the fort itself was flatter and more spread out than I anticipated, and I think I was expecting something more European--a high-walled, turreted castle looming out of the countryside. Perhaps it was because the massive fortifications were on a headland and so took advantage of natural height instead of building upward in the European fashion. Instead of worn and lichen-encrusted rock walls, there was lots of clean stonework in a good state of repair and we walked through echoing tunnels, wandered the battlements, looking out over the edge to the ocean or standing in one of the little domed garitas that were rather like stone guard boxes. We also visited the city of San Juan, but my father complained that it was too much like an American city for his taste. Still, we took in the sights and bought some small souvenirs before going back to the ship.

The next morning we set sail once more and cruised along the north coast of Puerto Rico and then Hispaniola, rounding the 'upper jaw' of Haiti and round into the Golfe de la Gonâve. We docked in Port-au-Prince, the capital.

Haiti was then under the control of President Dr Francois 'Papa Doc' Duvalier and his feared private police, the Tonton Macoutes. The name Tonton Macoutes is the Creole for 'Uncle Gunnysack'. In local mythology, this bogeyman kidnaps naughty children in the night and stuffs them into his sack. By all accounts, his real-life successors, the private police, continued his work, making the political opposition of Papa Doc disappear in the night.

We did not stay long in this very poor city, but we visited a few markets and looked at some of the old buildings. The nation was Spanish first, then French, until the African slaves revolted and overthrew their oppressors, forming the first black nation in the early nineteenth century. Ruling themselves has not been much improvement over being ruled by others and Haiti has become the poorest nation in the Caribbean. All the wealth flows toward the corrupt government, leaving little for the people. My father was sure that some men in suits with dark glasses standing on a street corner were members of the Tonton Macoutes and only refrained from making loud provocative comments about them because my mother pleaded with him not to. We walked on a way and we heard shouts and saw people running. The streets emptied and a few minutes later a black car sped by, occupied by Tonton Macoutes and possibly some poor unfortunate stuffed into their proverbial gunnysack. For me, Haiti was colourful and exotic, but a little scary too. Besides, I had been filled with tales of Jamaica and I was impatient to get there, especially as we were now so close.

The last leg of our journey took us round the 'lower jaw' of Haiti and under the eastern part of Jamaica to Kingston Harbour. I stood on the rail to catch a first glimpse of my new home and my father pointed out the long sand spit called the Palisadoes, with the airport and the town of Port Royal on the end. He told me that it used to be a pirate den and the first capital of Jamaica until the great earthquake of 1692 destroyed it and sank buildings and streets beneath the sea. I had never experienced an earthquake, so I listened in awe and resolved to get my parents to take me there as soon as possible. I wanted to look down into the clear water and see the streets and buildings.

We docked and this time, instead of immediately heading out into the town to see the sights, we had to hang around to make sure all our luggage was unloaded. Finally, the last of our trunks and packing cases came off and my father organised for them to be stored until we had a house to move into. In the meantime, we were to go to a Guest House my father's insurance company had arranged for us. I can't remember the name of it but it was on the Old Hope Road toward the eastern hills. I was glued to the window of the taxi on the way there, soaking in the sights and staring in fascination at such novel sites as a pig foraging near huts made of sheet iron and cardboard, vultures squabbling over the carcass of some animal on the road, hordes of Jamaicans in colourful clothing, huge American cars, and the yawning red-earth gullies that bordered some of the roads. I couldn't wait to get out and explore.

We arrived at the guest house and were shown to our bungalow, set amidst bougainvillea and hibiscus bushes, coconut palms, Canna lilies and a whole lot of trees and shrubs I didn't know. My father got on the telephone to call his new boss, and my mother immediately started unpacking suitcases, so I went outside to start my exploring.

Those first moments to myself, on an island in the tropics, surrounded by new fauna and flora, overwhelmed me. I wandered around the lawns and gardens looking at the flowers, watching yellow, orange and white butterflies flitting by, listening to bird calls and trying to match them with movements in the trees, staring open-mouthed at the vultures wheeling overhead. I stood awestruck as a gorgeous hummingbird hovered by a flower, its bill inserted delicately into the floral tube while its wings blurred around it. Then in a flash of red and green and black it was off and I watched it go with a delighted grin on my face.

The owners of the guest house had a son of about my age, called Tom, and after some initial posturing, we became reasonably good friends. He took me to see his grandmother, a lovely old lady who fed us tea and biscuits and showed us her collection of stamps. My father had collected stamps and when I got interested, he passed his album over to me. The old lady's collection was of unmounted stamps loose in a shoebox, and she spread them out on her dining room table for us to look through. Tom had not been interested before but when he saw my enthusiasm, he started taking notice of these little scraps of paper.

The Jamaican stamps were fascinating and colourful and the old lady told me to pick some out as the start of my Jamaican collection. When I got home, I took out my album and stamp hinges and carefully added them to some new pages. My collection grew over the years until governments recognised that revenues could be generated by releasing stamps on every possible occasion. For a while, I continued my philatelic hobby, but I could not afford to buy every new issue and eventually I gave up.

I was not allowed to wander off by myself in those early days in Jamaica, but luckily the guest house grounds had enough to keep me occupied. As well as the gardens, there were the servants' quarters round the back shaded by tall breadfruit trees and some old ruined buildings half-hidden among the long grass and weeds. I have never been afraid of snakes, having kept adders at school in England, but my initial forays into the long grass precipitated my mother's ire until she was assured there were no harmful snakes on the island.

There were scorpions, however, and though I was disappointed about the snakes, I thought these little creatures would be a fascinating substitute. My first encounter with these scuttling arachnids happened within days of our arrival. I was on my belly in the long grass one evening, poking a stick into holes in the ground in the hope of disturbing something, when I felt a tickle on my bare leg. I reached down absently to scratch and felt something scuttle onto my hand. I looked--and leapt up, falling over backward in my haste to get away. The scorpion--for that is what had been climbing on me-- fell off and disappeared under a rock.

Tom later showed me how to find them and we would wander through the ruins, turning over the stones and poking at the little scorpions with a stick. They were pale, armed with pincers and an up-curved tail with a sting. I thought they were exciting but I was never tempted to pick them up, or get as close to them as I had that first time. Perhaps this was just as well as although none of them were dangerous, Tom told me their stings were painful.

Tom was not particularly interested in the wildlife, so after a few days he would be just as likely to leave me to my own devices as play with me. I was left to watch the geckos on the walls and ceilings by myself, to hunt for skinks in the leaf litter or marvel at the orange-throated *Anolis* lizards on the tree trunks. Occasionally I would catch one and hold it firmly as I studied it. The skinks would squirm in my hand, the geckos often dropping their tails in an effort to escape, but the Anolis lizards would open their mouths and hiss at me, exposing the bright pink flesh of their gullets. I watched stick insects and praying mantis and a number of other 'bugs' I did not recognise, but most of all I watched the butterflies. It was swiftly becoming apparent that Jamaica was a land of colourful butterflies and my early interest in these matters was about to bloom in this delightful tropical climate.

I had watched butterflies before, in Germany and England, and vividly remembered red admirals, peacocks, and painted ladies, but had not really collected them, at least not in any organised way, just haphazardly, as young boys do. Now, I could see myself becoming a collector of Lepidoptera (the order of animals that butterflies and moths belong to). It was to be a life-long interest.

Beginnings

Before I came to Jamaica, I knew next to nothing about it. I had looked for it in an atlas (this was long before the Internet had been conceived), and found it was one of the islands making up the Greater Antilles--Cuba, Hispaniola, Jamaica and Puerto Rico. On the map, it was a little blob in the Caribbean, coloured green and brown amidst blue seas and had three main cities--Kingston, Spanish Town, Montego Bay. It was famous for rum, sugar cane and pirates, but beyond that, this island that was to be my home was a complete mystery.

Luckily, my parents had invested in Aspinall's 'Pocket Guide to the West Indies'. I devoured this on the voyage from England, and dipped into it at frequent intervals to refresh my memory on one point or another. Aspinall told me it was twice the size of Lancashire, but as I didn't know the size of that county that fact wasn't very useful. One hundred and forty-eight miles (pre-metric days for me) in length and fifty-two miles wide at its widest was a little easier to get to grips with, and a million and a half people in that space told me the cities were likely to be crowded. That didn't worry me to much as I hoped to be out in the countryside a lot.

Jamaica is very mountainous and has many rivers and streams, though, of course, in a small island, none of them are very large or very long. I had occasion to take a raft trip down the Rio Grande in the eastern part of the island, but that's another story. I learned from Aspinall that the island is quite densely vegetated, though there are a lot of crops grown--things like coffee, sugar cane, bananas, coconuts, cocoa and spices. It seemed very exotic to me as I had come from Britain where fruits like bananas and coconuts were not common. I didn't know what sugar cane was and I was very surprised to find out it was really just a very tall grass. My father bought me a bundle of split sugar cane stems from a roadside stall and showed me how to pull the stem into strips and chew them, releasing a flood of sweet juice into my mouth. I have no doubt that chewing sugar cane enriched the dentists of the island.

Jamaica was discovered by Christopher Columbus in 1494 on his second voyage to the New World. The Spanish colonised the island, naming it St Jago, and completely ignoring the native Arawak Indian name of *Xaymaca*, meaning 'Isle of Springs'. The Spaniards almost wiped out the natives and had to import African slaves to work the plantations. Then the British took over, throwing the Spanish out in the 1650s and setting up Port Royal as their capital city. They imported more slaves as many of the Spanish ones had run away to the mountains. These runaways became known as 'The Maroons' and regularly raided the British settlements, until finally, around 1800, the British pacified the island, packing off many Maroons to Nova Scotia. I hate to think what they must have thought of that cold, inhospitable place.

The British divided the country up into three counties--Cornwall, Middlesex and Surrey--and a number of parishes also named after British places and saints. I always thought it strange to label one of my Jamaican butterflies as having been caught at say, San San Bay, in the parish of Portland, in the county of Surrey.

I think it was Jamaica that first instilled in me my love of words. I hadn't really noticed place names in England or Germany, except for perhaps chortling over the 'Rat' in the town of Ratingen where I went to school for a year. Reading Aspinall and looking at maps, I became entranced by the strange place names and sought out why they were named that way. I learned that 'Red Dirt', 'Stony Hill' and 'Long Mountain' were named after obvious landscape features, and that 'Bristol', 'Vauxhall' and 'Aberdeen' were named after places the settlers knew and missed. 'Wakefield', 'Harker's Hall' and 'Brown's Town' were named after people, but what was I to make of 'Quick Step', 'Look Behind', 'Duppy Gate', 'Corn Puss Gap', and 'Maggotty'?

It seems that the little town of Maggotty is not crawling with fly larvae, but was named after the birthplace of the missionary John Hutch when he preached in the area. 'Quick Step' and 'Look Behind' are both in the Cockpit country where the Maroons lived and relate to the attitude of the British soldiers when hunting these runaways. If you didn't look behind you and march quickly along the trails you were likely to end up dead. Duppy is the Jamaican word for ghost, so 'Duppy Gate' is a place where the ghost of an olden day British Officer is sometimes seen. 'Corn Puss Gap' is a bit stranger.

There is a story that a British surveyor got lost in the hills and was close to starving. He caught a wild cat, corned it and ate it.

Jamaica is also known for its pirates. Henry Morgan is perhaps the most famous one and he was at various times a pirate, a privateer--which is really just a pirate allowed to prey on enemy shipping, and an Admiral of the Royal Navy. Later, he was knighted and became Lieutenant Governor of Jamaica. When I heard that the island was so intimately connected with pirates, I got very excited because I had read comic books on pirates and buried treasure and was sure that if I looked hard enough, I would find a hidden trove. It was not to be, any more than my desire to find a *Tyrannosaurus* skull poking out of the ground during my walks in England had produced a dinosaur fossil. I did find a treasure though, a natural treasure--the wildlife of Jamaica.

I asked my friend Tom about butterflies in the first days at the Guest House, but he just shrugged his shoulders and suggested I ask a Jamaican. I did not know any, but approached the Jamaican gardener one day.

"Eh? W'at for yu wan' wit' bots?"

I was nonplussed and asked again.

He peered at me as if I was mad. "Bots, mon. W'at for yu wan' dem?"

I didn't know what he was talking about, but described a butterfly as best I could. I looked around and saw a small yellow butterfly dancing over the lawn, so I pointed at it.

"Bot," the gardener said, nodding.

Bot was obviously the Jamaican word for butterfly. "Are there many bots here?" I asked.

He stared at me, even more convinced I was mad. "Dere one bot," he said. "See dere?" He pointed at the little yellow butterfly now winging its way out of the garden.

"I mean, are there many butterflies...bots...in Jamaica? In Kingston?"

"Sumtime dere is, sumtime no. Bots in day, rot bots in nigh'."

Another word I didn't know. I puzzled it out--if a bot was a butterfly, then maybe a rot bot was a moth, particularly if nigh' meant night. I thanked the man and retreated, little the wiser. I found out later that both butterflies and moths are called 'bots' (bats) and that 'rot bots' (rat bats) were actually real bats. It was all very confusing for a naive little boy fresh out from England.

In the end, I had to go to the Institute of Jamaica in downtown Kingston for the answers to my many questions on butterflies. When I was there, it was a small, dingy building packed full of exhibits on all manner of things

Jamaican, but my main interest was in the field of animals so I didn't pay much attention to undoubtedly valuable items pertaining to the native Arawak Indians and the early history of the island. In fact, my main focus was on two large cabinets in a back room that housed the butterflies and moths of Jamaica.

I saw drawer after drawer full of wondrous and exotic species, some that looked vaguely familiar, like the little yellows and whites and blues that occur in many places, to large and beautiful butterflies in gaudy hues and others that were wonderfully camouflaged. The names meant little to me at first, but I asked the museum custodians and they humoured an inquisitive eleven-year-old who probably asked some fairly dumb questions.

There are about seventy species of butterfly on the island, over a hundred and thirty if you include subspecies, thirty-one of which are found nowhere else. Butterfly collectors used to come to Jamaica to collect specimens from the mid-1700s onward and I learnt that some of the great museums around the world own Jamaican butterflies. The custodians described places in Jamaica where various species were common, or could be seen, which was kind of them for I had no credentials to present as a serious collector. At the time, I didn't even have a butterfly net. I vowed, though, that I would visit every one of the sites they talked about and avail myself of their treasured inhabitants. Alas, I was but a small boy, and could only go where my parents took me. Even so, I managed quite well and caught some rare species and even two butterflies that should not even occur in Jamaica--but more of that later.

First of all, I had to prepare myself for the big adventure. I had owned a net of sorts in Germany, though it was flimsy and prone to breaking at the most inopportune times. I needed another one, stronger and more reliable. I searched out the materials I would need--a broom handle, a wire loop, fine mesh material--and my parents helped me put it together. It worked, after a fashion, and I was soon out hunting butterflies. The more I pursued them, the more I saw the flaws in my initial design. The broom handle was too heavy, the wire loop too small (being fashioned from a clothes hanger) and the fine mesh bag billowed out as I ran, slowing the swing of the net. Far more butterflies escaped than were captured, and after I had missed some particularly nice specimens, I took my net to the Institute to ask their advice.

The next incarnation of net was much better. I had a lightweight bamboo pole, a larger ring of stiff wire, and a coarser mesh that allowed the air to pass through while trapping all but the smallest insects. Every butterfly and moth that entered its folds remained behind. Now I was ready for some serious hunting.

Then another problem presented itself. I knew that professional butterfly collectors often used a cyanide jar to kill their specimens but I knew I would not be allowed one, so I had to find another method. Killing a butterfly is easy enough provided you are not too squeamish. You pinch the thorax (the part of the body that the wings and legs are attached to) firmly between forefinger and thumb, feeling the exoskeleton crackle and crunch, before placing the insect in a container. At home, you put a pin through the thorax and lay the wings out flat, holding them in place with thin strips of paper. The insect dries out and after a few days you can take the paper strips away, leaving the set insect with outspread wings. Later on I used proper setting boards and insect pins, but in the early days I just pinned them to a sheet of cork using sewing pins and stored my set and dried butterflies in a shoe box.

I discovered some other things that affect insect collections in the tropics--mould and pests. First, I discovered a grey mould all over my specimens and had to throw some out. After I moved them to a dryer place, mould was no longer a problem, but ants broke in and dismembered my precious trophies. I appealed to my father and he had some glass-topped mahogany cases made very cheaply, with a cork lining and secure hasp. I secured a small bag of mothballs in one corner, and now my fledgling insect collection could start to grow.

One of my early conquests was of the Tropical Silverspot, *Dione vanillae*. This is a beautiful orange-brown butterfly of moderate size, with a series of stunning silver spots on its underside that makes it look as if it had been spattered with molten metal. They are not particularly rare but their distribution is patchy and whenever I came across one, I just had to catch it. If it was in good condition, I added it to my collection; if not, I admired it and let it go.

The first time I saw the Silverspot (live, rather than in the Institute's cabinets), we had been invited round to visit some of my parents' friends also in the insurance business (I forget their names) and while the grownups talked inside, I was sent off to play with their two small girls. However, all they wanted to do was play with their dolls and teddybears, so I retrieved my net from the car and set off around their large garden to see what I could find. The family had dense plantings of trees and shrubs and though I saw a few butterflies, I could not swing my net effectively. I came out onto lawn and flowerbeds near the house, and many butterflies. I snared a few yellows and a White Peacock before spotting a lovely orange-brown butterfly whose underside gave me a thrill of excitement when it settled on a spike of flowers. It was unmistakeably a Silverspot.

I dashed forward and swung my net, missing the butterfly but ending up with broken stems and shattered flowers in the folds. I emptied them out and went in pursuit, swinging wildly, spraying flowers left and right and crushing others on the edge of the flowerbed with my feet as I over-reached myself. The Silverspot flew off, but a few moments later it, or another one was flitting over the flowerbed. I swung again, and this time I was successful, the butterfly tumbling into my net along with a double handful of broken flowers. I extracted it and gazed lovingly at the beautiful underside with its streaks and spots of silver metal.

"Max! What on earth are you doing?"

I turned to see my parents and their friends standing a dozen paces away with horrified expressions on their faces. I was still so thrilled with my capture I failed to see the damage I had wrought to the garden.

"I got a Silverspot, dad. Look." I held out the butterfly in my palm.

My father strode forward and gripped my arm, hauling me away from the flowerbeds. The butterfly dropped to the ground but I was not allowed to retrieve it. He pushed me in the direction of the driveway. "Get in the car."

I knew that tone. I saw the look of disappointment on my mother's face and that hurt me more than my father's anger, but I shivered, knowing what must follow.

My parents made their apologies and we drove home in silence. When my father had calmed down, I was reintroduced to his belt and spent the next hour or two alone in my room drying my tears and thinking about what I had done.

That evening, my parents sat me down and explained matters to me. I was to buy the lady whose garden I had wrecked some flower seedlings out of my pocket money, and I was to apologise to her and her husband in person. For a moment, it looked as though my father might go further and forbid me to collect butterflies any more, but my mother smoothed it over and I was allowed to continue my hobby provided I took care never to repeat my wanton actions.

"I promise," I said in a small voice.

The Silverspot I had captured was lost to me, but a month later I caught another, on a flowerbed in Hope Gardens, and I managed it without damaging the flowers (well, almost). As I became more experienced with my net, that early destruction of flowers and plants became a thing of the past. I could now creep close with my net poised and with a flick of my wrist, snare the butterfly as it hovered over a bloom, leaving the flower undamaged (sometimes).

Discovery

O ur house at 5 Carvalho Drive in the Kingston suburb of Half Way Tree was small but comfortable. My bedroom was also small but quite adequate for my purposes as I spent long hours outside and came to my room only to sleep or to mount my growing collection of Jamaican butterflies. The garden was almost bare when we moved in, with only a small ackee tree (*Blighia sapida*) and a row of *Plumbago* bushes underneath the front bedroom windows. My parents planted hibiscus bushes along one side of the drive and Canna lilies along the other. In front of the enclosed veranda with its wind-away awning, they set out a quarter circle of bougainvillea bushes which, in time, grew to monstrous proportions.

The ackee tree was new to me and its properties were carefully explained. It is a native of West Africa and has been used as a food plant over there for a long time. When slaves were brought across to work in the sugar plantations, the ackee was one of the plants brought across too. It produces pear- or bell-shaped fruit and the contents are poisonous until it fully ripens. It turns red, but is still unripe until it splits open into three segments, each with a large shiny black seed, at the base of which is a creamy yellow aril. This aril, or fleshy portion, is now edible, either raw or fried with rice and salt fish. I used to search the trees for ripe fruit and plunder the contents so if my mother wanted the cook to make a dish with ackee in it; she had to buy some from the markets. The tree had spreading branches on a short upright trunk and would have been a good climbing tree if it had not been infested with little black ants. My first venture into its branches was my last, and I had to strip off on the front lawn to divest myself of their swarming, stinging presence.

Plumbago became a favourite plant too. The leaves are sticky and rather unpleasant to touch, but it bears beautiful pale blue flowers. Blue is a relatively uncommon colour in flowers and I have always been attracted to them--*Plumbago, Lignum vitae*, cornflowers, convolvulus and forget-me-not. Large blue and grey Ground Lizards (*Ameiva dorsalis*) made their home under the bushes. They would come out and bask on the gravel path beside the *Plumbago* and I would devote many hours trying to catch them. I never did as they were always too fast and after a while I was content to just enjoy them at a distance.

Another oddity to our house was the bars on the windows. They were ornamental and painted cream, but they were bars nonetheless and at first it felt rather like we were in prison. When summer came we were glad of them though, as we could go out and leave the windows open, or catch the breezes on hot nights without fear of robbery. In the whole time we were in Jamaica, I only remember one attempted crime. I awoke one morning to find a long pole across my bed. Some would-be thief had taken our clothesline pole with the bent nail at the end and tried to hook my school bag from the chair on the far side of my bed. At some point, he had lost his grip and it had fallen into the room and across my bed, without wakening me. I stared at the pole lying across my bed, wondering what it meant, until I realised somebody had been trying to rob us. I leapt up and ran into my parent's bedroom, begging them to come and look. For me, the funny thing was that if he had succeeded, all he would have found in my bag was my homework.

We quickly learned that Jamaica is a very small island and that it is easy to get to interesting places in a short time. After a few initial forays around Kingston and out to the low hills to the east of the city where the coffee plantations lie on the skirts of the Blue Mountains, my parents turned their attentions to the North Coast. We were all interested in seeing what the island had to offer, so on many weekends we would head out, driving to a destination and staying the night, exploring the surrounding hills and bays.

Directly over the hills from Kingston lies the parish of St Mary and the road leads down to Annotto Bay. It was one of many white-sand beaches that litter the northern coast and the first we admired. We drove west and soon climbed to the town of Port Maria, which oddly enough is situated on a hill overlooking the sea. This town was one of the first the Spanish built in Jamaica and doubtless used the height of the hill for strategic reasons. They called their settlement Puerto Santa Maria, but the British changed its name to the present one and since then it has slipped in importance, becoming just another sleepy Jamaican town. We were new to Jamaica though, so we drank in the sights of sugar cane fields, palm trees and citrus.

I had a brand new butterfly net and I was eager to try it out, but I was also a bit diffident about running around waving it in full view of the populace. It would become a different matter when I grew used to the exercise, but for now I did not want to appear foolish, so as often as not I left it in the car when we walked through a banana plantation or stared in wonder at a pimento orchard.

Oracabessa lies a few miles further on and is another small town with a bit of history and a bit more that was to happen in the near future. When we first visited the town and its beaches in 1959, it was a quiet and pleasant place with lovely white sands, palm trees and cool stream mouths lined with mangroves, where the hills of the parish sweep down to the sea. Within a few years though, film-makers were to descend on the beaches and make them famous in the movie "Dr No", the first of the James Bond movies. We have actually picnicked on the beach where James Bond was soon to fight villains and seduce beautiful women. That was all in the future, though, and we searched for and found another place of interest, the home of Noel Coward, Firefly Estate. Of course, we could not go in, or even closely approach the house on its hill, but we gawked at the place where the famous personage lived.

Oracabessa also possesses a market, and we happened there on a market day when the streets were thronged with people and set about with stalls laden with the produce of the surrounding countryside. We walked among gaily-clothed people, hearing strange accents and incomprehensible words, smelling the richness of human sweat and a hundred scents and aromas that rose from the produce. Goats, cattle and chickens abounded. Butchers cut meat and displayed dismembered body parts, bakers had trays of fresh baked breads, enterprising young men sold sodas by the bottle or by the glass, or stood beside a mound of green coconuts and would, for a few pence, lop off the top with a machete and let you drink the delicious sweet water within.

Piles of fruit and vegetables covered trestle tables or lay in baskets on the ground--familiar ones like bananas, oranges, lemons, tomatoes, beans and potatoes--and less familiar ones like breadfruit, jackfruit, sugar cane cores, sapote and mango. It was fascinating and overwhelming, and my parents would always buy new fruits to try or buy some fresh baked bread and jerked meat for a picnic on the beach or beside a cool stream. Jamaica was a slow-paced country then, without the mad rush of tourists, and it was possible to enjoy a market without being importuned at every turn.

Ocho Rios is a few miles farther on and this little fishing village was also in the movie "Dr No" as the lair of the villain. Actually, his lair was really the bauxite works and jetty but most people were not to know that. The name of the village means 'Eight Rivers' but there are not eight rivers emptying into the sea at this point, so it is thought that the British mistook the name 'Ocho Rios' for the similar sounding 'Chorreras' which means waterfall. This is possible as the great Dunn's River Falls are close by.

Dunn's River Falls are where the Dunn River cascades down a thousand feet through pools and steps overhung by tropical forest before plunging under the coast road and into a lagoon on the beach. It is a wonderfully cool place to bathe or climb up through the forest with the rushing water close at hand, or picnic beside. We stopped there every time we went on the coast road, and in those days often had the place to ourselves. I remember the first time we were there--nobody else in sight, and little traffic on the road. We climbed the waterfall a little way and I took my net into the forests, eager to see what Jamaica had to offer. I was amazed by the huge Leafwing butterfly with its gorgeous dark brown and orange splotched wings and the cryptically coloured undersides that when the wings were folded, looked like an old dried leaf. I caught one and took it back to my parents, yelling with excitement at my wonderful capture.

Interesting spots dot the north coast and because of the small size of the island, it is only a few miles between one and the next. St Ann's Bay is a few miles on from Dunn's River and is the site of a Spanish settlement called Sevilla la Nueva. Just past it is Runaway Bay which apparently is the last point on the island to harbour the Spanish before they set sail and abandoned the island to the British. It is odd that this should be the last place for the Spanish, for the next bay to the west is Discovery Bay, which is supposed to be the place where Columbus landed on May 4, 1494. My father was interested in history and took us round all of the sights, pointing out that such-and-such a battle happened here, or so-and-so lived there. I'm afraid I paid little attention at the time, being more interested in the here-and-now abundance of butterflies than in dry accounts of the past. That has changed over the years and now history fascinates me so much I write about it. Perhaps it was my father's lectures in Jamaica that planted the seed.

Discovery Bay is also called Dry Harbour as it is the only bay not to have a stream or river running into it. The land is certainly quite dry too and there is a large grassy area inland from the beach. My father insisted on taking the first of no doubt many photographs of my Mum and me (and is on the cover of this book). She gazed off into the distance like Columbus spying out the New World, while I sat beside her clutching my net and waiting to be allowed to escape.

The butterflies in this open dry area were mainly whites and yellows and while I did not as yet recognise many of the species, I had great fun sprinting after them as they winged their way across the expanse of grass. I caught lovely large lemon yellow butterflies that reminded me of the European Brimstone, and whites that looked like nothing I had seen before. Others were deep sulphur yellow with small brown or purple scatterings on the underside. I caught what I could and stored them in an old envelope I kept in my pocket. I found that the butterflies' wings rubbed together and got damaged, so I knew I had to think of another way of keeping them safe. My father suggested a flat cigarette tin and said he thought he could get me one. My mother suggested making little envelopes out of squares of paper. I liked both ideas and applied them on future expeditions.

There were a lot of little butterflies in Discovery Bay and when I had the larger, showier species secured, I turned my attention to these--little yellow and white ones with wings edged in black, or with prominent black veins, small blues that danced over the grass or sat on shrubs rubbing their hind wings up and down. I caught these and added them to my collection, though I made another envelope for them out of scrap paper.

Birds were present throughout, though the only ones I was interested in at first were the hummingbirds. I thought their hovering and darting flight was marvellous and often broke off a butterfly chase to watch one feeding at a flower. My father pointed out the frigatebirds circling overhead, and took me to see them where they roosted. They are big black seabirds with long forked tails and long narrow wings, and the males have a huge red throat pouch that they inflate in the mating season. Their other name is Man-of-War birds as they have a habit of robbing other seabirds of their food. They sweep down on some unsuspecting gull or tern and rip the food from their beaks.

A few miles farther on is the town of Falmouth in the Parish of Trelawny, named after the Cornish birthplace of Sir William Trelawny, who was Governor of Jamaica from 1767 to 1772. It was for many years the main sugar exporting port for the island. Another ten or twelve miles on is Montego Bay which is Jamaica's second largest town and the main place where tourists arrive from America. I didn't like Montego Bay, as there was not much for me to do. My parents enjoyed the bars and restaurants and beaches, but sun and sand have never held a great attraction for me. I much prefer paths by streams where butterflies dance in sun-dappled glades. Doctor's Cave Beach was an exception, perhaps because we had to enter a cave to get there. A dim, rocky passage led to a secluded beach and shallow waters fed by mineral springs. As beaches go, it was very pleasant, and I spent happy hours there digging in the sand while my parents swam or lounged on the beach with cool drinks.

My father led us past Montego Bay, for his interests were always historical rather than touristy. The town of Lucea lies farther round the coast at the western end of the island. It has many old buildings and historical sites but the surrounding countryside is quite beautiful as many crops grow there. My father wanted to take us round to the westernmost tip at Negril, but the road was a shocker, and after a mile or two we found it washed out and had to turn back. We never managed to get back there and the western end of the island forever remains a mystery. On the way back past Montego Bay, my father detoured into the hills to an old ruined plantation house called Rose Hall.

The house and estate were reputed to be haunted and the burnt out shell of the Great House certainly looked as if ghosts were looking out the windows or stalking the overgrown grounds. My mother thought of herself as being slightly 'fey' and she shivered as she looked around.

"I don't like it, Jay," she said to my father.

My father grinned. "You know the legend of Annie Palmer, the White Witch of Rose Hall? She was one of the plantation owners' wives and had a terrible reputation for cruelty. She murdered at least one husband, tortured and killed many slaves, made lovers of others and practised voodoo arts. She was at last smothered in her bed by her slaves. It is said..." he lowered his voice and looked around. "That on the night she died this coal-black horse with three legs and fiery eyes..."

"A duppy," I cried out. "Three-legged horses are duppies. Cook said so."

"Exactly. Now, as I was saying, this three-legged coal-black horse with eyes of fire galloped up the long drive, past the slave quarters where women screamed and strong men trembled, to the Great Hall where the black soul of the White Witch mounted it and was carried off to hell, screaming."

My mother shuddered and I smiled uncertainly, thinking this was a thoroughly delicious story, but a bit scary all the same. "It's just a story though, isn't it, Dad?"

"Well, they say that on dark moonless nights, the horse still gallops down the long drive between the sugarcane fields and Annie Palmer still wails her piteous cries from its back." My father looked at me. "How about we come out here tonight and see if we can't see that wicked ghost?"

I nodded enthusiastically--after all, it was broad daylight and ghosts did not like sunlight. "We're not afraid of her," I said bravely. "She's just a silly old ghost and can't hurt us."

My mother stared past us toward the sea. "My goodness, what's that? Look."

We turned and saw the light cloud cover over the sea gather and twist about itself, whirling down toward the sea surface which whipped up into froth to meet it.

"It's a bloody waterspout," my father exclaimed.

"What's that?"

"A tornado, but over the water. I've never seen one before."

"It started as soon as you said those things about the White Witch."

"Coincidence."

My mother looked pale. "You shouldn't have said them, Jay."

My father laughed. "Well, Annie Palmer, old girl, I apologise for anything I might have said that offended you."

Within seconds the waterspout collapsed, and we left Rose Hall, driving down to our hotel in a slightly chastened mood. The waterspout was pure coincidence, my father assured us, but I thought it interesting from the point of view of timing and wondered whether there was more to ghosts than my father let on. Later that night he asked me again if I wanted to go back up to Rose Hall in the dark but I declined, saying I was tired. I don't think he believed me.

I decided I was going to ask our cook about other aspects of duppies when we got home, but by the time we got back to Kingston I had put thoughts of death and the afterlife behind me and was wrapped up once more in the concerns of life and especially in the many wonderful butterflies of Jamaica.

The Road to School

A s I have said, a few weeks after we arrived in Jamaica, we moved from the guest house to our own house at 5 Carvalho Drive in the suburb of Half Way Tree. This suburb was named for a crossroads that literally had a giant silk cotton tree growing there for many years, and in the old days of horse and carriage it was reckoned to be half way between the town of Old Kingston and outlying communities like Constant Spring and Stony Hill. Carvalho Drive was about half a mile away up Hope Road, heading northeast.

At about the same time as we moved in, I was enrolled in the Priory School, also on Hope Road. I was taken to see the Headmaster, Henry Fowler, an Oxford-educated Rhodes Scholar, who had founded the school about twenty years before. He was a nice man with a lively, erudite mind and I liked him immediately, though I was less enthusiastic about starting classes again.

The classrooms were a mixture of converted rooms in the old house that formed the school offices, of prefabricated buildings housing the laboratories or special needs subjects, and thatch-roofed buildings without walls where we could enjoy cool breezes and get distracted by everything happening around us. By and large, I enjoyed my couple of years at Priory, though most days I would rather have been out catching butterflies.

The length of Hope Road from home to school was only about half a mile and I could travel it in ten minutes without any problem. However, as there was so much to see and do on the way, I would commonly take half an hour to get there in the morning, and an hour or more to get home.

School started at eight o'clock and finished at one in the afternoon so we could avoid the heat of the day. It was cool when I left home and sometimes I would wait on the corner of Carvalho Drive for a friend, other times I would walk to school alone. There were mango trees on the corner of our road that spread deep shade and a crackly layer of dead leaves beneath. Fallen fruit would rot or be eaten by a multitude of creatures, tainting the air with a sickly smell for weeks after fruit fall. These mangoes were not the fibre-free varieties we enjoy today, but stringy and strongly flavoured, weeping with resins and stinking of turpentine. While I waited for my friend I would watch insects buzzing around the fallen fruit or follow the stealthy approach of lizards as they homed in on their own living food supply.

Then, with or without my friend, I would start for school. I had a few roads to cross, but the traffic on the side roads was usually light. The first was Waterloo Road and while I waited for a break in the traffic, I would gawk over the fence of the corner house. There was a scraggly tree near the fence, no more than ten feet high, with sparse leaves; and in the finer branches a pair of Vervain Hummingbirds had made their nest. These birds are reckoned the second smallest in the world, just slightly larger than the Cuban Bee Hummingbird.

The birds themselves were rather drab--browns and greens with a white front--but what they lacked in colour they made up for in character. They were fearless, and would fly at any bird that ventured too close to their tiny nest. Grey mockingbirds were common but no sooner would one land on the lawn that one of the Vervains would take off from the branch near the nest with whirring wings, and drive the intruder away, beating their wings around the larger bird's head. The hummingbird nest was tiny, no bigger than a doll's house teacup, soft and smooth inside and lined with spider silk and down feathers. Two minute white eggs lay in this receptacle and could be glimpsed whenever one of the parent birds left the nest. Sometimes, I would hoist myself up the fence and balance, limbs trembling with the effort, for a glimpse of these pearls.

I crossed the road and found a dead dog lying on the bare earth, just out of reach of the cars. It was a mangy, underfed dog that looked grateful to be beyond the troubles of life. Half a dozen dyspeptic undertakers stood around, in the form of 'John Crow', the ubiquitous turkey buzzard. Hunch-backed, garbed in black with bare, florid complexions, they watched and waited for the traffic to ease. I looked at them for a few minutes, hoping to see some action, but they just glanced nervously at me and shuffled their feet.

These birds are superbly graceful fliers, soaring effortlessly on outspread wings, riding the air currents and buoyed by the uprising thermals of the city, but on the ground they look shabby and ungainly.

I have watched these turkey buzzards circling, wings outspread on the warm air, gliding down one after the other onto a country road, to sit and regard some dead or dying animal. Then, plucking up their courage, they hopped flapping and screeching on their victim and ripped it to shreds.

The block between Waterloo Road and Kingsway was the most interesting part of the journey for me. Between the footpath and the road yawned a deep chasm where water run-off had gouged a channel several feet deep and many feet wide in the reddish soil. This gully contained all manner of wondrous things to interest a young boy--lizards and scorpions, rocks and clods of earth, and threaded through everything the detritus of regular floods, from coconuts to pieces of wood to furniture, and my attention would be torn between its treasures and the intriguing possibilities of the property alongside, for occupying most of the block was Devon House.

Devon House was the home of Jamaica's first black millionaire and in its heyday had been a luxurious home with resplendent gardens. By the time I was traipsing back and forth across its Hope Road frontage it had fallen into disrepair and its gardens were overgrown. As such, it was far more interesting to me. Bird life flourished in the undergrowth and butterflies flitted above the flowering shrubs. A few years later, developers would plan on building apartments but the Jamaican government stepped in and secured it for the nation. I like to think it is still there offering homes for the local wildlife.

On those school days when I was not delving the depths of the eroded gully, I scanned the fences and gateposts for moths. For some reason, moths liked the weathered wood and believed themselves to be invisible. I could move really close and even prod them with a stick or a finger to make them flash their hind wings at me.

This flash response is quite common. A moth often has two lines of defence against predators--the first is the statement 'I'm not here' and the second 'All right, I am here but I'm dangerous'. Moths roost with their wings flat and tuck their hind wings under their front ones, which are usually shades of brown and grey with streaks and patches and spots that often blend in with the substrate. This renders them almost invisible to the casual observer. If a predator (or a small boy) penetrates their first line of defence, many moths resort to a startle technique. These moths have brightly coloured hind wings--red, yellow, black and white. This sudden flash of colour will sometimes make a bird think twice, especially if the colour is patterned like a pair of staring eyes.

I found a long-winged moth on the Devon House gatepost. It had light fawn brown forewings and orangey-yellow hind wings, and I salivated when I saw it because it was a hawkmoth, a member of the family Sphingidae, and I have always had a special love for these burly insects. This one was a *Protambulyx strigilis*, and measured some four inches across its outspread wings--not particularly large but delicate and streamlined. I always carried a collecting jar in my school bag, so I caught it and killed it for later mounting. Although I killed my butterflies, and smaller moths, by pinching their thorax, this technique was not really suitable for larger moths like the hawkmoths. Their bodies are covered in fine hairs which rub off leaving unsightly bare patches if handled too roughly. I sometimes resorted to crushing the body if I had no other option, but the mounted moths never looked as good in my display cases. Hence the collecting jar, with cotton wool soaked in ethyl acetate--nail polish remover--which worked very well.

I hurried onward, having dawdled enough to make me late, but on the corner of Kingsway I caught sight of a Red-billed Streamertail, or Doctor Bird, and just had to stop and gawk. The Doctor Bird is the national bird of Jamaica and deservedly so. The male is a gorgeous green and black hummingbird, only a few inches in length, but two of its tail feathers are extraordinarily long, extending behind it like thin black streamers. This one was perching on a branch just inside a garden and every now and then would dart across to another branch where a female sat, hovering and swooping before returning to its perch. The female lacks the streamertails and the green feathers and is considerably less easy to see, which makes sense if you are sitting on eggs. I watched then for a few minutes before crossing Kingsway and running toward school, where I could hear the first bell ringing.

I crossed Queensway and burst through the bushes on the boundary of the school property, managing to make it to assembly just as the second bell went. I earned a shake of the head from one of the teachers, but nothing worse as Priory School did not believe in corporal punishment. It must have been the American influence. A lot of the kids there were American and one lovely young American girl with a beautiful long yellow flounced dress and a ponytail saw me and called out "Hi Poopsie!" I just blushed and looked away. I liked her but girls were like boys to my pre-adolescent mind--if they didn't like insects they were of dubious worth.

Classes started, and I drifted from one to another without really taking anything in. The only subject I really liked was Science, taken by Mrs Urquhart, an American teacher. She had a class full of boys and girls that were prepared to pay attention to her lessons, but had no special interest-- except for two boys, coincidentally both called Max. The other boy was called Max Wright and he liked butterflies too. In fact, he's the only other person called Max that I had ever met, though I have met a few dogs of that name.

English was another subject I enjoyed, though at times I had to struggle with the mass of rules that make up this complex and hybrid language. As I mastered its intricacies, I came to see the beauty of the written word and ventured to offer a silly poem or two to the School Magazine. In my final year they accepted two of them, and I like to think my writing career had its faltering start in that beautiful island.

Morning break arrived and we went out into the shade of the Poinciana trees. These are beautiful trees. It has delicate fern-like leaves and spectacular red, vermilion, orange, white and yellow flowers that it produces in a magnificent show at the beginning of summer. Beautiful though the flowers are, what attracted a crop of small boys more were the long flat seed pods that appeared toward the end of summer. They were about two foot long and two inches wide, dark brown and very tough, and they made excellent swords. Many are the vigorous sword-fights I have had with these rattling pods as I sought to board a pirate ship, fight a duel or repel a Saracen attack. Often, these bouts of cut and thrust would end with bruised ribs or sore knuckles, but it did not stop us.

Sometimes, particularly in the spring and autumn, Mrs Urquhart would come out to the playing fields with a pair of binoculars during break, or even after school. Nobody paid much attention, but the other Max and I would follow her and stand quietly beside her as she trained her binoculars into trees and shrubs or scoured the long grass in the fields behind.

"Please, Mrs Urquhart, what are you looking at?"

"Birds."

I looked in the direction she was, but could see nothing.

"What birds, Mrs Urquhart?"

"You see that bush at the edge of the playing field? There's a Bobolink in it. Here..." she passed me the binoculars. I had used my father's pair before, so I knew how to adjust them. The bush leapt into view and then swam in and out of focus. In the heart of it sat a small black and white bird.

32

"It's a migratory species," Mrs Urquhart said. "I've often seen them in the States, but they fly to South America for the winter and back again in the spring. Some of them fly right through Jamaica."

I passed the binoculars to Max Wright. "How do they find their way?"

"They fly by night and use the stars and the magnetic field of the earth."

"Wow."

"There are other species that migrate too," Mrs Urquhart said. "I saw a Baltimore Oriole last week--they're lovely birds, all black and vivid yellow. Sometimes there are grassquits in the fields, feeding on the seeds and insects."

"I saw a Doctor Bird on the way to school this morning," I said. "And a Vervain hummingbird and John Crows."

"They're everywhere," Max Wright said, a touch scornfully. "It's no big deal seeing them."

"Even a common bird can teach us things if we observe it carefully." Mrs Urquhart looked at us. "Do you boys like birds?"

Max Wright nodded. "Sure."

"Me too," I said, "But I like butterflies more."

Mrs Urquhart smiled. "Yes, I know about your butterflies, Max. However, there are some wonderful birds in Jamaica and I wondered if you two would like to come at some at my home in Newcastle. My husband and I have a few acres up there and there are lots of birds. Butterflies and moths too, but I couldn't allow you to catch them on our property. It would have to be observation only."

"When? Today?" Max Wright frowned.

"Not today, but soon. I would need to contact both lots of parents and check that you're allowed to come and visit."

"I'd like that, Mrs Urquhart," I said. Max Wright nodded his agreement.

School provided another interest once. In 1960, a film director--Peter Brook, I think--came to the school. We were told that a film was being made called 'Lord of the Flies' and that any eleven or twelve year olds interested could gather under the Poinciana trees. I and my friends duly appeared, excited at the prospect of becoming film stars, but the director took one look at us and said 'too old, too big'. He was after younger children and went elsewhere to find them. A promising acting career was cut short before it had begun.

The road home entailed similar distractions and provided lots of other things for boys to do, but with more time to indulge ourselves--in the dry season at least. The rainy season, May to October, brought with it downpours and flooding which altered the afternoon promenade. Rainy season implies lots of rain, we did not have days of solid rain. Clouds would gather through the morning, increasing the temperature and humidity, building up to a torrential downpour around noon to early afternoon, and then clearing to a fine evening. For an hour or three, the rain thundered down, rapidly turning the playing fields to sheets of water and spraying up from the roads. The footpaths would be muddy and slippery and the gullies beside the roads that carried the run-off were raging torrents of muddy water for a short time.

The road sloped down gently from school to home, and I loved rainy days and playing beside the swirling waters. Naturally, we made boats, fashioning them out of wood or plastic, or if nothing else lay to hand, using our imaginations and a stick to brave the raging cataracts of the Nile, or Amazon, or whatever river caught our fancy. I would arrive home soaked and muddy and with luck could sneak my wet things to the laundry unseen. The washing was done by our maid, so my mother would usually remain unaware of my escapades.

On dryer days, when the gully held only traces of moisture or the dry litter from passing vehicles, I would sometimes walk along its bed, turning over stones and searching out lizards and beetles. These I was usually content to capture, examine and release, but occasionally I would happen upon a caterpillar wandering forlornly over the red-brown earth and carry it home to see what it would become. Sometimes they pupated and hatched into moths, but mostly they wandered round and round the jar until they died or I took pity on them and let them go.

As the days went by, the corpse of the dog at the corner of Waterloo Road became little more than scattered bones and fur. Flies swarmed over the remains and, on edging closer, I could see carrion beetles seeking out sustenance on the scraps of flesh. A shadow swept over me and I looked up to see a single John Crow vulture drift past, the long wing feathers spilling air as he controlled his speed, and his bright red naked head swivelled to watch me. He flew over Waterloo Road and low over the garden on the corner. Two tiny things rose up from the scraggly tree, homing in on the soaring vulture like guided missiles. They were the Vervain Hummingbirds, defending their territory. The male rose above the vulture and descended, swooping close to its head with tiny claws extended as the female hit the tail feathers. John Crow sideslipped and with wings flapping ponderously, fled, with the hummingbirds pursuing until it was out of the garden air-space.

And so to home. I turned into Carvalho Drive and into number five. I shed my school bag and made myself a sandwich before grabbing my butterfly net and heading for the nearest bit of wasteland. I had spent quite enough time going to and coming from school, and now my time was my own. I could get back to butterfly hunting.

Hope Gardens

F
ar along Hope Road, past the Priory School, Government House, and the guest house where we stayed when we first arrived in Kingston, and nearly as far as the Mona Campus of the University of the West Indies, lay Hope Botanical Gardens. It was a place I frequented as often as I could persuade my parents to take me in the early days, and later on was a place I cycled to in my pursuit of butterflies.

Hope Gardens, as I knew it, comprised densely forested parts, open woods and lawns sprinkled with specimen trees and flower beds. There were two large ponds, covered in water lilies and lined with long grass, rushes and papyrus in which dwelled a multitude of frogs, and shoals of bright silver fish swam in its depths. The mud around the edges harboured snails and a plethora of insect larvae, well worth a look by a small boy.

The gardens were popular but they were never crowded. However, the men and women taking their leisure among the flowers and trees were very understanding of small boys armed with butterfly nets that chased their prey up and down the paths or leapt over flower beds and pounded across the grass. I caught many species in Hope Gardens, some of which were relatively uncommon, and it was one of my favourite places.

There were other things in Hope Gardens to keep me occupied besides butterflies. I had an interest in all aspects of biology and was not above tearing a flower to pieces to count its petals and anthers, or to delve into its inner workings. I looked for the nectaries that attracted birds and insects and sampled some of them myself. More by luck than good judgement, I managed to avoid truly poisonous flowers like oleander. I watched insects foraging in the flower beds--butterflies of course, unrolling their slender straw-like tongues to sip delicately at the floral banquet, or bees with their more forthright, bullying approach, pushing their way in and drinking greedily.

Some birds are nectar-feeders too, notably the hummingbirds. Three species of hummingbird were found in the Hope Gardens--the tiny Vervain and spectacular Streamertail or Doctor Bird, but also the Mango Hummingbird, having grey and black plumage with purple, blue and green highlights. This last hummingbird was less common than the others and better camouflaged in the shade, but they were there if you waited patiently by trumpet-flowered vines, though I didn't see one at Hope Gardens until much later. The Bananaquit was another nectar-feeder, though this small yellow, black and white bird could not hover while feeding. It would perch and thrust its long curved bill deep into the flower or else peck through the sides of the floral tube to access its sugary reward.

Peafowl frequented the Gardens and the stillness would every so often be racked by the mournful cries of these beautiful birds. Males unfurled their long 'eyed' tail feathers and strutted and stamped for the females, shaking their blue and green plumage in a shimmering display. The females would stand around and watch for a while before wandering off in search of something more appealing, like food. I suppose the males must sometimes have been successful in their courtship, for peachicks could sometimes be seen, scurrying after the peahens. At dusk, the peacocks would fly up into the treetops, long tails trailing behind them, and settle down for the night, uttering their chorus of cries once more. I would search the paths for the tail feathers but whenever I found them; my mother would make me throw them away.

"It's bad luck to have peacock feathers," she said.

"Mum," I groaned. "I'm not superstitious." However, I would still have to throw them away. My mother was funny that way and had a whole raft of little superstitions that I had to observe in her presence, like not putting my shoes on a table, not crossing knives on the dinner table, or throwing salt over my left shoulder if I spilt any.

Other birds were common in the Gardens too, but I seldom noticed the details if I had my net in hand. I do remember walking the roads and footpaths and have a pair of Pea Doves walking ahead of me, turning their heads to watch me as I got closer. At last, their nerve would break and they'd explode upward and forward, alighting again fifty yards away, ready to repeat the whole performance when I caught up. Other birds were present in abundance too. Swifts and swallows flew overhead, darting rapidly, capturing small insects on the wing, and unseen birds called in the undergrowth. Purple-black Anis and glossy jet-black grackles haunted the grassy swards, stalking back and forth with their eyes searching out the smallest morsel of food. Hawks cruised above, looking for rodents or lizards, occasionally mobbed by songbirds if they flew too close to the trees. Higher, turkey buzzards wheeled in the pale cloudless sky, waiting for something to die. By the ponds, water birds sought a living on the margins, sifting mud or hunting for frogs and small fish--herons and egrets, or ducks seeking a refuge from hunters. I noticed all these things, but few things distracted me from my passion for long.

Different butterflies occupy different habitats and the types that fly, feed and breed in open spaces are usually quite different from the ones that frequent forests. Hope Gardens had many habitats thrust close to one another, each vegetation type attracting a different suite of butterflies, though of course there was a certain amount of overlap. Chocolate and yellow *Colobura* (Banana Butterfly) and brown *Calisto* (Eyed Brown) occupied the deep shade in the forest sections, and black and yellow striped *Heliconius* (Zebra) and the brown and orange and palest blue *Adelpha* (Jamaican Admiral) danced in the dappled sunlight, while brown striped *Marpesia* (Daggerwing) and black swallowtails flitted along the paths with little flashes of colour.

The edges of the forest, particularly if there were flowerbeds close by, supported a profusion of species. Bright orange Julias, orange and silver-spotted *Dione*, yellow Thersites and black and yellow Andraemon swallowtails, a profusion of yellows and whites, tiny flutters of blue, zipping browns and oranges of skippers and darts, and the strong flights and glides of Danaid butterflies. I could wander out onto the lawns, far from flowers and trees and still find the little blue butterflies *Chlorostrymon* flying close to the turf, landing on tiny weed flowers, their jewelled hind wings rubbing against one another while they fed. The open ground harboured grass yellows too, a variety of the *Eurema* species as well as their white and sulphur cousins *Phoebis*, *Ascia*, *Kricogonia* and *Anteos*, though the larger Pierids were mostly just passing through. Little orange and white *Mestra dorcas* was here too, with the Buckeye, Tailed Skipper, Grizzled Skipper, and the White Peacock Butterfly. It took me a long time to learn the names of these butterflies, but the mind of a small boy is a sponge when it comes to things he is interested in--and I was certainly interested in butterflies.

I have always loved the orange and brown Danaids--the regal Monarch, *Danaus plexippus*; and its lesser cohorts the Queen, *Danaus gilippus*; the Soldier, *Danaus eresimus* and the Cleophile, *Danaus cleophile*. Danaids lay eggs on a variety of milkweeds and the caterpillars are voracious feeders. Along with their food, they ingest quantities of toxic chemicals which they store in their bodies. This makes them completely inedible and birds avoid them. The distastefulness is passed on to the adults and they can fly around with impunity, only being predated upon by small boys with large nets. As far as the butterflies are concerned, it is of little use being ill-tasting if every bird must learn the lesson afresh, so the butterflies and their larvae have adopted warning colouration. A bird soon realises that caterpillars with black, white and yellow stripes are not worth sampling and that adult butterflies that are orange and black with white spots on the body are likewise best left alone.

The Monarch, Queen, Soldier and Cleophile look very much alike and birds that have already experienced the horror of eating one of them will steer clear of anything that looks like them. This is called Mullerian mimicry and I learned about it from a curator at the Institute of Jamaica. The Monarch, Queen, Soldier and Cleophile are all bad-tasting and all benefit from looking like each other. Except for the Cleophile, I could find them all at Hope Gardens, though their occurrence was seasonal.

One other Monarch look-alike could sometimes be found here. The Danaid Eggfly, *Hypolimnas misippus*, has sexes that look quite different--the male is browny-black with large white spots on all four wings, but the female looks a bit like the Danaids. They feed on quite different plants though and are not foul-tasting to birds. However, because the female looks like a Monarch, birds tend to leave it alone. This mimicry of a tasty butterfly for a nasty-tasting one is called Batesian mimicry. I only ever saw this butterfly once, and it evaded my net.

I have never liked spiders and generally the presence of one was enough to send me walking swiftly away. However, I came to tolerate and even love the little crab spiders which abounded in the gardens. These gaily-hued spiders would hide in flowers and assume the colour of their surroundings-- pink, green, yellow or white--and capture insects as they alighted to feed. Jewel spiders were other interesting inhabitants. These small spiders spin webs but their bodies are covered in a spiny carapace that offers them some protection from birds. They are often brightly coloured too--black and white and yellow--and I would often run into one of their webs strung across a path. On the leaves of trees and shrubs roamed jumping spiders, again small, but a bit startling to a juvenile arachnophobe with their sudden movements. When I got used to them, I would watch them closely and admire their colours, their huge front legs and large eyes that looked forward. They would creep up on an insect, moving millimetre by millimetre until they were close enough and then leap, so fast I almost could not see them, and snare their prey. They had expressions that were almost intelligent and they seemed aware of my presence, shifting their legs nervously when I moved, so as to always face me.

I first came across the giant Marine Toad, *Bufo marinus*, in the Gardens. They are huge, warty creatures that raise their heads high and survey everything, seeming to categorise things into edible and dangerous. They would leap away from me, but if I was very quiet I could watch them forage for worms and beetles. I saw it eat a frog once and the stinking corpse of a baby bird, so I suppose they really will eat anything. If they are cornered and cannot escape, they gulp air and expand in size, hoping to scare off any potential predator. They have glands on the back of the neck that secrete a poison, so there are very few predators that have not learned to leave them alone. Man is their only threat and I regret to say I have seen young Jamaican men use them as footballs. A large toad reacted to discovery by puffing up and with every kick would try and make itself bigger, so that soon a soccer match was in progress with one of these unfortunate creatures acting as the ball.

Despite my love of butterflies, the ponds drew me too. What small boy can resist the pull of water, mud and slippery creatures? I often prowled the edges, my butterfly net doubling as a fishing net, slamming down over a frog or dipping into weed-choked waters after silvery slips of fish or even dredging up gobs of mud crawling with insect larvae and snails. I would hold my prize in a grubby hand and study each capture, marvelling at the feel of frog or fish, watching dragonfly larvae wriggling furiously in my palm in their efforts to escape, or the hesitant slip and slide of a snail over my finger as it sought to avoid the drying sun.

Sometimes, I would bring a jam-jar and lie on the turf with my chin in my hands and observe the antics of insect and fish. Water beetles would pop to the surface and swim frantically down again, a silvery air bubble clasped to their bodies before grasping a piece of weed and hanging in mid-water until their air ran out. Water spiders clung to a stem, their bodies silvered by an air bubble, and waited for prey to pass by. Dragonfly larvae sat in the mud, almost motionless while they waited for some hapless insect or tadpole. Then there would be a blur of movement and the hapless animal would be pierced or sucked dry by the predator's implacable jaws. Other insect larvae fed on tiny organisms in the mud and were more delicately constructed. Their limbs were longer and feathery gills fluttered beneath their abdomens as they sculled through the water. Fish hung in weed in the water column and darted out and back again, restless, their gill covers marking time with their gulping mouths. Silver and green scales caught the sun and reflected it back in shimmering patterns. I looked and I became greedy, wanting it for myself.

"Dad, can I have a fish tank?"

"For tropical fish? They're expensive, you know."

"No, just pond stuff. I'd catch it all myself."

"You'd be prepared to spend your pocket money on it, and look after it yourself?"

I nodded eagerly.

My father considered my request carefully and went out and bought me a large goldfish bowl measuring about two and a half foot across. It held a lot of water when full and was very heavy, so my father mounted it on a sturdy table in my bedroom where indirect light would fall on it. I could not wait to stock it, so on my next trip to the Gardens I took an array of containers, bringing back mud, insect larvae, weed, fish and frogs.

I tipped the mud in and then scrabbled about in the murky water anchoring the plants in place with rocks gleaned from the garden. I added half a dozen small fish and two frogs to the brew and stood back to admire my creation. I could not see much at first, but over the course of a few days, the water cleared and I could see my fish swimming back and forth, while my two frogs floated on the surface or dove to the bottom in a fresh flurry of mud when I came too close. It was wonderful.

Every time I went back to Hope Gardens, I took a jar and caught some more water creatures, adding them to my tank. The fish quickly ate the weeds and I had to bring in more. The insect larvae and snails disappeared--eaten by the fish probably--and the curved walls of the bowl turned green as algae bloomed. I loved it. Then the frogs stopped diving as I approached the tank. I investigated and found one floating bloated and soft on the surface. I gingerly fished it out and threw it in the garden, but although I looked, I could not find the other one. A rich aroma soon filled my room, encroaching on the rest of the house and I was forced to defend my tank.

"It's not my tank, Mum. Smell it. You'll see."

She did, and agreed that though it was a bit 'whiffy', it was not the source of the stink. That was tracked to my wardrobe and the rotting corpse of the other frog under it. Retching slightly, I disposed of this corpse in the garden also, and the maid disinfected my room. After that, I decided I would have no more frogs, just fish, as they stayed safely in their bowl. I went out and caught some more.

The bowl grew more crowded over a period of weeks and I was forced to scrape the sides regularly to keep them clear of algae. We went away to San San for a few days and before I left I dumped a handful of dried fish food in to keep my pets happy. A smell greeted me when I returned--not quite as revolting as the dead frog smell, but pretty bad. I found that the water in the bowl looked more like some bubbling soup than a pond of clear water. All my lovely fish were dead and bloated on the surface. This time I was physically sick, but when I recovered, I had to scoop out the bowl contents into a bucket, inducing fresh bouts of nausea, and carry it outside, being very careful not to slop any on the floor. I tipped it all out at the bottom of the garden, over-riding the complaints of the gardener. Then I took the bowl outside and scrubbed it clean before spraying more disinfectant around my room.

I never kept fish again in Jamaica, but prevailed on my parents to buy me a hamster instead. However, that is another story and has nothing to do with Hope Gardens.

A Butterfly by Any Other Name...

You may have noticed I have a certain love of, or dare I say propensity for, scientific names--those indigestible morsels of dead languages that scientists bandy about. I have thought about why this is and it is possible that is just the way my brain is wired. It may not even be a personal thing, as I have noticed many boys displaying a similar aptitude for dinosaurs at a very early age. Introduce a boy to pictures of creatures from a bygone age and within a short space of time he will be talking animatedly of 'Tyrannosaurus rex', Apatosaurus, Camarasaurus, Stegosaurus and Triceratops. Dinosaurs hold a fascination for young boys (myself included) and as there are seldom common names for these extinct creatures, one must, if one desires to discuss them with one's playmates, quickly grasp the pronunciation of their scientific names. On the other hand, my facility for these scientific names may owe more to a set of circumstances that governed my early life.

When I was sent to boarding school in England--Thorpe House Preparatory School for Boys in Gerrards Cross, Buckinghamshire--one of the languages I was forced to learn at the tender age of six was Latin. I was a dreadful scholar though. I'd happily sit in class reciting, with twenty other boys, 'amo--amas--amat--amamus--amatis--amant' and conjugating all the other common verbs. I'd repeat phrases; I'd wrestle with translations; I'd listen dreamily to learned dissertations from our erudite Classics Master on the Nominative, the Dative, the Genitive, the Accusative and all the other forms of Latin declension--but it all washed over my head like a warm meaningless tide.

But something must have stuck, some high tide mark, some drift line of detritus, of broken shells and dead jellyfish on the hidden beaches of my mind. I found, as my English vocabulary grew, that many English words have their basis in the Latin language and I recognised them, often being able to work out their meaning before I looked them up in my dictionary. I can also look at a Latin name, or a Latinised Greek one, and as often as not I can translate the dead language into a description of the beast.

However, recognition of Latin words was not the whole story. Early on, while perusing a book on microscopic pond life, I came across the trumpet animalcule. This is a tiny ciliated protist shaped like a trumpet and bears the name *Stentor*. I looked at the name and recognised it, but it took me several minutes to remember where I had seen the name. When I did, it gave me a delighted shock, for the name came from a translation of Homer's Iliad. During the Trojan War, the Greeks employed a herald with a very loud voice, so loud in fact that he was said to have the voice of fifty men. His name had been Stentor. (As an aside, Stentor is said to have lost his life after losing a shouting match with the god Hermes). I made the connection between a loud man and a trumpet (or megaphone) shaped protist. I rejoiced to discover that a scientist had been reading the same books I had. I was soon to find many other animal names that matched the heroes and gods of Greek and Roman literature, particularly when I became interested in butterflies.

My father owned a small library containing translations of Herodotus, Homer, Suetonius, Ovid, and Thucydides, and the works of Robert Graves, and he would let me delve into them. Well, the pages of those fascinating books abound in heroes and kings from both myth and history, and soon I was finding those same names cropping up whenever I looked at butterflies. An obvious example among the Jamaican fauna is the Blue Mountain swallowtail, *Papilio homerus*. This magnificent butterfly is the largest one in the New World, and it is fitting that it should be named after that giant of ancient literature--Homer.

There were others. *Papilio peleus* is named after Peleus, the father of Achilles; *Papilio thersites* after Thersites, the ugliest man in the Greek army (rather unfairly, I thought, as the butterfly is beautiful); *Battus polydamas* after Polydamas, a friend of the Trojan Prince Hector; and *Papilio thoas* after Thoas, another Greek warrior. Andraemon, Memnon, Apollo, Paris and Marcellinus have also loaned their names to swallowtail butterflies.

Looking further afield, Danaus was the brother of Aegyptus, a mythical king of Egypt, and gave his name to a group of beautiful orange, black and white butterflies--the Monarch and its relatives. Interestingly, the species name of the Monarch butterfly, *Danaus plexippus*, is named after one of the sons of King Aegyptus. *Calisto* is named for one of the lovers of Zeus, and the Daggerwing *Marpesia* for a Queen of the Amazons. *Dryas* and *Hamadryas* are nymphs from Greek mythology; *Vanessa* derives from the goddess of procreation, Phanessa; Dione for the mother of the goddess Aphrodite; and *Phoebis* (a bright yellow butterfly) for Phoebus, god of the sun.

There are a host of others, of course, named not only for the names of historical and mythological characters, but also for colours and patterns. There is a small orange-yellow British skipper butterfly called *Thymelicus flavus*. Flavus is the Latin for yellow and, for that matter the 'melicus' part of the name is Latin for honey. Another skipper, the American *Stallingsia maculosus* has forewings with a scattering of cream spots on a dark brown background. The name *maculosus* comes from the Latin word for 'spotted'.

The other thing you might have noticed in my accounts is the use of common names. Whereas I have had little difficulty with scientific names, my friends often stumbled over the complex syllables. We made up descriptive common names for some Jamaican butterflies, names that described them adequately for our own use. Leafwing was a handy name for *Historis odius*, and Tailed Leafwing for its relative *Historis acheronta*, but what we called the 'Banana butterfly', *Colobura dirce*, was usually referred to as a Zebra by other lepidopterists. Then again, we called the black and yellow striped *Heliconius charitonius* a 'Zebra' whereas it was sometimes called a 'Zebra Longwing', 'Longwing' or 'Tiger', depending on who you asked.

This, of course, is the best reason for using the scientific names. People may call the same butterfly by half a dozen different common names and not realise they are talking about the same creature, but use the scientific name and the confusion disappears. For instance, there is a beautiful butterfly that occurs in North America and Europe that is known as the 'Mourning Cloak', 'Camberwell Beauty', 'Grand Surprise', 'Willow Beauty', and 'White Petticoat'--and that's just among English speakers. The butterfly in question is *Nymphalis antiopa*.

The use of common names can be confusing not just for small boys but also for adult butterfly enthusiasts. When butterfly hunting and naming was first 'taking wing' in Britain, there were two species called the Golden Heath Eye and the Selvedge Heath Eye. They were later found to be female and male of the same species called the Gatekeeper. Then the name was changed to the Small Heath and the name Gatekeeper given to another butterfly that had been known as the Hedge Brown, Hedge Eye, or Large Heath. Confused? Let's take it a step further. The name Large Heath has since been given to a butterfly known as the Manchester Argus or Marsh Ringlet. Thank goodness for scientific names. The Gatekeeper (was the Large Heath) is *Pyronia tithonus*, the Small Heath (was the Gatekeeper) is *Coenonympha pamphilus*, and the Large Heath (was the Argus or Ringlet) is *Coenonympha tullia*. How much easier is that?

All this is but a brief explanation for the scattering of common and scientific names throughout my Jamaican Adventures. It is certainly easier to remember common names, but common names are merely tags of convenience that a person puts on a species and someone else will give it a different tag. The scientific name is the only real one, and those names owe their existence to the Latin language and the Classical writings of Rome and Greece. I had experience of both as I was growing up and I count myself fortunate. It has stood me in good stead during my life.

A Migration of Kites

I first met Steve Riley in early April of 1959, just after we moved to Jamaica, and he became my best friend. We were both effectively from single child families--I was an only child whereas he only had a baby sister. He felt self-conscious because of terrible scald scars on his neck and arms and I had not yet made many friends at school, so when we met, we both felt a need to bond. He was two years younger than me and as I was only eleven myself we generally played together as small boys do. We had bicycles but Steve was not allowed far from home alone, so I usually rode round to see him. What he did have was over a hundred large wooden blocks and an electric train set. Each toy by itself was fun, but together they were pure joy. Small boys often display destructive tendencies and we would construct elaborate constructions out of the blocks and then build the train tracks close to the key blocks so the edifice would collapse with a roar but with luck the train would race through unscathed.

We shared other hobbies--we both owned hamsters and collected stamps and, after his first visit to my house where he stared in fascination at my developing butterfly collection, he became an enthusiastic collector too. He asked his father to buy him a net, he bought a cork-lined mahogany box, and he later joined me in many forays around Jamaica.

In June of that first year though, that was still in the future. When we got together in those early days it was usually at his house as his mother liked to keep him close. He had a large front yard with a gravel drive, mowed lawns and flower beds, and a larger back one with several large breadfruit trees bounded by a tall and wild hedge. The grass grew longer at the back and we played in it, hiding from each other and letting our imaginations run riot. Jamaica is a fortunate island, having no poisonous snakes and only one or

47

two nasty spiders which were easy to avoid. We would sometimes come across small fawn-coloured scorpions under dry rocks, but the most deadly things we commonly encountered were wasps and bees.

One Saturday in June, Steve phoned to ask if I'd like to come round and play. My mother gave me permission, so I said I'd cycle round and would see him soon. Now, just two days before I had cycled somewhere with my butterfly net and had tangled the pole in my spokes, grazing my knees on the gravel of the road. So when I picked up my net I remembered my accident and left it behind. It was not going to be needed anyway, as Steve and I had not yet started our collecting expeditions.

I set off along Hope Road, heading for the Mona Estates where Steve lived. It was a long ride but traffic was light and it was a very pleasant sunny day. About half way there I saw a blue and black butterfly flit rapidly across my path and I wobbled as I turned my head to follow it. I hadn't the faintest idea what it was. I stopped and stared after it, trying to see where it had gone, but there was no sign and after a few minutes I went on.

I saw it again a minute later--or rather, another one, because I saw a second and then a third, crossing Hope Road from left to right. I stopped and looked to the left and spotted another one coming toward me. Again, I got that impression of blue and black as it sped past me. I waited and over the space of several minutes I saw another dozen cross the road within fifty yards of me. I started to get excited for this was a new species for me.

I looked back the way I had come, judging how long it would take me to cycle home and get my net. I decided it would take too long, and I should continue on to Steve's house and see if he had anything I could use to catch one--if they were still around, that is.

They were. By the time I cycled into their road I knew what the butterflies were, but not their name. I had seen one take a moment from its determined westerly course to visit some Ixora flowers in a garden. I jumped off my bike and ran into the garden, not caring that I was trespassing. I just had to see that butterfly up close. It hovered over the flowers and I saw it was a swallowtail butterfly, but much smaller than any of the other Jamaican species. It was striped zebra-fashion in black and pale blue and long sharp tails extended from its hind wings. Then it was off again, as if hurrying to catch up with its companions.

I knew I had to capture one for my collection, and now wished I had returned home for my net. I arrived at Steve's house and outlined what I had seen. We stood in his front garden for half an hour and saw nothing, but when we looked around the back it was a different story. High hedges surrounded the yards, but in the back there were several gaps in the vegetation and these blue swallowtails flitted through these gaps, dashed across the yard and along the opposite hedge until they found a gap, and then darted through and away.

"Wow," Steve said. "They're beautiful. Can we catch some?"

"That's what I want to do, but I didn't bring my net."

"You could go home and get it."

"It'd take me ages. They might have stopped by then."

"Then what?"

"I'll phone and ask my Mum to bring it to me."

Vain hope. I rang but my mother said she was busy and couldn't come. We wandered outside again and sat under a breadfruit tree and watched the lovely blue swallowtails fly past unhindered.

"Could we make a net?" Steve asked.

I thought about this. My father had bought me my net from a biological supply house in the United States, but it was a simple construction--a lightweight bamboo pole, a loop of stiff wire, and a fine-mesh cloth bag.

"We could try. I used to have one I made." I explained what we needed and we went into the house to look for the parts.

We found a mop and against the maid's protests, we took a hammer to the nail holding the head on and detached it. A coat hanger was bent out of shade and tied to the pole with string. Steve pleaded with his mother for an old pillowcase and we sat and considered how we were going to attach it. The best way would have been to sew it, but neither of us had the patience and skill to apply needle and thread, so we opted for large safety pins. We stood back and examined our creation, Steve with a big grin on his face and me with a sceptical frown. I knew what a net was supposed to look like. Still, it might serve its purpose and every swallowtail that passed was one fewer we would have an opportunity to catch. We hurried outside.

Steve graciously allowed me first use of the makeshift net. I positioned myself near a gap in the hedge and waited for the first blue swallowtail. It obliged me by appearing within a minute. I swung confidently, having captured many butterflies in the past, but the air filled the pillowcase and two things happened. The string tying the wire to the pole snapped under the strain, and the butterfly flew past as if I wasn't there. We went back to the kitchen and retied the string, winding more onto the pole until it was as firm as we could make it. Then we tried again.

"Your turn," I told Steve.

He got ready and swung the net valiantly as a swallowtail flew by. The net bent backward under the strain and the safety pins slipped, pulling the whole rim of the pillowcase round to one side. The material closed up and flapped ineffectually as the butterfly continued on its way unscathed. He threw down the net and kicked at a clump of grass. More repairs followed and gradually we honed our technique until the net stayed intact maybe three swipes out of five. We still did not catch anything though, as the pillowcase filled with air and we couldn't move it fast enough to overtake our fleet-winged prey. I even tried swiping head on, but the butterfly sort of bounced off the cushion of air and flew away. I wanted to cut holes in the pillowcase to let the air move through it, but Steve's mother vetoed the idea.

I held the net sideways with the pillowcase held above with one hand, and tried dropping it over the butterfly, but I was never fast enough. Steve got a tea towel from the kitchen and attempted to swat one. He came close, so I ditched the useless net and armed myself with another tea towel. For the next two hours we danced around Steve's back yard snapping our tea towels at those beautiful little blue jewels as they sped purposefully past us. Twice I managed to hit one a glancing blow, but it only flew off to one side even faster. Once, a tiny fragment of blue and black wing drifted down, but when I picked it up I was left with a transparent slip and a dusting of coloured scales on my fingers.

The sun lowered in the sky and the flood of butterflies dried up to a trickle and ceased. I stood disconsolately among the breadfruit trees searching for the vanished swallowtails for maybe half an hour before admitting they were gone.

"I'd better go home," I said.

"Will you come again tomorrow?" Steve asked. "With your net?"

"If I can."

I cycled home, keeping a sharp lookout for the blue swallowtails but saw nothing. I told my parents and asked if I could go round to Steve's again the next day. They said I could if his parents agreed, but when I phoned Steve, he told me his family were going out together. I determined I would hunt them by myself.

The next morning I was up with the first light, patrolling our street with my net in hand, but the blue swallowtails had vanished as if they had never existed. At ten o'clock my father called me in and said he had to go in to the office for an hour, and did I want to be dropped off at the Institute of

Jamaica for that time. I thought I could see the blue swallowtails in their collection, so I agreed.

The cabinet of butterflies at the Institute contained only a handful of the creatures neatly arrayed on their pins with wings spread out. I saw that their name was *Graphium marcellinus*, but I was grateful for the common name appended to the label--the Jamaican Kite Swallowtail. I went looking for a curator and found a tall grey-haired man wearing an Institute jacket.

"Excuse me, sir, can you tell me about the Jamaican Kite Swallowtail?"

The old man smiled down at me. "You're the boy who's always in here looking at the butterflies, aren't you?" When I nodded, he went on. "Aren't you interested in our other exhibits?"

"Well, yes sir, but mostly butterflies."

"And now you've become interested in the Kite?"

"Yes sir."

"What do you want to know?"

"I saw a lot of them flying yesterday, all in one direction, but there are none today. Will they be back?"

"Were they, by George? What direction were they flying?"

I thought for a moment. "Er, west, I think. Across the Hope Road."

"Wait here," the man said. "I have to make a phone call but then I'll tell you all I know."

He walked off rapidly, turning down a dimly lit hallway and leaving me looking at a display of Arawak Indian bows and arrows. The Arawak people were the native inhabitants of Jamaica and other islands in the Caribbean when Christopher Columbus arrived here in 1494. Their society was destroyed by the Europeans but their descendants still live in some of the islands. I examined the displays without much enthusiasm, wondering how long the man would be on the telephone.

At last he returned and smiled at me. "Sorry to be so long, but that was exciting news you had. I was at work all day yesterday, so I didn't see the migration myself, but I called up some people I know and one of them saw it."

"Migration? What's that?"

"That's what they call it when a lot of one type of butterfly--well, any animal really--moves in a deliberate manner from one place to another. The monarch butterfly is perhaps the most famous migrating butterfly, moving from Mexico to Canada and back every year, but lots of butterflies do it. The Jamaican Kite Swallowtail is one."

"Wow. So they do that every year? I've only been out here a few months and I've never even seen a Kite before."

"No they don't. The Kites only migrate at infrequent intervals. I've only ever seen one migration, back in 1952, but I'm told there was one in 1945 and before that in 1892. When they fly through, it may be for a day or a week. If you haven't seen any today it probably means it's over. Still, you should think yourself very privileged to have seen a migration. Did you catch any of them?"

I shook my head. "No, I left my net at home. My friend Steve and I tried catching them but they were too fast."

"That's a pity," the man said. "Still, if you are in Jamaica long enough you may see another one and have better luck with the net."

I thought about this. "Where are they found when they aren't migrating?"

The tall man scratched his head. "No one really knows. You may be lucky enough to find single Kites in other years, but they're rare. They've been seen in the Cockpit Country. Nobody knows what habitat they like or what plant their caterpillars eat." He grinned and ruffled my hair. "There's a job for you when you grow up. Find out where they live and what they eat and you'll be famous."

I thanked the man and went to the entrance lobby to wait for my father. I was absolutely crushed by the news that the migration of Kites might have been a once in a lifetime event and I'd missed out in catching one. If only I had gone home for my net.

The Jamaican Kite Swallowtails didn't migrate again while I was in Jamaica, and I never saw one flying around though you can be sure I looked. That might have been the end of the story for me, but two days later, when I was cycling home from school, I saw something by the side of the road and stopped to take a look. It was a dead Kite Swallowtail being dragged along by little black ants. I picked it up and dusted off the indignant scavengers. They had eaten out the body, reducing the magnificent butterfly to a shell and dried wings, but I cupped it in one hand and walked my bike home, jubilant.

It is the only example I have of *Graphium marcellinus* in my collection, and though strictly I did not collect it, I am still proud of it. Its colours have faded over the years, but the sight of it brings back those intense feelings of initial excitement, later disappointment and eventual triumph.

Jack's Hill Tails

I found Jack's Hill quite by accident, though I later found out it is quite a famous butterfly collecting site. My parents were out for a drive and I tagged along, happy to sit in the back seat of our Austin and stare out at the countryside. Sometimes we would stop at a small hill restaurant for lunch and my parents would sit and drink wine on the veranda and I'd wander around looking at the flowering shrubs with their escort of hummingbirds or watch the gaudy-throated *Anolis* lizards on the tree trunks or chase the blue and grey Ground Lizards down gravel paths until they disappeared under bushes. Other times, we would just stop by the side of the road under the shade of a tree and enjoy a cool soda drink.

On this particular day, we had explored the dry and dusty hills to the east of Kingston and were heading homeward over a modest ridge known as Jack's Hill. We stopped near the top where the road widened to include a narrow lookout and saw the city spread out beneath us. A few minutes looking at the scenery were enough for me, so I left my parents enjoying the view and, arming myself with a stick, went exploring.

The air was dusty and filled with an indefinable fragrance of red earth and spices. The sun beat down on dry vegetation splashed by the occasional small red and yellow flowers I had come to recognise as *Lantana*. Butterflies often visited these blooms so I paid them special attention and was rewarded by sightings of the little yellow and white butterflies, *Eurema daira* and *Eurema lisa*, and one of the cloudless sulphur butterflies, but I could not be sure of its identity without catching it. I did not have my net with me. I also saw what I'm fairly sure was a Church's skipper, but it only alighted for a moment before flying off. It might have been the commoner tailed skipper and again, I was angry at myself for forgetting my net.

53

"Max, time to go," my mother called, so I turned back toward the car and as I turned, I saw it--a huge black and yellow butterfly flying straight down the hillside toward me and over the road at about head height before disappearing over some low scrubby trees below the road.

I gaped; sure I had seen the legendary Homerus swallowtail. I let out a scream of excitement and went running back to my parents babbling about my sighting. They listened patiently, and my father even consented to be dragged back to the spot so I could show him exactly where it had flown and where I was standing and how I could have caught it if only I had brought my net.

My father smiled. "That'll teach you to forget it. Now come on, we have to get home." I followed him back to the car, walking backward, hoping to catch another glimpse of this fabulous creature.

On the way home, I pleaded with my father to bring me back up to Jack's Hill, this time with my net, but he shook his head.

"There's not much up here; it's too dry. You can't expect me to sit in the car all day while you run around the hillside."

"You could drop me off and pick me up later."

"Max, you're only eleven," my mother said. "You're far too young to be out here alone."

"Aw, Mum, I'd be fine. What could happen if I stayed near the road?"

All my father would say further on the matter was, "We'll see."

The following Saturday I asked to be dropped off at the Institute of Jamaica in downtown Kingston. My memories of the building were of almost deserted rooms filled with all the treasures a young boy could desire. I often went there with my friend Steve Riley, but this time I went alone. My parents dropped me off at the museum and said they pick me up in an hour's time. I went straight to the butterfly cabinets and pulled out the glass-topped drawer containing the swallowtails.

I gazed avariciously at the Homerus swallowtails, trying to decide if the creature I had glimpsed at Jack's Hill could be the same as this magnificent butterfly. *Papilio homerus* is a huge butterfly with a bold pattern of black and yellow with hints of blue and red scales on its hind wings. I thirsted for the opportunity to catch one of my own.

An older Jamaican entered the room and smiled when he saw me. I recognised the Institute of Jamaica armband he wore and plucked up the courage to talk to him.

"Please, sir, do you know much about butterflies?"

"Perhaps," he replied. "What do you want to know?"

"I think I saw a Homerus at Jack's Hill last week. Could it have been one?"

The man asked me to describe exactly what I saw and what the surrounding countryside was like. When I finished, he stroked his chin thoughtfully. "I'm sorry to disappoint you," he said, "But I don't think it was Homerus. It is too dry at Jack's Hill and Homerus flies slowly, following streams or the edge of forest."

My face fell. "Oh. I really thought it was."

"Well, there is another swallowtail it might be, and while it is perhaps not as lovely as Homerus, it is nearly as difficult to find."

"What is it, sir?"

"*Papilio thersites*." He opened another drawer in the cabinet.

I saw several large yellow swallowtails under a label that identified them as Thersites. "But they're yellow," I said. "The one I saw had a lot of black as well."

"The Thersites swallowtail is sexually dimorphic," the man said. He saw my look of incomprehension and explained. "The males and females look completely different. All those yellow ones are males and fairly common--I'm sure you've seen them around Kingston--but these big black and yellow ones here..." He pointed. "...are females. I think you might have seen one of those up at Jack's Hill."

I examined the pinned specimens of female *P. thersites* carefully, and admitted to myself that what I saw on Jack's Hill could have been one of them. This beautiful swallowtail was smaller than the Homerus and with finer, more delicate looking wings. It was mostly black in colour with thin bands of yellow and scallops of blue and red on its hind wings. I looked from female to male and back again, marvelling at the difference between the genders.

"I suppose it must have been one of these." Disappointment tinged my voice.

"Don't be too upset," the man said with a laugh. "If you can catch a female Thersites it would be a big feather in your cap. Imagine how a male and female together will look in your collection." He left me looking at the butterflies and went off to do whatever it was I had diverted him from.

My parents picked me up from the museum and I immediately asked my father if I could go up to Jack's Hill again.

"There's female Thersites up there and the man at the museum said I should try to get one."

"Did he indeed? I'll have to have a word with him about leading my son astray."

I could see a faint smile on my father's face so I did not worry too much that he'd carry through his threat. "Please, Dad. Mum?"

"I think it's too dangerous to be wandering alone. If you're with him, Jay, I won't worry." (Jay was my father's first name, short for James. My first name is James also, but I'm called Max, short for Maxwell which is my middle name.)

"All right," my father said. "Next Saturday we'll go up for an hour. How's that?"

"Great, Dad. Thanks."

Next Saturday, we drove up to the Jack's Hill Road lookout. I literally hurled myself from the car, butterfly net in hand, and my father had to call me back and admonish me to keep to the sides of the road and look both ways before crossing. I was never to run out after a butterfly and... By this point I was squirming and darting surreptitious glances along the roadside in case my quarry was even then flying by. My father evidently saw my discomfort, for he finished his lecture telling me I had an hour and to listen for the beep of the car horn when it was time to go home.

I dashed off and started patrolling the sides of the road, scouring the dry hillsides for movement and intensely studying the small patches of *Lantana* flowers. I caught a few small butterflies that I already had in my collection-- Satyrs, Barred Sulphurs, Hairstreaks and saw a few skippers of whose identity I could not be sure--but did not even see a swallowtail. The minutes marched by and though I did not have a watch, I knew that my hour would be up soon. I started to think about how I could draw my time out.

My father was a man who would brook no nonsense or blatant time-wasting, but he would accept a reasonable excuse. If I was within sight of the car when my time was up, I would have to return immediately, but if I was out of sight, I might be able to plead uncertainty when the car horn sounded. After all, there was a little traffic on the hill road; a car horn could be somebody else. I was dicing with a belt across my backside if I misjudged it too badly, but I thought it worth the risk.

I sauntered off up the road and was soon out of sight of the lookout. A hundred yards or so further on, I came to a dirt road that angled off across the hillside and caught a glimpse of a house further along the road. I set off along it, eyes peeled for swallowtails. Fifty yards along the road, the dry scrub and bracken on the hillside ended and a patch of thin woodland intersected the cutting.

As I reached it, a flash of yellow caught my eye and I flicked my net out almost without thinking. Something hit the folds of material and started thrashing about. I folded the net over and dropped it to the ground, leaping on my prize. It was a male Thersites, but in such bad condition I felt sorry for it, so I let it go. The panicked insect raced back up the hill and disappeared from sight, but the capture had raised my hopes. *Papilio thersites* was on Jack's Hill and I reasoned that if a male was here, a female might be too.

A horn beeped in the distance, and a few moments later it sounded again. I uttered the worst swear word I knew--'Bother'--and started back toward the main road. By the time I reached it, my father was getting heavy-handed on the horn so I quickened my pace, though I still managed to snag a Julia just before I got back to the car. I saw my father's expression and decided to get in first.

"Sorry, Dad, I was so far away--there's a road up there and a little patch of forest and there was a Thersites, and I caught it but it was so badly damaged I let it go and I'm sure there are others up there and..."

"All right, all right, you're here now. Hop in and show me what you caught." He peered at my little collecting tin and asked the names of a couple of the showier ones. I told him, and after a few minutes he was smiling. I risked a question.

"Could I come up again, Dad? That road looked like a really good place. There's even a house along there so I'd be safe. You could drop me off and pick me up a couple of hours later."

My father just looked at me. "We'll see," was all he said.

He must have decided I would be safe enough as he took me back up to Jack's Hill two weeks later. When he dropped me off at the bottom of the side road he said, "The house up there belongs to a Mr and Mrs Chambers. I've spoken with them on the telephone. If you're in trouble, go to them, but otherwise don't bother them. I'll be back in..." He looked at his watch. "...three hours and twenty minutes--at two o'clock."

I waved goodbye and turned to survey my little kingdom, planning how I was going to examine every bit of it, and imagining the wonderful species I would catch, including the female Thersites.

If it was that, I reminded myself.

First I walked the length of the road, passing the white-walled Chambers' house on the uphill side near the end. I looked up at the blank windows but saw neither Mr nor Mrs, so continued to the end and looked over the crushed and buried vegetation where the road grader had pushed the excess dirt and gravel. There were a scattering of *Lantana* bushes growing in the disturbed soil but I saw no butterflies.

I walked back past the house, examining the edges of the scrubby woodland below and above the road and was rewarded with a glimpse of a brown butterfly in the treetops. At least there were some butterflies here; it was not a complete waste of time. By the time I reached the main road I had seen a dozen more, but nothing I did not already have. I caught a couple, sweeping my net gently over skippers nectaring on Jamaican vervain plants by the roadside, just to keep my hand and eye in for the main event.

The edges of the woodland seemed the most promising area so I scrambled up the bank and pushed my way through the thick bracken fern that covered the hillside. I saw small yellow *Eurema* and little brown Satyrs within the woodland and pressed on, confident that I was on the right track. The ferns gave way to scrubby vegetation and I hauled myself up onto a grass-covered ridge with a dense patch of *Lantana* bushes where the upper edge of the woodland nudged the ridge.

Butterflies abounded--little blues and yellows, large yellows and whites, darting skippers, lazy swallowtails and colourful flashes from a variety of nymphs. I even saw a Jamaican Admiral and a Leafwing. I later learned that many butterflies display behaviour called 'hilltopping', in which males gather on hill tops and ridges. At the time, I was just amazed and started catching everything I could. I only kept a fraction of what I caught because I was looking for the best specimens, and my tin only filled slowly.

After an hour or two (judged by the position of the sun), I was hot and thirsty and had collected everything I wanted from the butterflies on offer. I wondered whether to wait in case something else turned up or go looking elsewhere. I still wanted my female Thersites, which had not put in an appearance, but in the end, thirst tipped the balance. I slipped and ran down the hill slope to the road and trudged along to the house, where I knocked on the door until the Chambers' Jamaican maid answered.

"Hello," I said. "May I have a drink of water please?"

The woman looked at me with suspicion written in every line of her face. "Wha' you wan', eh?"

"Water. May I have a drink of water please?" I mimed the action of raising a glass to my lips. "Mr and Mrs Chambers said I could." Well, I suppose thirst could be viewed as trouble.

"Mizz Chambers no' here. Go 'way." She closed the door.

I wondered whether to try again and then noticed a garden tap. *They won't mind, surely?* I turned it on, splashing cool water over my face and hair, drinking great draughts of it, before the front door burst open and the maid came running out holding a broom.

"Yu go 'way, or I call p'lice," she yelled.

I grabbed my net and ran back onto the road and, as she followed me out, I dashed away toward the main road.

Well, that settles it, I thought. *I can't walk up and down the road now; I'll have to go back up to the ridge.* I didn't want to risk the police being called. I shuddered as I imagined my father's response to his son being arrested.

I scrambled to the top again and looked around, conscious that time was passing and my father would be back soon. There was no change in the types of butterflies foraging around the *Lantana*, so I walked along the ridge top, hoping to find something else. I saw only the usual Satyrs, skippers and grass yellows until I came to a steep-sided gully that ran down to the main road which I could just see through gaps in the trees. The gully itself was so steep that the canopy of trees growing in the bottom of it was at my height on the ridge and no more than three or four paces away. One of the trees was covered in tiny white blossoms, but I had no idea as to its identity. However, butterflies obviously liked it, as several were flitting around the canopy, foraging for nectar.

I started drooling. I could see some Danaids and three types of swallowtail--a *Papilio pelaus*, a *Battus polydamas* and a male Thersites. I edged closer to the drop and stretched my net out, but I could only reach the outermost patches of flowers. I stood ready and stared at the butterflies as they hopped and flitted over the blossoms, now coming closer, now drifting away. Minutes drifted by. The male Thersites flew off. I saw a nice Queen and snagged it, transferring it to my collecting tin with my eyes still peeled for new visitors.

Two black swallowtails with yellow flashes swooped down the gully and hovered over the flowering tree and my heart lurched. One was the 'Orange Dog' swallowtail, *Papilio andraemon*, but the other was a female Thersites-- there was no doubt in my mind. I shouted with excitement and edged out as far as I dared, but keeping my net to one side so as not to alarm them. I waited; fidgeting with impatience as the two butterflies slowly worked their way across the canopy, the Thersites closer to me.

A car horn blew--my father had arrived to pick me up, and I knew I had only a few minutes grace. I looked away, through the trees to the main road and then back to the canopy. The female Thersites inched closer, wings fluttering as its proboscis delved into the little white flowers. It was at a clump I had judged to be at the outermost reach of my net. The horn blew again, impatiently, distracting me once more and I knew time had run out. I swept my net around, leaning as far out as I could. The butterflies lifted away in alarm, but as I overbalanced I saw my net envelop the nearer one.

I fell with a yell, clutching the handle of my net as I plummeted through the canopy, hitting branches on the way down and landing on stony soil and tree roots at the bottom. Pain flared in my ankles and I put my hand up to my face, feeling blood trickling from a gash on my forehead. Then I saw my prize struggling in the folds of the net and I forgot my wounds. I leaned over and pinched the thorax of the beautiful swallowtail before transferring its still-twitching body reverently to a collecting tin that was dented from my fall but still intact.

I heard my father calling and shouted back, before hobbling down the gully to where it debouched on the main road a mere twenty yards from the side road where my father had parked.

"I got it," I said with a grin, holding up my tin triumphantly.

My father stared in horror at my blood-smeared face, a rip in my shirt and leaves in my untidy hair, but as soon as he found out I was mostly uninjured, he laughed. "Who's been dragging you through the bushes?"

"I fell through a tree, Dad, but I got it--a female Thersites."

"Good boy. Now hop in and we'll see if we can't make you look a bit more presentable before we get home. Your mother will have a fit if she sees you like that."

I tidied myself and washed the blood off my face with some water in a bottle in the car's boot and as we drove home I opened up my collecting tin to gloat over my capture. I gently eased first a pencil and then a finger between its folded wings and slowly opened them, my mouth falling open as I recognised the pattern of yellow and black on its unblemished wings. It was the Andraemon, not the female Thersites. I sifted frantically through the other paper envelopes in my tin, but I knew already that it was not there. Somehow, when the car's horn sounded and I turned my head, I had mixed up the butterflies and caught the wrong one.

I felt like crying, but as I looked at the dusting of yellow and black scales on my fingers I realised that a *Papilio andraemon*, particularly in such good condition, was worth having. The butterfly would not have died in vain as it would join my collection and I would be proud of it. A female Thersites would come later, I was sure.

I did not tell my parents of my mistake, and my father did not ask after it, having other things on his mind, I suppose. He took me back up to Jack's Hill several times over the next year, both by myself and with my friend Steve Riley, but I never saw another female Thersites. I had had my chance and missed it, but I preferred that to never having seen one at all.

Port Royal

"I have to go out to the airport to collect a package. Want to come?"

It was the school holidays and I had nothing much planned. My best friend Steven Riley was away and I had been contemplating cycling up to the Hope Gardens and trawling through the flowerbeds for new butterflies. My father's question interested me.

"Where's the airport?"

"Out on the Palisadoes."

The Palisadoes was a long sandy spit that ran out to where the old pirate haven of Port Royal had sat. The spit almost enclosed the large sheltered harbour that had helped Kingston become one of the most prized of British possessions in the West Indies. I had never been out there and knew nothing of its vegetation or butterfly riches.

"Can I bring my net?"

My father shrugged. "If you want, but I don't know how much time we'll have for catching butterflies."

We drove south through Kingston and then east along the coast road to the little town of Harbour View. I was bubbling with excitement, staring out over the dashboard at the sandy spit that was looming up on our right. The turnoff was signposted and soon we were cruising along the narrow two-lane road with the Caribbean Sea on our left and the white-capped harbour on our right. In places, the spit was so narrow I could have thrown a rock from harbour to sea, and the scrubby vegetation narrowed to a thin strip along the road sandwiched between two beaches. I kept my eyes peeled for butterflies but saw nothing.

Abruptly, the spit widened out into broad flat land spotted with mangrove-lined lagoons. I saw an aeroplane approaching over the harbour, its wings rocking and dipping as it came into land. I have always had a love of air travel, having flown from the age of six in the 'Viscount' and 'Elizabethan' of British European Airways, from Dusseldorf in Germany to London and back again at the start and end of each school term. As I grew older and 'more responsible' (aged eight to ten), I even travelled alone. I craned my neck to keep the plane in view as it crabbed toward the runway, a puff of smoke erupting from its tyres as it touched down.

"Can we stay and watch the planes land and takeoff?" I asked.

"I thought you wanted to catch butterflies?"

"Well, yes, but I like planes too."

"I'll be a few minutes collecting my package, so you can watch from the observation deck while you wait."

We parked and entered the airport building. My father found the stairs to the observation deck and pointed the way. I raced off and found myself a position in the open air where I could see the runway and the tarmac where two or three planes were parked, loading and unloading freight and passengers. I stared at everything, but especially at a huge aircraft off to one side. People were boarding it, walking across the tarmac and climbing sets of stairs set against doors at the front and back.

"Excuse me, sir," I asked a man standing nearby. "Do you know what type of plane that is?"

The man looked and said, "It's a Boeing 707. Never seen one before?"

I shook my head and went back to the railing, devouring the details of this '707'. It was long and sleek with swept-back wings and two large pods under each wing. There were no propellers, so I knew this must be a jet. I'd heard of jets before, of course, and remembered the British de Havilland 'Comet', especially the crashes that plagued that aircraft. I wondered whether this '707' was any safer.

My father arrived, with a thick envelope under his arm. "Ready to go?"

I pointed at the jet and told him what it was. "Passengers have just finished boarding," I explained. "Can we wait and watch it take off? Please? It shouldn't be long."

We waited and watched as the stairs were pulled away and the doors closed. The jet sat there for several minutes and then a whining noise gradually grew louder and a gust of hot air swirled over us. It started moving and taxied around the end of the terminal building toward the runway.

"I can't see it anymore," I cried. "Can we go down and watch?"

"Be patient, Max." My father smiled and pointed. "We can see the runway from here, so we'll be able to see it take off."

More waiting. We could hear the muted whine of the jet engines but couldn't understand why nothing was happening. I started fidgeting. My father tapped me on the shoulder and pointed out over the harbour to where another propeller-driven plane was slowly approaching.

"They're waiting for that plane to land first."

We watched the other plane land and taxi off the runway toward the terminal. As it cleared the main strip an escalating roar washed over us. I automatically looked up at the clear sky before realising it was the '707' taking off. It came into view, accelerating so fast down the runway I opened my mouth in astonishment, and just before it reached the end, tilted back and leapt into the air, climbing steeply over the sea. Trails of smoke issued from its four engines, shredding and dissipating in the stiff breeze. The jet, already small, banked to the right and headed back toward the land, still climbing as the wind made the roar of its takeoff rise and fall. I yelled with the excitement of it all and several people looked round. My father ushered me away and we descended through the terminal to the car park.

"That was fabulous," I said. "I'd love to go on one."

"Maybe one day. Now, do you want to try your hand at butterflying or go to Port Royal?"

"Um, both?"

"Port Royal it is."

I was only a little disappointed as I had found out a lot about Port Royal from reading Aspinall and other books, and from exhibits in the Institute of Jamaica. After Britain had ousted the Spanish from the island in the 1650s, the provisional capital had been set up at Port Royal on the end of the Palisadoes. The port of Kingston attracted pirates, especially such characters as Henry Morgan and 'Calico Jack' Rackham, and it soon became a den of thieves and drunkards where murders were committed daily. In 1692, a massive earthquake hit, destroying the town and killing half the population. A good part of the town sank into the sea and it was said that when the wind and sea conditions were right, you could still hear bells tolling beneath the waves. I wasn't sure I believed that last part, but I was excited at the prospect of going there.

Port Royal lay only a few miles past the airport, so it did not take us long to get there. There wasn't much to see at first. The town may have had a rich and interesting history, but when we visited, it was little more than a fishing village with a few stalls selling souvenirs. That was fine with my father as he loathed touristy places, preferring to delve into the history of a place at his leisure. Today, he had an impatient little boy in tow, so he probably didn't expect too much.

We parked where the main road came to an end. My father advised me to leave my butterfly net in the car and his expression made me disinclined to argue the point. He strode off up the nearest street with me trotting behind, looking this way and that. The spit of land is only about a third of a mile wide at that point, so it did not take us long to reach the harbour's edge. I gazed expectantly at the choppy water, hoping to see bits of buildings poking up above the water. I was disappointed--the streets did not even run down into the sea.

"I thought there would be more to see," I said.

"It's been over two hundred and fifty years, Max. They cleaned up and rebuilt, so you won't see anything obvious. We should go along to Fort Charles. I hear they have a museum there."

We walked along the foreshore, past shanty shops selling cold drinks and jerked meat, then angled over onto the narrow beach where fishermen were repairing nets and painting boats. Fort Charles itself was a bit of a let-down, though I'm not really sure what I was expecting--a stone castle bristling with guns or a pirate den, I think. Either way, it displayed little of the fire and romance of those days. Tired brickwork and more modern whitewashed buildings greeted us. There were guns--cannon--but only a few, pointing at nothing in particular.

We went into the little museum but I quickly lost interest, thinking how much better it would be if it had displays of butterflies rather than old bottles, pottery and a few corroded instruments hauled from the harbour by divers. My father insisted on dragging me round the exhibits and reading out some of the information displayed on plaques and posters. I found out that although the earthquake of 1692 was most famous for destroying Port Royal, the town had been rebuilt and then destroyed again in another earthquake in 1907.

I yawned, thinking of butterflies. "Can we go now?"

"This is history, Max, and more than that, it even relates to our family a little bit."

I perked up. Our family had been pirates? I stared at the display in front of me.

"The fort was built in the 1650s and was originally called Fort Cromwell, its name being changed later to Fort Charles when Charles II came to the throne," my father read out. "You've heard of Oliver Cromwell?"

"Mmm...a pirate?" I hazarded.

My father snorted. "What do they teach you at school? Oliver Cromwell was Lord Protector of England. He, and others, overthrew the monarchy and made England a Republic for a few years. One of our ancestors, Major-General Robert Overton was one of Cromwell's Generals. I have a book at home, by Maurice Ashley, which deals with this period in history. It even has a chapter on our ancestor. I'll let you read it, if you take care of it."

So I was not descended from a fierce buccaneer of the Spanish Main after all. I tried to look enthusiastic. I faithfully read the chapter on Robert Overton but wasn't too impressed with the man. He seemed to change his mind and allegiance a lot. My father gave me the book when I left Jamaica (more of that later) and I still have it in my overcrowded bookshelves.

I suffered through the rest of the museum tour, fidgeting and staring through the windows at the blue skies and palm trees, and eventually we walked out into the bright sunshine.

"Where now, Dad? Butterflies?"

"Let's finish with the history of the place first."

Back through the streets of Port Royal we went, to Church Street, where we found St Peter's Church and a particular gravestone that had been referred to in the museum. This was the grave of Lewis Galdy, who had been caught in the great earthquake and miraculously survived. We stood and looked at the cracked and stained tombstone with its carved skull and waves.

'Here Lies the Body of LEWIS GALDY who departed this Life at Port Royal on the 22$^\text{d}$ December 1739 Aged 80. He was Born at Montpelier in France but left that Country for his Religion and came to settle in this Island where He was swallowed up in the Great Earthquake in the Year 1692 and By the Providence of God was by another Shock thrown into the Sea and Miraculously saved by swimming until a Boat took him up. He Lived many Years after in great Reputation. Beloved by all and much Lamented at his Death.'

"They've misspelled 'Lies'," I said.

"That's how they spelled it in those days." My father looked around at the small graveyard and church for a few moments, and then sighed. "Come on, Max, one more stop and you can indulge your hobby."

"Where to?"

"Gallows Point." He smiled down at me. "Is that exciting enough for you?"

"They hanged pirates there? Wow!"

We retraced our steps, past Fort Charles and on toward the end of the Palisadoes sand spit. My father asked me if I was thirsty and I nodded, so we stopped at a stall and bought two sodas from the man's icebox. The cold, sweet fizzy liquid was welcome and we drank as we walked. My father belched loudly and I giggled, forcing out one myself. It was a moment of camaraderie that I treasured.

The streets ended and we crossed some open land toward the mudflats and dense mangrove stands. My father gestured toward the vegetation.

"We can't go in there, but that's where the gallows would have stood."

I stared, screwing up my eyes in concentration as I tried to imagine what a gallows looked like. I swallowed, thinking of a man choking to death at the end of a rope. Their crimes must have been dreadful to be punished like that.

"The infamous pirates Charles Vane and 'Calico Jack' Rackham were hanged here, along with many others," my father said. "Happily, those days are far behind us."

Just then, a rather tattered and faded butterfly flew past and I turned to stare after it. I didn't know what it was, but it looked a little like a Painted Lady, but most likely the American species rather than the European one I was used to. I wanted it and took a step forward before I remembered I had left my net in the car.

My father saw how my attention had been distracted and sighed. "You know, Max," he said, "There'll come a day when you'll wish you'd paid more attention to the rich history of these islands."

I only half heard him. "Can I go butterflying now?"

We returned to the car and I retrieved my net. While my father sat in the car listening to the radio and drinking another soda, I returned to the wasteland and searched for the Painted Lady. It had vanished, perhaps winging its way across to Kingston, but I did find a couple of other butterflies. Nothing special--a Pygmy Blue or two and a White Small Sulphur, *Eurema messalina*. I already had the Sulphur, so I let it go. I did not have the Pygmy Blue and debated whether to add it to my collection or not. In the end, I didn't, not because I didn't want it, but because it was so very small. I liked bigger butterflies anyway and the very small ones were difficult to set out--difficult for a young clumsy boy anyway. I walked away and later regretted it as I was never able to find it again.

I happily returned to butterflying in Kingston without a care, but my father was right. Years later, I developed a thirst for history and wished that I had made more of my opportunities of experiencing it first-hand in the remnants of pirate-haunted Port Royal.

Blood & Bananas

I had seen the Banana Butterfly many times in Hope Gardens in Kingston, but never managed to catch one there. They fly fast and erratically in the denser wooded areas and seem to disappear when they get close to tree trunks. After a while I found that they alighted on rough-barked trees like mangoes and sat head down in the shade camouflaged by their striped undersides. They were very alert and I seldom got close enough even to swing my net in a futile effort before they sped off into the shadows.

The butterfly itself is *Colobura dirce*, but because of the curve of bright yellow splashed on the dark brown upper surface, I and my butterfly collecting friends called it the Banana Butterfly. Later, I found out that Jamaicans often called it by this same name because it frequented banana plantations, drawn to the sweet smell of ripe and rotting fruit.

My first encounter with a Banana Butterfly was soon after our arrival in Kingston. My parents have always liked parks and Hope Gardens was recommended to us. We drove up the long park entrance to the car park and set off on foot. In those early days I had not yet become an avid collector of butterflies but was content to trot along after my parents as they admired the flower beds and stately specimen trees and mounds of profusely flowering bougainvillea. There were peacocks crying mournfully in the wooded areas and many species of birds that I could not identify. I loved the hummingbirds though and could watch them all day as they dipped and hovered, sipping nectar from gaudily coloured flowers.

There were butterflies too, but on my first visit to the Gardens could do little more than classify them according to colour. Actually, colour is a good way to classify butterflies anyway. Yellow and white ones are often members of the family called Pieridae, little blue ones belong to the family Lycaenidae, large gaudy ones with tails on their hind wings are Papilionidae or 'swallowtails', and little fast-moving brown and orange insects are the Hesperiidae, commonly called 'darts' or 'swifts'. The most obvious butterflies, to my unpractised eyes at least, were members of the fifth great butterfly family, the Nymphalidae or nymphs. They could not be easily categorized by colour as they were every possible colour, but they were mostly medium-sized butterflies with a bold, brash nature, and were found everywhere. There are exceptions to all these family generalisations, but they are a good starting point if you are learning about butterflies.

I had come across nymphs before I went to Jamaica, having seen red admirals, tortoiseshells, peacocks and painted ladies swarm around buddleia bushes in Germany, and spotted the same butterflies and a few others in England--brown ones with eyes on their wings--the wall, the meadow brown and speckled wood.

Here in Hope Gardens I saw black and yellow-striped heliconids, long-winged orange Julias, silver-streaked Diones, swift-flying dagger wings, the stately monarch and the leaf butterflies that flitted through the undergrowth in shades of orange only to disappear from sight as they alighted in a bush. The Banana Butterfly is another nymph, but at that time was only glimpsed.

As with most of the butterflies I saw, I visited the Institute of Jamaica and made a bee-line for the butterfly cabinets, staring for hours over the glass-fronted shelves, intermittently wiping away drool as I daydreamed about one day catching each elusive species.

My father was a busy man, being manager of an insurance company, but he made time for his family, and was sometimes willing to ferry me and a friend to various places so we could rush around with butterfly nets if I asked him. Occasionally, he volunteered to take us.

"Max, I have to take some papers round to a client in Yallahs. Do you want to come? We could have lunch at some shady spot afterward and you could hunt butterflies."

"Sounds great, Dad. Where's Yallahs?"

"East along the coast from Kingston."

I called my best butterflying buddy, Steve who, as I have said, was a couple of years younger than me, and made him the offer. After asking his mother, he quickly accepted. We picked him up on the way and Dad drove us down to the coast road and headed east toward Yallahs.

The coast road in those days was narrow and did not carry much traffic. The day was warm but a cooling breeze blew in from the sea, and we two boys wound our windows down and leaned out, soaking in the sights and sounds and smells. The Blue Mountains are in the eastern part of the island, and the land rose steeply from the coast, allowing only a thin strip of land for our passage.

We passed through small towns labelled with imaginative names like 'Six Mile', 'Eleven Mile' and 'Bull Pen' and happened upon the town of Yallahs by mid-morning. Dad found the address of the person he had to deliver the papers to, and we waited in the car, checking over our equipment. Not that we had much to check over--our equipment consisted of a white muslin butterfly net, a few paper folders and a tin for storing our dead butterflies. In my case it was a dark blue Player's Navy Cut cigarette tin. The folders were small squares of paper folded into overlapping triangular envelopes for isolating each butterfly we caught. If we did not store them separately, they would rub against each other and get damaged.

My father emerged from the house and we set off to find a suitable place to lunch and hunt butterflies. The coast road from Kingston to Yallahs had not included many likely butterfly spots so we prevailed on my father to drive us further round the island.

We came to a stretch of road where the land rose steeply, covered in vegetation, with short roads leading off the main one. My father said the place was known as Green Wall. He stopped at a few places and Steve and I got out investigating for a few minutes, but none of the sites showed much promise so we persuaded my father to carry on round the coast.

A few miles further on, we found what we thought might be the perfect spot--a small stream fell down the steep hillside and gathered its strength in a small grass-lined pool before rushing under the road to the sea. A grassy patch encouraged little yellow and blue butterflies, and a grove of mango trees promised other insect treasures. My father pulled off the road and we piled out with our nets.

"Hey, where're you going?" my father asked. "It's time for lunch."

"Please dad, just a few minutes. We have to see what's here."

He let us go with a smile and settled down on a blanket in the shadow of the car to read his newspaper while Steve and I explored our little kingdom. The little yellow and blue butterflies proved to be common ones that we already had in our collections, so we explored the stream banks, hoping for nymphs in the lush vegetation. We saw a few brown butterflies but nothing came near enough for us to even swing a net at, so we climbed back up to look at the mango grove.

The air was cool and shadowed beneath the heavy foliage and nothing moved as we crunched slowly through the leaf litter. Then a flash of yellow, instantly vanishing, caught our attention. We moved deeper into the grove and saw it again, a flit, a flash, disappearing on a tree trunk.

"It's a Banana," Steve called out excitedly. He ran forward, net raised and slashed at the butterfly as it whipped past him and away.

We followed, and disturbed it again. I was nearest this time so I crept up on it and swung at it as it sat head down on the trunk of a large mango tree. My net crashed into the trunk and it slipped to one side and flitted off. This time, another Banana Butterfly rose from a nearby tree and intercepted ours, the two insects spiralling upward into the branches as if dog-fighting. After a bit they came down again and the hunt was on as we tracked down a butterfly apiece.

I shut out everything around me, grasping my net firmly in both hands and creeping through the leaf litter after my quarry. It would sit head-down on a tree trunk and apparently watch me as I inched closer, waiting until the last moment before flitting off to another trunk. After a few fruitless stalks, I wondered if it could see the white of my net too plainly, so I held it behind my back until I got close enough to swipe at it. A miss. I tried again and missed again.

"Max, Steve, lunch time!"

I bit my lip in frustration. I could put off answering my father for a few minutes but I hated the thought of giving up on my butterfly after all my trouble. Just then, Steve uttered a cry of triumph.

"Got it!" he yelled.

I cursed innocuously, not having learned any juicier language yet and edged closer to my own butterfly. Just before I swung my net, I had a thought. Every time I had swung and missed, the butterfly had escaped over the top of my net. Perhaps I should try something different. I lowered the net and moved it closer until it was just below the butterfly on the trunk, with the open mouth facing up. I took a deep breath, concentrating hard on my quarry.

"Look, Max, look! I got one." Steve came hurrying toward me and I saw a quick flash of yellow as the butterfly slapped its wings open, launching itself into the air. I snapped my net upward, despairingly, and saw the butterfly enveloped by the folds of material. I leapt forward with a triumphant yell and pinched the butterfly's thorax between thumb and forefinger. I gently removed it from the net and examined it, Steve peering over my shoulder.

"It's a beauty," he said. "Almost unmarked."

"What's yours like?"

"A bit tatty, but it'll do until I can get another one." Steve showed me his own prize, and I gloated over my own catch.

"Lunch!" my father called again, so we hurried back to the clearing with our prizes.

Dad had set out a blanket and a wicker lunch basket with a cooked chicken, some salad and bread and butter. We made ourselves sandwiches and sat around chewing and admiring our Banana Butterflies. We recounted each chase in the smallest detail, exaggerating our own cunning and patience with each telling. Steve closed the lid of his tin and tucked it away in the car, but I kept mine open, feasting my eyes hungrily on the perfect shape of its wings and its bright, fresh colours. I imagined how I was going to mount it, and how it would look in my fledgling collection.

"Who's for some Coke?" my father said, brandishing a large glass bottle of the beverage. We chorused our affirmations and my father searched the picnic basket for the bottle opener and then, frowning, the boot of the car and the glove box--to no avail.

"Never mind," he said. "I can open it on the bumper."

Steve and I came to watch and my father's first effort was tentative and unsuccessful. He muttered and positioned the bottle cap near the lip of the bumper and poised the heel of his left hand above it.

"Dad," I said. "We don't need it. Let's wait until we get to a shop and buy an opener."

"Yes," Steve agreed. "That looks dangerous."

Dad laughed and brought his hand down sharply. Nothing happened, the cap staying firmly in place. He tried again, harder. The neck of the bottle shattered and his hand continued down, impaling itself on the glass shards. He dropped the bottle and I watched curiously as the spilling Coke mixed with my father's blood.

"Max, get a towel from the car." My father spoke calmly, eyeing the blood that was now pouring from a deep gash at the base of his thumb. I grabbed one, a large white fluffy towel, and he wrapped it tightly around his hand. Within seconds, the white towel bloomed patches of red.

"Throw everything in the car," he ordered. "I've got to get to a doctor or a hospital."

We hurried to obey, throwing blanket and basket, scraps of food and our nets into the boot and piling into the car as my father started up. He turned the vehicle and burst out onto the road, heading back toward Yallahs.

Within a mile or so, the towel wrapped around my father's hand was soaked in blood and was starting to drip onto the floor, as well as smearing the gearstick. We found another one and wrapped it gingerly around his gushing hand.

"There's no hospital in Yallahs," my father muttered. "I can't last until we get back to Kingston, so I'll have to find a doctor. God knows where, though."

"You'll have to ask somebody," I said. "Maybe the man you visited in Yallahs?"

My father nodded and concentrated on driving. He looked very pale and he was showing some difficulty driving a steady course. As we reached the outskirts of Yallahs, he stopped and leaned out of the window.

"Doctor?" he asked a passing man. "Do you know where...?"

"Down dere, mon," the man said, pointing.

"What street?"

The man shrugged. "Don' know. D'ers 'erbal woman. Secon' or t'ird one, I t'ink."

Dad nodded his thanks and let in the clutch, lurching up the street in the indicated direction, but stopped again when he saw a couple talking on a street corner.

"Is there a doctor here?" He held up his bloodied hand.

The woman gasped. "Not in Yallahs. Go t'rough to Poor Man's Corner and Somerset Street on lef'. Don' know the number. Doc' Edwar's."

"Thanks," my father called, already pulling out into the road.

We reached Poor Man's Corner only a mile or so further on and found Somerset Street, though we had to ask again before we found the doctor's surgery. Steve and I sat glumly outside on the step while my father was ushered inside. We were too worried to even explore our surroundings or even to talk, so I spent the next hour watching the *Anolis* lizards on the trunk of a breadfruit tree that shaded the surgery. They were the same lizards that frequented the trees at home, so I learned nothing new, but it was a good way of keeping my mind off the sight of my father apparently bleeding to death.

He emerged from the surgery pale and shaky with a huge bandage around his left hand. I ran to him and hugged him, while Steve just stared round-eyed.

"Does...does it hurt, sir?" Steve whispered.

My father smiled. "Not now. The doctor gave me a pain-killer before he sewed me up. I'll be fine."

We drove home slowly and it was not until we unpacked the car that I found I had left my Player's tobacco tin with my precious Banana Butterfly back at the picnic site at Green Wall. In our hurry to get my father to a doctor, I had completely forgotten the open tin which was probably still sitting on the grass. I told my father and he shook his head.

"I'm not driving all the way back there just for a butterfly, Max."

I bit my lip and nodded. "Yes, Dad."

He must have relented because a week later he handed me my blue cigarette tin at dinner. "I found this," he said. "Nothing in it though. I guess the ants must have got your butterfly."

I never returned to Green Wall, but I did manage to capture another almost-perfect specimen of the Banana Butterfly in the Hope Gardens a few months later. Even though it is not that first *Colobura dirce*, the sight of it still brings back memories of that blood-soaked day when my father almost bled to death.

Leafwing

"**L**eave it alone, I caught it!"
The words took me by surprise, as my friend Steve had always deferred to me on matters relating to butterflies.

"Get back, it's in my net, it belongs to me."

I looked at him and gaped. The butterfly was quite plainly not in his net but rather in mine, as the nets lay in a tangle on the road. Steve stood defiantly over them with a determined look on his face, his muscles tensed as if ready for a fight.

Now how on earth do two people get so excited over a butterfly? I should explain that we were youngsters, twelve and ten years old, and small things can seem of great importance to young boys in the grip of a favourite hobby. Actually, the butterfly itself was no small thing, as I'll get to in a moment.

Steve had always been my best friend. In the year I'd been in Kingston, I had found myself on the outer edge of what passed for a social life in the local school. I had a passion for collecting butterflies since the age of six in Germany, and a tropical island with all its exotic wild life was pure heaven for me. Few other children my age shared my passion though. In fact, Steve was almost the only person who took an interest in what I was doing. For a while he just tagged along behind me, talking about anything that came into his head. Then he started to get interested in what I was doing. He made himself a net and started catching his own.

We were never what you might call 'knowledgeable' about the local butterflies, but we recognised most of the common ones, and even what plants attracted some of the larger and gaudier species. Whenever we could, we would visit the Institute of Jamaica, a small, dark building in the middle of

Kingston. It had, I suppose, quite a reasonable selection of preserved wildlife of the island, and a number of artefacts of the now extinct Arawak Indians. What attracted us though, were two cabinets tucked away in a back room. Opening these would reveal hundreds of the most wonderful butterflies in glass-topped drawers, and we would spend hours looking at them and thirsting to own them. Whenever we caught a new species, we would be down there trying to match it to one in the collection.

It was here that we became familiar with some of Jamaica's rarities. The Blue Mountain Swallowtail, *Papilio homerus*, was one we gazed longingly at, but it was only found in a very restricted locale, so it wasn't likely we would be able to catch it. Others were more accessible and it was these we concentrated on; memorizing their colours and patterns. Latin names were a bit of a mouthful for most of our friends, but we made common names out of them that we could bandy about, and impress our parents. Size was another thing that impressed us. The larger the butterfly the better we liked it. One large brown and orange butterfly caught our attention early. It was called *Historis odius*, but its common name was Leafwing as the underside of a resting butterfly looked exactly like a dead leaf. It was a swift flyer, usually found around treetops, but it had one weakness. It loved rotting fruit, and could often be found under mango trees where it could be caught as it fed on the fermenting juices. Over the next few months, we managed to catch a few of these, and we became more interested in one of its relatives, *Historis acheronta*. Now this was a bit of a mouthful for common usage, but as it looked similar to the Leafwing, with two little tails on its hind wings, we called it the Tailed Leafwing. It had similar habits to the Leafwing, but was less common. This was our next target.

One day in late summer, my mother casually mentioned that we were all going up to San San Bay for a short holiday.

"Do you want to bring one of your friends?"

"Yes please--Steve," I said automatically, already thinking about what butterflies were to be found on the northeast coast.

We always stayed in small cottages at a resort called San San near the town of Port Antonio. These little cottages were surrounded by neatly arranged lawns and gardens and each had their own little scallop of beach. Palm trees provided shade, and hibiscus and bougainvillea hedges gave us privacy and colour. Fireflies blazed in the shrubbery at night. The butterfly fauna around the manicured gardens of the cottages was a bit sparse though, so we would need to look further afield.

After settling in and scouting the beach and paths nearby, Steve and I grabbed our nets and headed out. Crossing the main road we struck off into the low hills behind the resort. As we went inland, the dense vegetation of the coastal fringe changed and became sparser. It became drier too, and soon we were trudging up a dusty road with the summer sun hot on our heads. Grassy fields stretched on either side of us, with occasional patches of scrub or small trees. The countryside was deserted, save for a single turkey buzzard wheeling far above us in the burnt blue sky.

We saw nothing new, or even particularly interesting in the way of butterflies. A few small grass yellow butterflies wavered among the long grass at the side of the road, and a Soldier or two glided across the fields. We were contemplating turning back, when we spotted a large clump of mango trees up ahead, straddling the dusty road. We decided we would walk as far as the trees then rest a bit before turning back.

The shade beneath the trees was welcome after the sun, and we sat and tossed sticks at the *Anolis* lizards on the tree trunks. The sickly-sweet smell of rotting mangoes was strong. A flicker of yellow caught my attention. I got up, dusted off my shorts, and investigated.

"Banana!" I yelled. Steve leapt up and joined me, net at the ready.

It was a 'Banana' butterfly, *Colobura dirce*, a lovely dark brown one with a vivid yellow splash across its front wing. The underside was beautifully camouflaged, and at rest it blended into the tree trunk. Only when it flew did the yellow flash and catch the eye. Now this species is hard to catch, not only because it's hard to see when it's at rest, but also because it's difficult to get it into a net. You can either slam the net over it, risking breaking your net, or try sweeping close to the trunk, hoping to scare it into flight and capturing it as it takes off. We spent a vigorous ten minutes pursuing it around the grove, before I managed to trap it against a trunk. I killed it by squeezing its thorax and carefully placed it in my collecting tin.

Though we both had them in our collections, Steve was quite envious of my catch and we looked around for others. We spotted another, but lost it. Then Steve spotted a large brown butterfly, cunningly camouflaged, on a branch high above us. It looked like a Leafwing, so we threw sticks at it to get it to fly. If a butterfly is out of reach, there are two possible solutions. One is to wait patiently for it to fly nearer, but that is asking a lot of small boys eager for the chase. The other is to persuade it to move without actually chasing it off. We opted for this latter method, and it worked, after a fashion.

The butterfly dropped, flew rapidly between us and disappeared down the road. Something didn't look quite right about it though.

"I think that was a Tailed Leafwing," I breathed. "Its colour wasn't right, and it flew kinda funny."

"Oh, wow! Wouldn't that be something? Come on then, let's look for it!"

So we ran off in the direction it had disappeared, but it became obvious very quickly that we weren't going to find it out in the bright sun. We returned slowly to the shade of the trees, looking wistfully over our shoulders.

"Perhaps it'll come back," Steve said. "Leafwings sometimes do."

"Maybe. Let's spread out and have a look."

A minute later Steve cried out and swept frantically with his net. Something dark flitted past me before I could react. It disappeared out into the open again.

"It was the Tailed again! It did come back."

We stood at the edge of the shade looking excitedly down the road. After a few uneventful minutes, our attention wandered, and we started drifting around the edges of the mango grove. As I did so, I spotted a dark butterfly flying rapidly towards me across the grass.

"There it is," I cried, as it rushed by me. It flew up into the branches, settling just out of reach. It slowly opened and closed its wings, showing us the rich browns and amber of its upper surface. The tails were not apparent, but this was definitely not an ordinary Leafwing.

"It really is a Tailed," said Steve. "How are we going to catch it?"

"Well, one of us could throw something at it while the other one has a net ready."

"So who's going to have the net then?"

We looked at each other. We both wanted it, and we gripped our nets tighter. Neither of us was prepared to give up our chance at this rarity.

"I suppose we could take it in turns, but who'll go first?"

"I guess I will," I said.

"Okay, but you have to throw it close. No just chucking a stick and saying that's your turn done."

I gave him my best withering look and put my net down. My first throw made the butterfly twitch. Then it was Steve's turn. His throw came close, but it didn't move. My next one made it take off, swirling past my head and off into the open again.

We cursed and ran after it, but it disappeared. I walked back to where I had a view of the grassy fields, and was soon rewarded by the sight of it coming closer again. I knew approximately where it would enter the grove and positioned myself. Steve stood a few paces to my left. The Tailed Leafwing flew in straight and strong slightly to my right, perfectly positioned for my sweep, then at the last moment, faltered and swung to my left. My net was already moving though, and all I could do was despairingly follow the butterfly round as it flew between us. Steve let out a yell and threw his arm out in front of it, and both nets crashed together, before flying out of our hands into a jumble on the road.

"Damn!" I yelled. "I had it, why did you do that?"

"It was mine," Steve screamed back. "It was flying into my net."

"Well, it's gone now, and after that, I doubt it'll be back."

I went over to the nets, but as I reached down to pick mine up, a fluttering caught my eye.

"It's in the net!" I leapt forward, putting my hand over the folds of netting.

That's when our friendship faltered. Steve's reaction took me completely by surprise, and my delight at the capture slowly drained away as I saw him standing over me as I knelt with my hand over the struggling butterfly.

"Leave it alone, I caught it!"

"No, you didn't."

"Get back, it's in my net, it belongs to me."

"What?"

"I'm warning you," he said. "That's my butterfly. I caught it, and you're not taking it away."

I eased back onto my heels and looked up at him. Steve is smaller than me but wiry and quick. I knew that if it came to a fight, my extra height and weight would help me, but I didn't want to fight him. We had been best friends for a long time.

"But, Steve, the butterfly isn't in your net; it's under both of them." I looked quickly to check and saw that it was lying pressed against the dusty road with two wings under his net, but two wings and the body under mine. I reckoned that gave me a greater claim. I pressed my thumb against its body, feeling the crackle as I crushed its thorax, then picked it up.

Steve stepped forward and pushed me, hard. I sat down on the road with a thump, letting the butterfly fall from my hand. He looked down at me and I was astonished to see his face screwed up and quivering with emotion.

"It's mine," he repeated. I knew then that I had a choice. I could claim the Tailed Leafwing, or I could keep a friend, but I couldn't have both. I looked at him silently, then said quietly, "Go on then, it's yours. You want it more than I do."

His face twisted as he struggled for control, then he picked up the small corpse and cradled it lovingly in his hand.

I got up and dusted myself off. Retrieving my net, I said, "Come on, I'm going back." I set off down the road, but after a few paces looked round. Steve was still standing over his net, unmoving. I went back and looked searchingly at him.

"What's wrong?"

He mumbled something.

"What?"

"It's...it's not mine. You were right, it was more in your net, and it should be yours."

"Doesn't matter," I said. "If you really want it, you can have it."

"No. This is the first one we've seen, and you caught it. Well, most of it. You should have it. I'll have the next one we catch."

I smiled. "Okay. The next one we catch is yours. And I bet it'll be in better condition than this one." I lifted the tattered body from his hand and slipped it into my tin.

We turned and started for home. We were both quiet, thinking our own thoughts. I felt excited at the prospect of pinning out this rare addition to my collection, but not as excited as I thought I should have been. Perhaps it was the realisation that my friend Steve did in fact have a claim on it. I didn't want a butterfly at the cost of our friendship, but I couldn't reject his gift. I thought for a moment, then said,

"Steve, I caught a nice *Marpesia* dagger-wing the other day. Would you like it?"

His look of pure joy told me our friendship was intact, and with a grin, I slapped him on the shoulder, laughed, and raced off down the road.

Just the other day, over fifty years later, I came across that battered specimen of a Tailed Leafwing. Looking at it immediately brought to mind Steve's face, that hot, dusty day in Jamaica, the thrill and the pain of its capture once again. Beside it in the box was a dagger-wing. Not the perfect specimen I had given to my friend, but a rather ragged one that was all I had been able to capture as a replacement. Though the butterflies themselves have little intrinsic value, they serve as an aide-memoire of days far removed in time and a valuable reminder of the importance of friendship, a reminder that will last far longer than the butterflies themselves.

Strawberry Hill

There is an old legend that when Christopher Columbus returned to Spain and was asked by Queen Isabella to describe Jamaica, he took a piece of parchment in his hand and crumpled it to indicate the mountainous terrain. Nowhere on the island is this more apparent than in the eastern part, where the John Crow and Blue Mountain ranges soar to heights of over seven thousand feet. You can see these magnificent ranges from Kingston, which nestles on the coastal plain at their feet, the land rising steeply into forested hills. The climate is different too from the dry sweltering plains, being both wetter and cooler. Naturally, the wildlife also differs and it was an area I looked to often from our home in Kingston. The ranges really did look blue, and it may be that this was because of volatile plant oils in the air, or dust, or the nature of the vegetation. Whatever the reason, I looked at these mountains and wanted to go there.

On especially hot weekends, my parents would drive into the foothills and look for a picturesque tavern or restaurant where they could enjoy a few cool hours over drinks while I wandered the local roads or sat with them, ice-cold Pepsi in hand. I was never a particularly troublesome child, often being content to just sit quietly and listen to the adults talk, but sometimes my parents wanted some time alone and my hobby was the perfect activity to allow this. Net in hand, and collecting tin in my back pocket, I would set off along lonely roads or on dirt paths on the hillsides to see what I could find.

The air was filled with an indefinable aroma, compounded of acrid dust that was kicked up from the unpaved roads and a variety of plants and spices each leaking their particular volatiles into the cool air. Over it all were the cries of unseen birds and as often as not the damp touch of fog as it clung to the upper slopes, deadening the sound and lending an air of unease to the lonely roads. Coffee is grown in this region, producing the world-famous Blue Mountain brand, and the coffee shrubs with their sprays of red berries are often shaded by pimento trees, providing a second crop for the farmer. I think the pimento spice smell was a large part of the mountain aroma.

There are roads out of Kingston that head east into the mountains and the coffee growing areas, but the one we took most often was the windy road that crossed the ranges to Buff Bay on the north coast. We seldom went all the way over, but instead visited towns like Gordon Vale, The Cooperage, Irish Town and Redlight, before ending our journey at Newcastle and the Hardwar Gap beneath Catherine's Peak. There were plenty of butterflying sites along the way and my parents were happy to dally beside a cool stream or in the shade of roadside trees with a glass of wine or fruit juice while I charged about madly with my butterfly net.

Down around Irish Town, the vegetation was on the borderline between the dryer temperate forest and the lush, wet tropical forest. It was an excellent site to see butterflies and I collected there whenever my parents took that road. Above the town is Strawberry Hill, which has since become a tourist spot. At the time I was there, it was relatively unspoiled and the views were free. The edges of the roads and gaps in the forest were often lined with ginger lilies and I could always be sure of seeing hummingbirds--Streamertail and Vervain.

Butterflies swarmed there too, and I collected grass yellows, skippers and blues by the roadsides, together with many of the nymph species I was used to from Kingston. There were less common species too, but I had to hunt for those. Leaving my parents ensconced with a book and a drink to hand, I would find a track through the undergrowth and set off to explore.

Sometimes I would head upward, aiming for the summit of one of the hills where I could be sure of finding male butterflies. I was aware of the phenomenon known as 'hilltopping', where the males of many species congregate, waiting for passing females. Other times, I would stick to the slopes, looking for a track that cut across the hillside, hoping for both genders feeding on some flowering shrub.

There were a few species I knew were up here that I did not have, among them being the Jamaican Albatross (a butterfly, not the bird), the Clearwing, and *Lucinia cadma*. I set off to find them. The track crossed the hillside through open forest not much taller than me. The day was fine, but the altitude cooled the air and mist hung low over the peaks, only allowing the sunlight through in patches. I came across flowering shrubs but upon examination they yielded flies, wasps and small beetles, none of which I was interested in. A stream tumbled down the slope across my path in a jumble of rocks and I had to pick my way carefully to the bottom, where I was faced with the choice of taking the path back up the slope on the other side or investigating the streambed. I went with the latter as the trees arced over the tiny rivulet making a gloomy tunnel that looked intriguing.

I went downhill, treading carefully on boulders or splashing through shallow pools, while keeping my eyes peeled for movement. I found a small rip in the canopy with sunlight angling through and found three Zebra butterflies (*Heliconius charitonius*) drifting back and forth. They flicked and glided on black and yellow-striped wings, and stayed high, out of my reach. I looked wistfully at them but went on after a few minutes as I already had them in my collection.

The stream angled downward more steeply and I took greater care as I moved from rock to rock. Soon, I came to a drop off, where the tiny stream plunged many feet down a steep bank and I decided I wasn't going to risk a descent. I looked out at the view of distant Kingston and the tops of the trees before starting back up the stream, but a tiny movement caught my eye. Something flickered in the shadows, crossing an open space and disappearing. I watched, and it happened again, but I didn't know what it was. I edged closer and was rewarded by another gentle fluttering, equally hard to decipher. I stared into the shadows, wondering what it could be. The thing it most resembled was a damselfly but it flew differently.

Then I realised it was a Clearwing, *Greta diaphane*. I shivered with delight for this was the first time I had seen one and I desperately wanted it in my collection. The problem was that I was balanced on boulders in a streambed in the forest and the place I had seen these butterflies was a dozen feet above me up the steep sides of the stream. I examined the slope and slowly worked my way upward, hanging onto saplings and roots, inching into a position where I thought I might have a chance of capturing a Clearwing should it appear. I waited, and after a few minutes, the flicker came again. It passed a few feet in front of me, within reach, but as I moved my net I overbalanced and just saved myself from a fall by grabbing a small tree.

I eased myself back down into the streambed and found a comfortable seat amongst the tangled roots and leaf litter, prepared to wait for another Clearwing to appear. I sat and scanned the vegetation, the rocks, and the minute patches of sky I could see, not really knowing what I was looking for and hoping I would recognise it when I saw it. Minutes passed and I became conscious of a tickling sensation under my shirt. I tried to ignore it, then I scratched, but that only made it worse. Then something stung me and I yelped, lifting my shirt and examining my chest. I saw a small reddish ant lift its abdomen and thrust its stinger into me again.

The pain was only a pinprick, but I jumped up and swatted the offending insect, but its nest-mates were out in force, stinging my back, neck and legs. I quickly stripped off and danced around, brushing the little things off. After several minutes, during which I had to turn my clothes inside out to find the last of the ants, I got dressed again and resumed my wait for a Clearwing.

I climbed back up to the place where I'd seen one before, and considered my problem. Perhaps if I waited for one to settle, I could creep up on it at my leisure. I watched the next one carefully, making no effort to capture it. It flew to a bush nearby and...vanished. I stared at the bush and the last place I had seen it, but it was as if the butterfly had never existed. I frowned. *It must be there. I saw it land and it hasn't taken off again. Right...* I crept forward, fixing my gaze on a dead leaf close to the spot that I thought the Clearwing had landed. Inch by inch, I transferred my feet across the loose soil and stone of the slope until I was braced against two saplings within an arm's reach of the bush. I still could not see the butterfly, but I knew it was there and I thought I knew roughly where it was. I took a deep breath and calmed myself, lined up the net...and swung.

My net crashed into the bush and I lost my footing, falling heavily and sliding down the slope, ending up painfully on the boulders in the stream bed. For a few seconds I just lay there, and then I leapt to my feet and retrieved my net from where it lay, wedged between two trees a few feet above me. I frantically searched the folds of material, but there was nothing in the net except a couple of small spiders and several leaves. I looked around quickly but saw nothing. I swore volubly--a 'bother', a 'darn', and I even guiltily risked a 'damn'. I sat down to wait for the *Greta* to return, but half an hour later I was still waiting. I didn't want to admit it, but I'd had my chance and blown it. I sighed, and with many a backward glance, climbed back up to the original track.

A few hundred yards across the hillside, the vegetation changed, becoming dryer and more stunted. I think this was because the underlying rock came closer to the surface, leaving a thinner layer of soil for plants to grip. At any rate, there was more space between the plants and more butterflies about. I saw at least three species of grass yellow, a couple of blues, a white or two and a handful of skippers--all of which I disregarded.

These common butterflies were not what I had come here to catch. I had missed the Clearwing, but there were others I wanted. However, I always was a sucker for size--a *Phoebis sennae* flew past and I was after it. I already had it in my collection but they are lovely sulphur-coloured butterflies and I found them hard to resist.

I crashed through the undergrowth, following the sulphur across the slope and made a series of frantic swipes at it. It evaded my net with ease and sailed out over the drop, leaving me to trudge back to the path, cursing under my breath and vowing that I would not be tempted by another butterfly I already had. Ten minutes later, I was off again, this time after a Pelaus swallowtail. After a chase of a few minutes, it stopped to refresh itself at some blossoms and I caught it. Its wings were ragged though, so I let it go and watched it make a hasty escape. I thought the blossoms worth staking out and caught a nice male Angled Sulphur, *Anteos maerula*, a few minutes later, but seeing nothing else, I went back to the path and continued my quest.

The track petered out a few hundred yards further on and I turned back. I found a patch of weed flowers--yellow and red *Lantana* and purple *Stachytarpheta* mainly--a little off the track, and waited for the blossoms to entice passing insects. I saw the usual species, and a nice Buckeye which I bagged, and then a lovely Silverspot (*Dione vanillae*) arrived. I already had one, but I admired its rich orange and black upper wing surfaces and the silver splashes on the underside as it wandered over the *Lantana* blooms, dipping its proboscis into the nectaries. I couldn't resist, so I caught it and slipped it gently into my collecting tin.

Another half hour passed and I heard my father tapping the horn of the car. We had agreed that when my parents were ready to leave they would sound a series of toots ten minutes before they packed up. I knew I had ten minutes to get back but could possibly stretch it to fifteen if I was prepared to try my father's patience. There was very little happening around the flower patch, so I started back along the track, moving slowly, in the hope that I might still see something interesting. I crossed the stream and looked wistfully down the tunnel of the stream bed. I would willingly risk being late for the sake of another crack at the Clearwing, but nothing moved in the dappled sunlight. I sighed and continued back to the road.

As I stepped out onto the road I saw a flutter of orange near my feet and without thinking, dropped my net over it. I picked up the folds and looked at my capture and my mouth dropped open--it was a *Lucinia cadma*. I trembled

87

with excitement as I brought it out. It was not particularly rare, but it was localised and I'd never stumbled across it before. I carefully slipped it into my collecting tin and waved at my parents as they put their folding chairs into the car. They would not have to sound another reminder for me. I started back down the road and another *Lucinia* flew in front of me. I dashed after it, swung my net smartly and I had it in my net--two in as many minutes. I was bubbling with excitement when I got in the car, and showed my captures.

"I thought we'd go on up the road a bit," my father said. "Perhaps as far as Hardwar Gap if it stays fine."

We continued winding on up into the hills, heading for the gap in the Blue Mountains where the road runs over into Portland Parish. As we ascended, the mist came lower, shutting out the view. My father debated whether it was worth going past Newcastle as we were not going to see much. He pulled over in the large parade ground and we walked over to examine the cannon and the insignia of the troops who had been stationed there. In the old days, when the British Army had troops stationed in Jamaica, yellow fever killed many men, but the authorities noticed that more people died on the coastal plains than in the hills, so they had barracks built at elevation. One such outpost was Newcastle. There is a large stone wall with the insignia, but all I can remember is the West Yorkshire and the Fifth Fusiliers, though many others were included on that roll of honour. I climbed onto the small cannon at the base of the wall and sat astride it with my butterfly net while my father took a picture.

The sun came out while we were in Newcastle and my father agreed to drive on a few more miles to Hardwar Gap on the crest of the Grand Divide. It only took us a few minutes and the mist withdrew enough that my parents decided to stop and admire the view. This gave me a fresh opportunity to catch butterflies, but the vegetation was very different up here. This was a real forest, many-layered, lush and dim beneath the canopy. Large trees reared up, festooned with epiphytes--orchids, bromeliads, vines--and fallen logs were festive under an array of fungi. I saw very few butterflies in the dense forest, but I heard birds that were equally invisible.

Dominating the scene was the sound of a flute whistling and trilling that I thought came from the rufous-throated solitaire, though I never caught sight of it. I could also hear a haunting, mournful 'woo-woo' that echoed out of the mist that I was fairly certain came from the Mountain Witch, a grey and rufous tinted dove. I had seen this bird before, lower down the hills, walking along the road with its head pumping back and forth. There was a movement in the trees above me and I glimpsed a grey and white bird. It uttered a shrill cry when it saw me and I thought it was a White-eyed Thrush. I followed it with my eyes as it flew and saw a very black bird foraging amongst the bromeliads high up on a tree. I couldn't think what this was unless it was a Jamaican Blackbird. I knew these were found up here, but I also knew they were relatively rare, so if that's what it was I was fortunate to see one.

My father called. The mist was closing in again and my parents were ready to descend the hills. I would gladly have stayed in the mountain forest for the rest of the day, whether the sun shone or the mist wrapped everything in its damp embrace, but the choice was not mine. Besides, I was sure we'd be back again and I could explore more next time. I got in the car and we drove back down to dry and sunny Kingston, leaving the different world of the Blue Mountains behind us.

A Pound of Butterflies

My father was exceedingly athletic, not on the sporting field as such, but he believed that a man should be physically fit as well as mentally competent. He had little control over my school reports except to rail at my lack of commitment and progress, occasionally taking his belt to me, but he made greater efforts to cultivate my sporting abilities, encouraging me into every manly venture. Alas, the only venture I was really interested in was collecting butterflies, though I toyed with other things.

I had loved cricket from the age of four and had even made a minor name for myself in my English school as an all-rounder. However, cricket proved to be merely a hobby rather than a passion when a bouncer connected with my bat one day in Jamaica and smashed up into my eye socket, knocking me to the ground in a daze. I never recovered from that shock and found myself unable to face fast balls, so I let this sporting endeavour pass away.

My father found another outlet for what he was sure was an inherited talent for sport by enrolling me in boxing classes. The school had recently invested in the 'noble' art of pugilism and was looking for interested participants. I was dubious, as I was a shy boy and avoided fights, but I did not want to disappoint my father (again). The organisers were new to the sport and managed to mismatch the contenders in each bout. I was put in with a friend who was a head shorter than me and even more reluctant to inflict pain on somebody he knew. Encouraged by the howling of the bloodthirsty mob of teachers, kids and parents, I pounded my friend into submission until they rang the bell to end his suffering. My friend was crying and I could think of nothing else but comforting him, though he shrank from my efforts. I realised I had done something dreadful but did not know how to heal the wounds.

The school was delighted with the success of my first bout and quickly decided on a second. This time they erred the other way and matched me against a bruiser who proceeded to pound me into the canvas. I was led weeping from the ring and never stepped back inside it. I told my father I was happy just to chase butterflies, but he would hear none of it.

Horse riding was his next idea. My father had been an officer in a cavalry regiment in England before the Second World War and I have photographs of him astride his charger with sabre in hand. He looked very dashing and I think he had visions of me doing similar things. He enrolled me in a riding school and took me down for my first lesson. The owner of the riding school quickly summed up the pale, shy child in front of her and assigned me to a placid grey mare called Lady Jane. I mounted this huge animal, with assistance, and sat perched precariously at a great height, frozen in the saddle. After a while I relaxed, as Lady Jane seemed equally wary about this little thing sitting atop her. She stood and waited for instructions, as did I.

Finally, when all the other horses were walking around in a great dusty circle, the instructor showed me how to coax my horse into motion. Lady Jane walked slowly round while I clung to the reins and saddle rigidly. I was afraid that my slightest movement would precipitate an ignominious and possibly painful fall. After a few turns, we were told how to make our horses trot, but thankfully, Lady Jane was disinclined to exert herself, and I spent a relatively pleasant half hour sitting astride a plodding mare while others trotted past.

"How was your ride?" my mother asked when we got home.

"All right, I suppose," I replied without enthusiasm. "The horse was nice."

"They gave him a bloody broken-down mare," my father said. "You can be sure I'll be having a word with them."

He was as good as his word and the next Saturday, when we returned to the riding school, I found to my disappointment Lady Jane had been given to some other lucky child. I was led to a colossal stallion, my father having no doubt informed the owner that his son came from cavalry stock and needed a mount to match his (my father's) expectations.

Lady Jane had two speeds--stationary and walking. This horse, whose name has been, without regret, expunged from my memory, also had two speeds--stock-still and full gallop. I think I did two circuits while the other horses were just starting to amble. The instructor saw my plight and matched her horse's speed to mine and brought it under control. Prising my rigid hands from the beast's mane, I was lifted trembling from the stallion's back and delivered to my silent father. He said nothing on the way home, but I knew that I had failed him again.

For a while, my father gave up on teaching me some manly skill and allowed me to develop my butterfly skills. He took me to the Institute of Jamaica to identify my captures, transported me and my friends on butterfly hunting trips, and even had glass-fronted mahogany boxes made to house my collection. He remained stoical at the sight of his only son and heir running around the countryside waving a butterfly net making, in his eyes, a fool of himself.

Though we lived in Kingston, nowhere in Jamaica is very far away. We would often drive up into the mountains or across to the North Coast and find some secluded beach or waterfall, relaxing beside pure streams, enjoying a picnic in the shade, and swimming in the warm shallow seas. Or at least, my parents swam as I splashed around in the shallows like a beached porpoise. My father was an accomplished swimmer and would forge out through the surf to the fringing reefs and sometimes even dive down. My mother stayed close in and could swim well enough, but I could not manage more than one or two breast strokes in water so shallow my knees scraped the sand.

I just did not want my head to go under water and I panicked if I felt myself even marginally out of my depth. My lack of ability frustrated my father and in the evenings I sometimes overheard my parents discussing me.

"Damn it, Cyn (Cynthia was my mother's name), everybody needs to know how to swim," my father said.

"He will; just give him time."

"How much longer am I supposed to give him? We gave him swimming lessons in England without the slightest success."

"At least he's enjoying himself."

A few more cocktails would be sipped as my parents enjoyed the tropic evening on our veranda. I sat inside, reading one of the books from my father's book cabinet. 'The Greek Myths' was one of my favourites, but I also enjoyed 'The Iliad', 'The Aeneid' and 'Gibbon's Decline and Fall of the Roman Empire' as well as Herodotus 'The Histories' and Thucydides 'The Peloponnesian War'. In later years I bought my own copies and read them all again, but for now I raided my father's small library.

"It was that damn experience in Malaya that damaged him," my father muttered. I stopped reading and listened carefully.

"Malaya? You mean the Lawtons?"

My father nodded. "Damn fool thought every child was the same as his own aquatic brats and threw him in the swimming pool. He sank like a stone and if I hadn't been there he might have drowned."

"But he didn't, Jay. You were there, and thank God you were."

"You have to wonder if the incident didn't damage him somehow--I don't know--psychologically."

"He was only a baby. He couldn't remember anything."

"So explain why he's scared of water. Damn it, we live in the perfect spot for swimming and he just chases after those bloody butterflies of his."

"It's a harmless hobby," my mother said placatingly. "He'll swim when he wants to. He just needs an incentive."

"I've already tried my belt," my father grumbled. "But even that's not incentive enough."

"Perhaps a reward for swimming instead of a punishment for not," my mother reasoned.

I went back to my book, but I thought about what my parents had said. Maybe I could work this to my advantage. I considered my vague idea more closely and thought it might work. If it did, my butterfly collection would increase in size and my father would have a son he might be proud of.

I broached the idea to my mother first. I waited until we were alone in the house and took out a little booklet I had. I sat at the dining room table and studied it so hard and so quietly she looked up from her magazines.

"What are you doing, darling?"

"Looking at this list of butterflies for sale," I replied. "It's from England and it has lots of mounted or papered butterflies from around the world. They're quite cheap--well, some of them are."

"That's nice."

"Do you think dad would buy me some?"

"Maybe for your birthday."

That was still months away, and I hoped that might be an additional gift.

"Maybe I could earn it," I said.

Mum looked at me. "Earn it how?"

"I could do something he really wants, like...like...swimming."

"Ask him."

I thought about broaching the topic with my father. "Could you ask him?"

"I can mention it to him, Max, but you'll have to talk to him."

A couple of days later my father raised the subject at the dinner table.

"Your mother tells me you want me to bribe you to swim."

"Er, not exactly, Dad. I thought maybe you'd buy me some butterflies if I learned to swim."

"How do you buy butterflies?"

I showed him my booklet and he leafed through it, noting the prices on each page in shillings and pence.

"You'll learn to swim if I buy you a butterfly?" he asked. "Which butterfly?"

"You have to buy at least a pound's worth," I pointed out. "It says so right there."

My father read the paragraph on ordering. "A pound's worth of butterflies for learning to swim?"

"Yes, but my choice of butterflies."

He nodded. "All right, but I have a couple of conditions of my own. I want you to apply yourself to this, no shirking. Also, when you have learned to swim and have your butterflies, I want you to keep swimming, keep getting stronger."

I nodded, but then asked, "How far do I have to swim for you to agree I've learned?"

My father thought about this for a few moments. "A length of the swimming pool at the Liguanea Club."

I grimaced. "How about two widths?"

My father smiled. "Then you'll just swim in the shallow end where you can put your foot down. Practice there by all means, but to win your butterflies you must swim out over deep water."

I accepted glumly and went to my room to think about it. If I wanted my butterflies, I was going to have to conquer my fear of water sufficiently to brave the deep water with its invisible horrors. I shivered at the thought but put my fears to one side and opened my booklet again. I took an exercise book and started making a list of the British butterflies I wanted. A red admiral cost three pence and a peacock cost four pence, but a Camberwell beauty would set me back five whole shillings and a swallowtail even more. I had to juggle my desire for quantity with my greed for rarities, and made several lists, crossing some out, adding others, until my finalised order list came to exactly one pound. Now to earn them.

We went to the Liguanea Club again that weekend. The Liguanea club is one of the oldest and most select private clubs in Jamaica. It has a golf course, tennis courts, squash courts, a swimming pool and lovely shaded verandas where families can enjoy drinks or a meal. My favourite drink was grape soda in a tall glass with crushed ice and a straw. Later on, after I had left Jamaica, I learned that scenes from the James Bond film 'Dr No' had been shot here.

The swimming pool was large and surrounded by paving where lounge chairs sat like altars to the sun god, laden with oiled offerings of flesh. Large trees at the shallow end offered shade for others and my parents often sat here while I splashed about in waist deep water. I changed into my swimming trunks and got in, sinking down on bended knees until just my head and shoulders remained above water. I looked across the pool and groaned at how far away the other side looked. I studiously ignored the deep end. Perhaps it wasn't really so far. I maintained my bent posture and slowly walked across the pool, making believe I was swimming. No, it really wasn't very far after all, I decided.

I knew the motions for the breaststroke, but it was too daunting to launch out across the pool, so I went out a few feet from the steps, turned, lowered myself into position and threw myself forward. A great wave of water washed out in all directions, and I found myself clutching the steps, a big grin on my face. I tried it again, this time making an effort to move my arms in a proper swimming stroke. That worked too, and over the course of the next hour I found I could manage several strokes across part of the shallow end as long as I was heading for the safety of the steps. I could not pluck up the courage to head away from the steps despite the bottom of the pool being no more than a leg-length away, but I was happy with the start I had made. My father said nothing on the way home but that was all right--we had an agreement.

Over the next few weeks I grew steadily bolder until I was managing at least half a width. I found something else to help me. The pool had a gutter around the edge just above the water line and if I swam close to the edge and lost my nerve, I could put out a hand and grab the gutter. Soon, I was doing a full width with the gutter on my right side. I was less confident grabbing hold with my left hand, so successive crossings of the pool were in the same direction--anticlockwise. I'd get out and run back to the other side before starting my next crossing. No matter, I was getting there, and I was now making full crossings without having to reach for the gutter.

As I grew more confident, I found I could change direction, veering slightly to left or right. I would ease away from the side of the pool then back again, weaving a zig-zag course over twenty yards of shallow water. I showed my father my accomplishments, but he only reminded me that I had to swim a length, not a width.

Then one day, unremarkable in other ways, I set off across the pool and as I neared the far side, I started veering to the left until I found myself slowly forging down the length of the pool, the gutter an arm length away. The water changed from pale blue to a deeper shade and I knew I was out of my depth--but I could see the far end of the pool getting nearer and nearer. I was doing it.

I reached the ladder at the far end bubbling with excitement and accomplishment. I hauled myself out and ran back down to where my mother was sunbathing and my father was reading a book.

"I did it, I did it, Dad. First across the pool like I always do but then I changed and went up the pool."

My father looked up from his book. "What was that, Max?"

"I swam a length, without stopping or holding on," I said proudly. "Actually a width and a length non-stop, but..."

"Well, let's see you do it again."

"But I get my butterflies, don't I?"

"If you swim it again."

"You said I only had to swim one length for it to count."

"If you've swum it once, you'll be able to do it again."

I looked aghast, my lips trembling. I felt betrayed. "You said one length."

"And now I'm saying you need to do it again," he said impatiently. "Go on."

I have no doubt most kids would have swum a length again to prove themselves to their fathers, but I just felt hurt that he had gone back on his word. I sat on the pool steps until he lost interest and then I got out and changed back into my clothes. I never went into that swimming pool again and I never swam another stroke.

Of course, I also never got my pound's worth of butterflies, just the weight of more paternal disappointment loaded on my young shoulders. I told myself it did not matter and concentrated on catching Jamaican butterflies. It would have been nice to have some British ones--and a father's pride--but I was learning that for some things, the cost was too high.

Years later, as an adult, I bought a range of British butterflies from the same supplier though at greatly inflated prices. I often open up the two small cases I store them in and gaze at their familiar forms. They stir in me a mix of emotions--pride in ownership, wonder at the beautiful colours and patterns, and sadness. If I could live my life again, I think I'd swim that second length of the Liguanea pool, please my father and claim the prize, but I cannot turn back time. The burden of a father's disappointment in his son and a son's disappointment in his father, are all that remain with me from that episode.

San San Bay

My parents were firm believers in experiencing everything a country has to offer and we did not stay in Kingston all the time. We would often make day trips up into the hills to the east, travelling up to Mavis Bank, or else north to Castleton Gardens, or westward to Spanish Town. For weekends, or in the holidays, we made longer trips, mostly to the unspoiled beaches of the north coast. While my parents swam or sat on deckchairs, sipping on drinks and relaxing, I would be wandering the roads with my net, curious to see what was there.

One of our favourite places was a small resort on the northeast coast a little past Port Antonio, called San San Bay. In those days it was idyllic; a handful of villas set on small but private plots of land, each with its own postage-stamp sized beach. The palms leaned out over the white sand and warm shallow water and hibiscus and bougainvillea hedges protected the privacy of immaculately tended lawns and secluded patios. The villas were serviced and we could order meals that would be served candlelit on the patio in the evening and we were serenaded by the gentle shushing sound of wavelets on the beach, and treated to a faery dance of fireflies, winking green and yellow as they drifted across the lawns or settled in the shrubs. Little frogs called unseen in the shrubbery--high-pitched peeps and trills, with an occasional deep-throated creak as if an unlubricated door swung open somewhere. It was a magical place and I looked forward to our visits there.

Another eagerly anticipated pastime was butterfly hunting. The species found on the moister north coast were often quite different from those found around the capital city of Kingston, on the dry southern coast. Butterflies there often frequented dry open grassland or scrub, though many forest species came to the well-watered gardens of the Hope Botanical

Gardens. San San Bay provided me with access to different butterfly habitats and I could wander shaded roads, climb into the dryer hills or clamber up fern-choked streams to see what danced in the sunlit forest openings.

The first time we came to San San it was early in our stay in Jamaica and I was unaware of the different butterflies that flew on the north coast. I wallowed in the shallow sea, watching silver fish darting around me, or sat on cool grass in the shade and sipped coconut milk direct from the shell. There were plenty of other things to catch the attention of a small boy and I eagerly tracked blue and grey ground lizards as they skittered along gravel paths, tried to catch the orange-throated *Anolis* lizards as they bobbed their heads on tree trunks or marvelled at the iridescent plumage of vibrating hummingbirds that came to flowers and feeders around the villas.

My second visit took me into the hills behind the resort where I caught a Tailed Leafwing with my friend Steve, but on our third visit, I became more adventurous and, net in hand, went exploring on my own. The sea-strand was narrow and quickly led onto other properties so I gave that up, walking up the drive to where it met the main coast road. From here I had choices. Turning right would take me toward Port Antonio, but I did not want towns and people, I wanted the lonely places where the butterflies flew undisturbed. I turned left and wandered along the grassy verges of the road, my net at the ready. There was very little traffic and I could concentrate on my hunting-- unfortunately, there was little of interest--a few grass yellows and sulphurs, a few hairstreaks, skippers and nymphs, but all ones that I already had in my collection.

I found a drain beside the road that had a small amount of flowing water in it. It disappeared under the road in a pipe and emerged into a swampy piece of land near the sea. I went the other way, following the tiny freshet until I found its source in a soak where water apparently drained off the hillside. The wire fence bordering the road was strained and warped at that point and I clambered over and pushed through the vegetation toward an open space I could just make out. There I found that the source of the water was a tiny stream that paralleled the road for a space before plunging through to the sea a little farther on.

I followed the water course upstream, skirting mud and dense vegetation until I emerged in a tiny glade where butterflies floated and sunned themselves on rocks and leaves. Among others, I saw the Banana Butterfly, *Colobura dirce*; the Leafwing, *Historis odius*; and the Jamaican Admiral, *Adelpha abyla*, as I looked around. *Colobura* quickly flitted off into the vegetation, so I turned my attention to the Leafwing. I think most small boys are attracted to large butterflies and *Historis* is a pleasantly chunky butterfly measuring several inches across its spread wings. It is a velvety brown on top with a large orange patch, but beneath it is more subdued in colour, with patches and streaks and spots that camouflage it rather well. One perched head down on a tree trunk near the water, but as I crept closer I saw that its wings were ragged around the edges, so I left it alone.

The Jamaican Admiral was sitting on a boulder in the sun, wings held open to catch the warmth. Its brown wings also had a small orange patch, but both fore and hind wings sported the palest of pale blue stripes that angled inward toward the butterfly's abdomen. It was a gorgeous creature and in good condition, so I proceeded to stalk it. When I was close enough to swing my net, I flicked the white material as I started to sweep, with the intention of startling it into the air. I have found that butterflies on rocks can be hard to catch as the net may hit the rock if you aim too low or miss entirely if you aim too high. I timed this sweep just right and the mouth of my net swept over the rock as the Admiral leapt skyward. It disappeared into the folds of the material with a soft but satisfying thwack and I quickly folded the net to prevent its escape. I killed it and transferred it to my collecting tin, feeling very pleased with myself.

I continued up the tiny stream. The vegetation thinned as the land rose, and I soon emerged onto grassland. There were more butterflies here, skimming the edges of the forest or twinkling over the grass like yellow and blue and brown snowflakes. I wandered among them for a while, catching several but only keeping a few. I found a nice Queen and a Crescent Spot and saw a *Heliconius* gliding through the shadows on the forest edge, but nothing of great interest to me. I walked back along the forest edge until I came to the dirt road leading up the hill toward the stand of mango trees where Steve and I had found our Tailed Leafwing. Instead of following it to see what now lay beneath the mango trees, I turned back toward the coast and when I reached the road I found myself very close to the San San Villas.

Lunch was nearly ready when I got back, and over a light meal, my parents informed me of the afternoon's activity.

"We're going to Boston Beach," my father said.

"Where's that?"

"About five miles further along the coast. We can also see the Blue Hole which is on the way."

"What's the Blue Hole?" I asked.

"It's a very deep bay, almost land-locked," my mother said.

"And is reputed to be bottomless with things living in it that drag unwary swimmers under," my father added with a straight face.

"Jay, don't fill his head with nonsense."

"No monsters," my father said with a laugh, "But it is deep. Not bottomless though."

We set off after lunch, and I decided to bring my camera with me instead of my net. The Blue Hole was impressive, yellow-green at the edges, rapidly dropping off to the blue depths within yards of shore. We saw it with a blue sky overhead which probably helped, and the shore lined with forest. For such a beautiful place there were very few people around. I took a picture and my father took a few colour snaps, trying to capture the vivid blue of the water and the green of the vegetation.

We drove on to Boston Beach, and despite its undoubted beauty and relatively untouched white sands, it did not particularly appeal to me. I think I have mentioned elsewhere that swimming is not one of my pleasures. I don't mind wallowing in warm shallow water or wandering along the sea-strand looking for shells, but after a while I got bored and just sat in the shade until my parents had had enough.

Dad took us back via the back roads, and we would have gone the long way round, winding up into the hills, but we came upon a washed out section that had not yet been repaired and we turned back. We happened upon a village called Nonsuch, an unparalleled name for such an ordinary place; and another called Sherwood Forest. This made my father grin as before the war, he had belonged to a regiment called the Sherwood Foresters (Nottinghamshire and Derbyshire). He said it was nothing like he remembered.

We were nearly back at San San when we were flagged down by a policeman. There had been an accident up ahead, he said, and politely asked us to wait a few minutes while the road was cleared. My father pulled over and we opened the doors, enjoying the cool shade under an avenue of trees. I wandered up and down the verge, not really looking for or finding anything, until I saw a tiny flash of green. Green is an uncommon colour in butterflies so I paid attention and it was soon repeated. A small butterfly with wings of metallic green flitted low over the verge and settled, disappearing from my sight as it did so. I looked closer, but could not see it, so I knew it must be well camouflaged.

"Max, time to go."

I looked round quickly and saw that the few cars pulled over under the trees were starting to move. "Just a moment, Dad." I quickly turned back to the verge and whacked at the herbs with a stick. The metallic green butterfly flew off and I stared after it hungrily. I didn't know what it was, but I wanted it.

I carefully watched as we drove back the last mile or so to the Villas, imprinting the features of the road in my memory. It was too late in the afternoon to do anything, but I resolved to go there the next day. I only had the one chance as that would be the last day of our short holiday.

That night I searched my memory for any hint of what the butterfly might be. I visualised the butterfly cabinet at the Institute of Jamaica, and imagined myself opening each drawer. I could safely ignore the swallowtails, the Pierids and skippers, and probably the Lycaenids as well. Several members of the 'Blue' family have green on their wings, but usually on the under surface, whereas the one I had seen had metallic green on top. By elimination, that made it a nymph of some sort. I tried to imagine the drawers of nymphs and the names I had seen and one name whispered in my ear--*Dynamine*. It frustrated me that I could not put a picture to the name, but if it was an unfamiliar nymph, that was good enough for now. I would call it *Dynamine* until I learned its real name.

Next morning, after a hurried breakfast of pawpaw and toast on the patio, I gathered my net and collecting tin and headed for the door. My father stopped me before I could escape.

"Where are you off to?"

I was evasive as I wasn't sure my father would let me walk two miles up the main road. "I found a stream on the other side of the road yesterday."

"All right, but respect other people's property. Be back by lunch time."

As soon as I was out of sight, I ran up the drive to the road and then walked quickly along it. I looked carefully back to make sure I wasn't observed, and then hurried round the first bend in the road. If my father saw me soon, I could always claim I was just wandering and lost track of the distance, but if he found out I had gone miles away, I'd be reacquainting myself with his belt, and that was definitely something to be avoided.

It took me nearly an hour to reach the spot where I'd seen the green butterfly as I had to move carefully in places because of traffic and I was also delayed while I tried to catch a Pelaus swallowtail. It eluded me, and cost me several minutes. At last I was in the right place and looked around expectantly, hoping to see them in abundance. I saw a small black and white butterfly with a flash of blue but ignored it, telling myself it was just a 'Blue', whereas I was after *Dynamine*. There were no green butterflies, so I walked slowly up the verge for a hundred yards or so, until the shade of the trees gave way to bright open grass and little yellow butterflies. I walked back on the other side without any greater luck.

I was starting to think that the green butterfly was a sport, a mutation, and that there had only ever been one of them, and it was now gone. I uttered a heartfelt 'Bother!' and turned my attention to the black, white and blue Lycaenid I'd spotted earlier. After a little searching, I saw one and netted it without difficulty. I killed it and opened it up gently. It was about the size of a grass yellow, but had black wings with a broad white stripe running from front to back in the middle of each wing. The area closest to the body had a metallic blue sheen. The underside was camouflaged in tones of russet and white in lines and circles. I had never seen it before and carefully tucked it into a paper triangle in my collecting tin.

I caught another one after a few minutes and, having two safely in my possession, watched the next one I saw and managed to keep it in view as it settled. I marvelled that the pattern on its underside could camouflage it so well, and looked around in the vegetation for others. Now that I knew what I was looking for, I found them. I sat quietly and enjoyed their presence.

The position of the sun told me it was getting close to noon and I would have to start back very soon. I promised myself one more walk along the length of the verge to look for *Dynamine*, and then I would go home. As I got up, one of the roosting butterflies took off and I gaped at the flash of metallic green. I raced after it, a car beeping its horn at me as I ran on the edge of the gravel, and slammed my net over it. Trembling with excitement, I killed it and took it out. Disappointment washed over me as I saw the pattern on the underside--it was one of the black and white blues. I looked through the net again, but I had apparently missed the green and netted the blue. I put the specimen in my tin and walked the length of the verge twice, but did not see the green again. I turned for home feeling most despondent.

I saw something else fluttering in the shadows as I was about to leave, but I had no time to investigate. I thought it was one of the black and white blues, but it seemed to be missing the white band. Further, I could have sworn I saw red on its underside. *Never mind*, I thought. I intended to return for the green so maybe I could look for this one too.

I was late for lunch, but not too late, and as I was obviously excited by my catches, my father said nothing. I was prevented from going out again that afternoon as we were all going to dinner at a restaurant in Port Antonio on our last night and my mother insisted I rest in the afternoon. I gave in with as good a grace as I could muster and went to my room to mount my few catches from the morning.

I got out my setting board and pins and cut some thin strips of paper. Then I opened my first triangle and took out the butterfly I was calling the 'Black and White Blue'. I gently opened its wings and inserted a pin through its thorax, wishing I had some proper entomological pins instead of ordinary sewing ones. I positioned the insect on the board and proceeded to push the wings flat with strips of paper, securing them with pins, before delicately teasing the wings into their final position. When the butterfly dried out, the wings would stay in this position after I removed the paper strips. I took my second specimen out and repeated the procedure, but when I opened the wings, I gasped. It was a green *Dynamine*, not a Black and White Blue. I put it down and stared at it, almost afraid it would vanish if I took my eyes off it.

After I bit, I started thinking. The underside of the butterfly looked almost identical to the Blue. I took out my third specimen, checked it was a Black and White Blue, and then compared the undersides. Yes, they were very similar, if not identical. What did this mean, I asked myself. I recalled a curator at the Institute telling me about sexual dimorphism and explaining that this meant the male and female looked different. Perhaps *Dynamine* was sexually dimorphic. If that was the case, I suddenly had three specimens where a few minutes ago I thought I had none. I finished setting my captures, feeling very pleased with myself.

When we returned to Kingston, I paid a visit to the Institute of Jamaica and looked for their specimens of *Dynamine*. I learned that its full name was *Dynamine egaea* and that the green one was the male and the Black and White Blue was the female. When I had absorbed all I could, I went in search of a curator and asked him about the other butterfly I had glimpsed at San San Bay.

"It was like a female *Dynamine*," I said, "But had no white on the upper surface and had some red underneath."

The man thought for a bit. "It doesn't sound like any Jamaican butterfly I know."

I got excited. "You think it might be a new species?"

He laughed. "Who knows, but you'll need to catch one first."

I vowed I would do that, the very next time we went to San San Bay.

Blue Mountain Mist

When my parents first told me about their planned weekend trip up into the Blue Mountains I was excited and asked whether my friend Steve could come. Unfortunately, this was just before he went off to boarding school in Mandeville, and his parents wanted him around. I really commiserated with Steve, as I had spent time in a British boarding school, but for some reason he was quite looking forward to it. He would have liked to come with me to the Blue Mountains, but it was impossible. So my trip to those blue-tinted peaks would have to be a solitary affair. I thought initially we would be heading up to Newcastle as we had done before, but my mother said we were going the other way and that my father was interested in climbing Blue Mountain Peak. I couldn't really see the point in that effort, but I was willing to come along because the Homerus swallowtail lived there and I really, really wanted one of them.

The Homerus swallowtail, *Papilio homerus*, is the largest butterfly in the Americas and the second largest in the world. It is a robust creature with black and yellow patterned wings and prominent spatulate tails and the only places it is found is in the foothills of the Blue Mountains and in the Cockpit Country at the other end of the island. This magnificent butterfly is a strong flyer and can be found cruising along the edges of dense forest or perching high up in the canopy. I would be lucky to see one and luckier still to be in a position to catch one, but I was going into its territory and I was determined to give a good account of myself.

Thus, one hot weekend, we left Kingston, passing through the Mona Valley and motoring up to The Cooperage in the cool foothills of the Blue Mountains. Instead of taking our usual route up past Irish Town to

Newcastle and the Hardwar Gap however, we took the right hand turn along the ridges toward Mavis Bank and the Blue Mountain Peak itself.

Mavis Bank is a small township that has grown up around a coffee farm and its factory. I had heard of Jamaica Blue Mountain coffee before I ever went there, but knew nothing about it except what my parents said in my presence. When we went to Mavis Bank, I learned more about it. For instance, I found out that not all coffee grown in the Blue Mountains actually bears the famous name. That honour belongs solely to beans grown between elevations of 3,000 and 5,500 feet. Between 1,500 and 3,000 feet it can only be called Jamaica High Mountain, and below 1,500 feet it is called Jamaica Low Mountain.

I got to tour the factory at Mavis Bank, and we sampled the fresh brewed coffee and savoured the Tia Maria liqueur made from it. Of course, I did not get to drink the liqueur, though my parents allowed me a small taste. I did not particularly like either the liqueur or the coffee, but at least I got to try it at the source.

The coffee bushes themselves are unprepossessing plants, the only thing that elevates them above the ordinary are the lovely sprays of bright red fruit. These fruit contain the coffee 'bean' of course, and it is not just people that seek them. Birds abound in the plantations and especially on the forest edges where they can forage the cultivated land as well as the undisturbed vegetation. I saw several species but probably heard many more as a lot of the birds were quite secretive.

It was a beautiful day when we arrived, and we made ourselves comfortable in our little chalet before going to the restaurant for lunch. I can't remember what we had, but my parents enjoyed a fresh cup of local coffee while I looked around. I had left my butterfly net in the chalet rather than lug it to the restaurant and I debated whether I should go back for it. This would involve asking my father for the key though, and I did not want to make a nuisance of myself this early in the trip, so I hoped I would not see anything to make me regret my decision.

The land around the chalets was artfully landscaped to offer privacy as well as restful views of hills, forests and plantations. There were flower beds, but not many as the owners had obviously opted for low-maintenance grounds. Gravel and paved paths connected the buildings, lined with low shrubs, and I searched diligently, though unsuccessfully, for lizards. I did come across an old Jamaican gardener though, kneeling by a flower bed, weeding.

"Hello," I said.

The old man looked back at me cautiously. "I done come he'p yu, young mon?"

I shook my head. "What are you doing?" That was a dumb question.

He waved vaguely at the flower bed. "I trash dem weeds."

I nodded, trying to think of something sensible to say. Then I remembered the Homerus swallowtail and thought he might be able to help me. "Er, have you seen any butterflies around here?"

"W'at dem?"

"Butterflies." I looked around and spotted a grass yellow flying across the lawn. I pointed. "Like that one, but bigger."

"Ah, w'at yu want wit' dem?"

"I catch them," I said.

"Yu ketch bots? W'at for yu do wit' dem?"

I have found that many Jamaicans lump things together. Anything that lives in the sea is 'fish', any meat you eat is 'jerk' and anything that flies is either a bird or a bat. I had come across the word 'bot' before as butterflies were classed as a bat, or 'bot'.

"I, er, collect them. I pin them in boxes for people to look at."

"Yu put pins in dem? Don' dey hurt?"

"I... I kill them first."

"Yu kill bots, put pins in dem, and show dem? Yu one warra-warra y'uth." He shook his head and turned back to his work. I blushed uncomfortably as 'warra-warra' stands in for a swear word when a person is being polite. The gardener obviously didn't think highly of me.

I turned to go and then decided to have one last try. "Have you seen any really big butterflies...bots...around here? Big black and yellow ones?"

He spoke without turning round. "Dere's big bots all round. Yu look, yu see; yu ketch, yu kill; no fash me."

I walked quietly away. I had made no friend there for some reason. I went back to our chalet and sat on the step until my parents got back from lunch. They said they were going to have a rest for an hour before going to the coffee factory, so I said I'd take my net and see what I could find.

I avoided the garden because I felt a bit ashamed of meeting the old gardener again, and hurried out onto the road and went downhill. On the way there I had seen several spots that looked interesting and I was eager to see what butterflies inhabited Mavis Bank. A few hundred yards down the road, I came to the first of these spots--a small open field bordered by pimento and coffee shrubs. I climbed the gate and walked through the grass, paying special attention to any flowering plants I came across. There was very little in the field. I saw a few small blue butterflies and a grass yellow, but nothing that interested me until I came close to the far edge. A small milkweed plant struggled to raise its leaves above the grass, and on its stems I found two small caterpillars.

Milkweed is a plant with narrow lance-shaped leaves and a copious white sap that is toxic for most animals but a few creatures like Danaid caterpillars can eat the leaves with impunity. These caterpillars had black and white stripes around their bodies and yellow spots on the black. In addition, it had six thin black fleshy filaments that rose from its body, two near the front, two near the back, and two about two-thirds of the way back. These features told me it was a Danaid butterfly caterpillar and probably one in particular-- the Queen, *Danaus gilippus*. I wanted the caterpillars but I had nothing to carry them in.

I had raised caterpillars with moderate success in the past. It was endlessly fascinating to watch the little caterpillars munch their way through leaves, eventually growing so much they got too big for their skins. Then they'd stop and split the old skin, shrugging it off like an old suit and revealing a shiny new one underneath. This happens four or five times before they pupate and eventually become butterflies. There are problems involved in rearing caterpillars. They are sensitive to air conditions--too little moisture and they dry out and die, too much and they die of mould. Bacteria can rot them from within, and tiny parasitic wasps and flies can attack them. If they survive all this, you are rewarded by the sight of a pristine new butterfly.

If you are a butterfly collector, you want good specimens, and the way to get perfect ones is to rear them yourself. I had done this in the past and I certainly would not turn down the opportunity to rear two Queen caterpillars to adulthood and add them to my collection. However, I did not have a container to carry them in, and I lacked a reliable source of milkweed. Most caterpillars will only eat specific plants and I knew these Queens would only eat milkweed. If I couldn't give them the right diet, they would starve. Regretfully, I left them where they were.

My next stop was half a mile further down the main road. A small stream tumbled down the hillside and through a culvert, continuing on down the slope through a tangle of vegetation. The upper section was more open and I thought I could negotiate the bed. I pushed my way upstream, swinging overhanging branches out of the way and stepping carefully over rounded boulders. After ten minutes, I came to an open space where the stream had encountered a depression in the hillside and formed a large, still pool. Dragonflies and damselflies danced above the surface and I looked at them very closely in the hope that I would find the Clearwing, *Greta diaphane*. I had missed this butterfly before on Strawberry Hill and I was eager for another encounter. It was not to be, however, and the Odonatan insects danced above the pool unmolested.

Nothing else was disturbed by my passage, so I returned to the road and made my way back to the chalets. I wasn't too disconsolate about catching nothing as I was after relatively uncommon butterflies. I was used to returning empty-handed. I just hoped that I would see them later.

My parents were almost ready to go out when I got back, so I quickly washed and had a Pepsi to refresh myself. I wanted to bring my butterfly net but my father forbade it.

"We're going to look around a factory and plantation, not run riot with a net."

Ah well. The factory tour was interesting. We saw the bins of freshly harvested beans, the pulping vats and the sorting tables, the drying tables, the roasting ovens and the grinding. My parents inhaled the rich aroma of the coffee and sampled tiny cups of flavoursome coffee as we watched the finished product being packed into bags. Afterward, we and four other people were escorted through one of the plantations where we saw the coffee bushes protected by a canopy of pimento trees. The guide explained everything to us, but my interest was snatched away by little green butterflies flitting through the sun-dappled shade. I recognised them as *Dynamine egaea* males, which I had captured at San San Bay on the northeast coast. I was surprised to see them here and I wished I had my net with me. I have seldom spent a day with my butterfly net either in hand or close by and not had a single capture to show for it, but I was determined to do better the next day.

The next day dawned cloudy and dull, but my father was all fired up. He had arranged for a vehicle to pick him and another man up from Mavis Bank and take them through to Whitfield Hall, from where a hike of a few hours would bring them to the Blue Mountain Peak. I asked to go with him as I had visions of the Homerus Swallowtail abounding there. He frowned, but agreed provisionally, providing I was prepared to wait for him at the Hall if the guide said the trek would be too hard for me. I agreed willingly, and a little after eight in the morning, we piled into a converted army jeep and headed out on the winding dirt roads for Whitfield Hall at the base of Blue Mountain.

The cloud descended as we neared the mountain, and it was raining by the time we got to the Hall. A guide met us and shook his head when my father asked about an ascent.

"Sorry sir, but the forecast is rain. I wouldn't try it for another three days at least."

My father scowled, but there was nothing he could do. He and the other man from Mavis Bank repaired to the bar while I sat on the veranda and looked out at the mist-obscured forest and plantations. As well as the weather, my butterflying expedition also looked like it was going to be a washout. I sighed and propped my net up against the veranda railing and wandered round the building, staying under cover. At one point the wooden veranda receded into shadow and I spotted a wide-bodied moth nestling up under the eaves. I could see it was a hawkmoth, but not what type. I dragged a chair over to the wall and stood on it, gazing up at the moth.

Now that I was closer, I could appreciate its beauty. Its wings were dark grey, mottled with lighter grey that gave it the appearance of being part of a lichen-covered branch--except it stood out on the faded wood of the wall. I reached up gingerly and nudged it gently with a fore-finger. The moth reacted by swinging its wings forward a fraction, revealing dark grey underwings and splashes of yellow along its tapered abdomen. I recognised it as *Manduca rustica*, and I did not have it in my collection.

I got down from the chair and thought about how I could capture it. There was not enough room to use my net. I could carefully press my thumb to its thorax and crush it against the wall, but although I had successfully used this method before, it sometimes damaged the insect by rubbing off the hair covering the body. The best way would be to place a jam jar over it, slide a piece of card under the jar, trapping the moth inside and then pop the whole thing into the ice-box of a refrigerator. The freezing temperatures would send the cold-blooded insect into torpor and kill it painlessly. The only trouble with this method was I did not have a jam jar and anyway, I could not see the owners of Whitfield Hall allowing a small boy to put insects in their refrigerator.

I would have to use the crush method after all. I got back up on the chair and positioned myself on tip-toe, reaching up so my right thumb was poised above the moth's thorax. I hesitated, knowing I had to press firmly, dead centre, else I risked considerable damage to the specimen. As I started my thumb down, I heard my father...

"Max, come on, we're leaving...Max..."

My thumb slipped as I half-turned my head, and the moth squirmed when I rubbed the hair off its thorax. It dropped and spread its wings and I made a futile grab for it as it whirred past me, out from under the veranda, and off into the rain. I jumped down from the chair and ran to the railing, staring after my prize.

"Max, there you are. Come on, we're heading back to Mavis Bank."

I retrieved my net and followed, wishing I was back home in Kingston. This trip was shaping up to be my worst ever. The rain eased before long, and half way back to Mavis Bank it stopped altogether, a few weak rays of sunshine struggling through the cloud cover. It was late in the afternoon by the time we got back, but I went out with my net anyway, determined I was not going to leave empty-handed. There was very little around, but I found a nice grass yellow, *Eurema messalina*, and gratefully slid it into my collecting tin where it sat in solitary splendour.

We were driving back to Kingston next day after checking out around ten in the morning, so I was up early. I looked out at a misty, overcast day and just knew there would be nothing flying for at least an hour or two, so I left my net behind and walked down the road. Mist hung tenaciously to the forest and plantations and the heavy aromatic scents of spices clung to me, while the mournful cries of birds echoed unseen from the hillsides. I walked a few hundred yards before turning back, tiny droplets of moisture covering my clothing. Then as I trudged back toward the chalet and breakfast, something big and black flew out of the mist toward me. It came fast down the road and it only took a moment for me to realise this was not a bird or a bat, but a true 'bot'. It swept past me, and all I had was a glimpse of black wings, and then it was gone.

"Homerus," I squeaked, and after one last look into the mist, I turned and ran for the chalet. I burst in to find my father drinking coffee and my mother packing our suitcases. "Homerus," I shouted, gesturing to the door. "I saw one. It flew right by me." I looked at my mother, and then at my father. "Homerus," I repeated.

"Well you won't catch it standing here," my father observed.

I grabbed my net and ran out, pounding down the road to where I had seen the ultimate prize. All that met my eager gaze was the ragged wisps of mist clinging to the trees. A ruddy quail dove mocked me from the forest with its booming and repetitive 'ooo-ah' call. I roamed the roads and soaked my shoes and socks in the wet grass beside them, but the Homerus swallowtail eluded me. The sun rose, warming the mist and thinning it and all of a sudden I saw my 'bot' again, flapping around a ruined shed in a field. I raced over, my eyes fixed on the large black-winged insect and as I got within striking distance I swept my net toward it. Even as the 'bot' crashed into my net, I knew something was wrong--this was not *Papilio homerus*.

I isolated it in my net and stared down through the material at what I had caught. It was a Noctuid moth, a male Black Witch, *Ascalapha odorata*, sometimes known as the 'duppy' or ghost moth. I grimaced and eased it out of my net, holding its quivering body gently but firmly in my fingers while I debated what to do with it. I did not have it in my collection, but this was a very battered specimen, with many chips and chunks missing from the edges of its wings. I wanted to keep it, but I also recognised this desire had something to do with my desperation at having caught nothing but a single grass yellow all weekend. I smiled and opened my fingers, letting it beat its way frantically into the sky.

I walked back up to the chalet, wondering if my earlier sighting had not been Homerus either. Thinking back, I could not recall seeing any yellow on it and the way it flew was unlike the measured beats of a large swallowtail.

"Did you get it?" my mother asked.

I shook my head. "No, it was a large moth."

I changed my wet socks and shoes and climbed into the car. On the road back to Kingston I turned in my seat and looked back to the Blue Mountains and the Mist, vowing I would return and capture a Homerus swallowtail. It could not elude me forever.

Shanty Town Oranges

When Steve Riley went off to boarding school in Mandeville, Max Wright became my sole butterflying buddy. Initially we met because we were the only two boys with the name 'Max' in the school, and we happened to both be in Mrs Urquhart's biology class. We both loved butterflies, so it was natural that we would go out collecting together.

The other Max was a much more self-assured boy though an 'only child' like me. I'm not sure what his father did for a living but he was away a lot and his mother had an active social life, leaving Max to amuse himself. He used to go out exploring, investigating places many boys his age would not dream of going, and on occasion taking me places I did not dare tell my parents about. His love for butterflies was a more theoretical love than mine, and would often leave his net at home, just noting down the places he saw butterflies and going back later to collect them if they interested him. Sometimes, when I went round to visit him, he'd ask what species I was looking for, and if he'd seen one, he'd lead me to the place.

Once when I cycled round to his house, my butterfly net strapped to the bar of my bike, I told him about the Pierid butterflies I had and the ones I had yet to collect. Pierid butterflies are mostly yellows and whites, with variable amounts of black pigment and occasionally orange or red.

"I caught a brimstone near King's House last week," I said. "It was a bit tatty but the only one I've seen recently."

I should explain that my friends' knowledge of the proper names of butterflies was less than perfect, so we all made up common names that described them. I've already related how we called *Colobura dirce* the Banana Butterfly; well, the brimstone was really *Anteos maerula*.

"Yeah, I've seen a few," Max said, "But nowhere special. I think you just have to be lucky enough to be in the right place at the right time."

"Do you think they migrate?" I was thinking about the blue swallowtail migration I had witnessed.

Max shrugged. "Who knows? Possibly--they're strong fliers."

"So what are we going to do today?" I asked.

"Depends. What are you after?"

"I'm always looking for a Homerus," I said with a laugh. "Otherwise, I suppose some of the grass yellows. I've got Dainty Sulphur and a Barred Sulphur, but there are others I haven't even seen let alone collected."

"What about the tailed orange?"

"You've seen one of those? They're supposed to be rare. Where'd you see it?"

He made a vague, non-committal sound. "You interested?"

"Of course."

Max hesitated. "It could be, well not exactly dangerous, but it could be scary."

"What do you mean?"

"How well do you get on with Jamaicans?"

I frowned, wondering what he was talking about. We had a Jamaican cook and a Jamaican gardener at home, and I knew a handful of Jamaican boys at school. My parents also knew Jamaicans socially and I'd been introduced to a few at my parents' cocktail and dinner parties before being bundled off to bed. "Okay, I guess. Why?"

"What about Rastas?"

Rasta is the common name for a Rastafarian. Rastafari is a way of life (some say a religion) based around the belief that the Ethiopian Emperor Haile Selassie (who was called Ras Tafari before he became emperor) is the resurrected Jesus Christ. They reject all Western culture and the white man, believing that Africa is where God (Jah) will establish his Kingdom on Earth. They smoke cannabis (ganja) as part of their worship, and as a result, are often intoxicated and sometimes violent. My father had warned me they were troublemakers and to stay away from them.

I had only ever come across one known Rastafarian, though of course I had seen them often enough. Once, as I cycled around the Kingston suburbs en route to my butterfly hunts, a bearded man with dreadlocked hair had stepped out in front of me and shaken his fist as I swerved past him.

"White man blood and fire!" he called after me as I pedalled away.

I considered Max's question in light of what I knew. "I don't know any," I said.

Max nodded. "All right. Just leave any talking to me."

Filled with trepidation, I followed Max outside and we set off on our bicycles. We headed north and west, heading into the poorer areas of Kingston, eventually stopping at the end of a dirt road where grass and scrubland stretched away in front of us. We chained our bikes to a small tree, out of sight of any passers-by, and set off with our nets at the ready.

There was a small patch of scrub at the end of the road, with *Lantana* growing wild around its edges and we saw a number of butterflies, but nothing out of the ordinary. I saw a couple of grass yellows too, Dainty Sulphurs--I caught them just to make sure, but released them.

Max pointed the way we should go and we set off across rolling grassland. The sun was high but the air was not hot, merely pleasantly warm with a fresh breeze and dry with an acrid dusty smell where rain had ripped gullies in the red earth. There were butterflies here too, but smaller ones easily missed if you were not looking for them. Small blues were in abundance and I collected a few--Hewitson's Hairstreaks, Jamaican Blues and a Hanno Blue. There were even a few little orange and white butterflies. I netted one and satisfied myself it was a Dorcas. I let it go as I already had one in good condition. Grass yellows, the objects of our expedition, were less abundant, and I found only the commoner species. I commented on the fact.

"Don't worry," Max said. "There's a better place. We'll get there soon."

We came to a deep gully gouged in the red soil. Several small Jamaican children dressed only in ragged shorts were playing in and around it. Some of them ran off when they saw us but a few of the older bolder ones approached.

"Wha' fo' dem nets?" demanded one of them. "Der don' be no wate' heh. Don' be no fish heh."

Max explained that we were looking for butterflies.

"Wha' fo' yu ketch dem? Dey's goo' t' jerk?"

This was a little harder to explain, and after a few minutes of describing how we killed them and put a pin in them, spreading their wings out to dry and keeping them in boxes, the boys seemed as confused as before.

"Jesum piece," exclaimed their spokesboy, "Dis fool fool white bwoy disrespec' I an' I wi' dis shi'. Lessee yu net." He stuck out his hand.

Max turned to me and said, "Let them see your net."

Reluctantly, I handed it over. The boy examined it minutely, rubbing the material between finger and thumb, and testing the flex of the shaft. He passed it to another boy, who also regarded it solemnly before giving it onward. One or two of the boys swept the net experimentally through the air and as the last boy was testing it, a Monarch butterfly flew by. The first boy grabbed the net and charged after the insect, slamming the net over a small bush. The butterfly flew off unscathed while the boy shrugged and handed the net back to me. I took it back with a grimace and started picking bits of twig and leaf out of the mesh.

The boy now confronted Max. "Sho' I an' I how yu ketch dese t'ings."

Max nodded and looked around, spotting a slow-moving Jamaica Queen, *Danaus gilippus*. He moved casually into position and as it flitted past, swept his net around and neatly bagged it, to exclamations of wonder from his audience. As the boys crowded round, Max carefully took the Queen out of the net and held its wings open with his thumb, showing it to all of them.

"Yu now kill it?"

Max shook his head. "I already have one." He opened his hand and tossed the butterfly lightly into the air, watching it as it flew off.

"Yu sho' respec', mon. Wha' t'ing yu done ketch?"

"It is a little butterfly, about an inch across, maybe a little more, orange in colour. I have seen it around here before."

"I and I he'p yu done ketch," the boy assured him. He stood aside for Max and me, but before we had gone more than a few paces we heard a shout and saw four youths racing toward us. They took the boy aside and engaged in some rapid conversation in Rasta patois that I could not follow. However, we were not left in doubt for very long.

"Yu come wit' I and I," said the youth.

"Where to?" Max asked.

"Yu on Rastaman tu'f. Yu ask p'mishun."

The youths did not touch us, but we were left in no doubt that we had to accompany them back to the village. Max smiled reassuringly at me but I thought I detected worry in his eyes.

"Just let me do the talking," he whispered. I had no argument with that as I had difficulty understanding their patois questions, let alone formulating a reply.

They led us a few hundred yards to a ramshackle array of corrugated iron, wood and plastic that was their shanty town. Many people gathered, mostly men and boys, though there was a scattering of women and toddlers in the background. The youths and men were bearded and sported dreadlocked hair with red and green and yellow and black banded caps. Our escort led us to an old Rasta man sitting in the shade of a Poinciana tree, and told him why they had brought us.

The old man looked us over carefully, his bloodshot eyes gauging us. "Wha'for yu done come Rastaman place, lil' white pickney?"

"We...we came to catch butterflies," Max said.

The man looked around the circle of faces and then back to us. "Der done none in Rastaman place. Wha'for dose?" He gestured at our nets.

"We catch butterflies with these," Max replied. He demonstrated with a sweep of his net and I followed suit.

The old man laughed. "Deh don' ketch fish; mi t'ink dese white pickney done be fish."

The villagers roared with laughter and several made thrusting motions with their hips. I took a step closer to my friend and quavered, "Wh... what's happening?"

Before Max could reply, the old man waved a hand and the laughter and gesturing died away. "Breathe easy, mon," he instructed us. "Be level. Yu fava duppy. Yu fluffy but yu no tink. Yu take yu doops an' go do yu ting." He took out a pipe and something that looked like tobacco and proceeded to fill it. "Do yu ting," he repeated, waving his hand in dismissal.

"I think we can go," Max said.

We turned and the circle of men and boys opened to let us through. We walked back the way we had come and several of the smaller boys followed us or trotted alongside, chattering amongst themselves. I walked fast and Max told me to slow down, the elder had said we could go ahead and 'do our thing', catching butterflies.

"I didn't understand half of what he said," I complained. "Did he call us fish?"

"A fish is...well, it's a homosexual."

"What's that?"

Max looked uncomfortable. "I'm not quite sure, but..." He shook his head. "Never mind. It's not important."

"What about 'doops'?

"Friend, I think."

"He said duppy. Did he mean ghosts?"

"He meant we looked frightened."

"And fluffy?"

"I think it means we look well-fed compared to a lot of these kids."

I smiled. "I suppose we are. Are we safe now?"

"Probably, but perhaps we should just call it a day and go home."

I looked around at the grasslands and scrub raked by red earth gullies and of the tailed orange butterflies which might be out here.

"We should go look for the oranges. If we leave now, we might never come back, and the old man said we could."

"He'll be smoking his ganja by now too, and may change his mind...but, okay... let's give it a go. This way."

Max led the way, scrambling down into a large gully and up the other side, setting off across the grassy wasteland. It took us another half hour walking and the Rasta boys dropped away by dribs and drabs as they saw little happening, so we were all alone when we started to see grass yellows again. We were near a road and houses again, and water was obviously seeping from a drain because the grass was longer and greener. Small flowers bloomed in the grass and little blues danced among them. I didn't bother with the blues, being more concerned with seeing that flit of orange that might signal the presence of the tailed orange, *Eurema proterpia*.

I saw a small yellow and black butterfly and netted it, identified it as a Little Sulphur and released it again. Little yellow and white Barred Sulphurs were caught and let loose, while I prowled up and down the area of green grass. A Buckeye caught my eye with its distinctive flight, alighting and spreading its wings for a few moments before flying on. I saw a White Peacock too, but ignored it, my gaze travelling over the grass and searching the tiny clumps of flowers, looking for the tell-tale orange of our quarry. Other butterflies are orange, but I thought I would recognise the tailed orange if it put in an appearance.

I saw a Dorcas and another and then... yes! It flew like a grass yellow, but larger and orangey-brown. It must be. I yelled and set off after it. It flew down the wide depression of the drain and over the lip into a large gully. By the time I got to the edge, it had disappeared. I prowled along the perimeter, searching hungrily for a sign but after a hundred yards, turned back. I reasoned that while the butterfly had flown into the gully, there was no reason to suppose it was still here, whereas I had seen it in the drain.

Max called. "There's one coming toward you."

I ran and arrived in time to see a tailed orange fly over the lip and drop into the gully, just like the other one. This one flew up the gully and I followed on the rim, debating whether to jump down into it or wait for it to fly out. Then it did something that decided me: it started up the far side of the gully. Seeing it get away, I leapt down without thinking and found I had misjudged the distance. I landed awkwardly in a welter of red dust and soil, and rolled to the bottom, my net flying off in the opposite direction.

I picked myself up hurriedly, looking for the tailed orange and saw it, no more than twenty yards away, feeding on a scraggly stalk of *Stachytarpheta*-- Jamaican Vervain. I limped to my net and picked it up, checking it for signs of damage with one eye while creeping closer to the butterfly.

Just before I got within striking range, it exhausted the nectaring possibilities of those few flowers and flitted off up the gully. I followed. It hovered at a number of clumps of vegetation but did not stop, moving onto the next as I approached. I picked up my pace almost getting close enough to make my move. The clumps of weed grew sparser and I could see a solitary Jamaican Vervain plant up ahead and then nothing. I knew that once it passed this plant it would fly off. As it alighted on the tall flowering stalk of the Vervain, I ran and threw my net over the plant, tripping and sprawling headlong as I did so. I scrambled forward and saw something fluttering in the folds. My heart hammered in my chest and my fingers trembled but I trapped the butterfly between two layers and firmly pinched its thorax between thumb and forefinger to kill it quickly.

I took it out of my net gently and cupped it in one hand, staring down at my first tailed orange. The edges of its wings were a little tattered, but it was unmistakeably *Eurema proterpia*.

The gully around me had narrowed as I ascended and I found that the grassy plain was not far above the level of my head. With my prize safely ensconced in my Player's cigarette tin, I scrambled up the dry earth bank and hauled myself onto the grass. I saw Max waving and set off toward him, grinning with the anticipation of showing him my catch. He duly admired my tatty tailed orange and then opened up his own collecting tin and showed me a beautiful pair of tailed oranges he had caught on the grassy slopes while I was scrabbling around in the dirt.

"They're a pair," Max informed me. "See this one with a heavy black rim to its wings? That's a female. This male has less black there but more along the front edge of its forewing."

I studied the differences and gently opened up my own specimen. "It's a male," I said.

Max agreed. "Come on, we'll look for another one for you."

We spent another hour scouring the slopes but did not so much as see another tailed orange. In the end, we gave up and started for home. Although I did not get another *Eurema proterpia* that day, I did catch another one a month or two later on wasteland near the Mona University. My second specimen was also a male, but in much better condition. It was also a lot easier to catch but it was the first one that stood out in my memory with its associations of shanty towns and Rastas.

Hellshire Hills

Southwest of Kingston and south of Spanish Town lies a bleak and desolate area near the coast that is known as the Hellshire Hills. They are dry because the underlying rock is limestone which drains quickly and also because they lie in the rain shadow of the Blue Mountains. The vegetation is known as subtropical dry forest and is relatively undisturbed as few people live here, frequenting only the coastal strip where white-sand beaches and secluded coves attract weekend visitors.

I was not much interested in the plants of the region, but I was eager to investigate its butterfly potential. However, its very bleakness and aridity put it low down on my parents' list of preferred destinations and it was over a year before I managed to visit it. My visit, when it happened, was accidental, and resulted from a visit to the former capital of Jamaica.

Spanish Town lies a little to the north of Hellshire, and used to be the capital city of Jamaica in the days when the island belonged to Spain. Initially it went by the name of Santiago de la Vega (and others), but after the British conquest in 1655, it was renamed. Although it was badly damaged during the conquest, so much so that Port Royal became the main British city, it remained the capital for another two hundred years, before that honour was handed over to Kingston, a mere thirteen miles to the east.

There was not much to see in Spanish Town unless you liked old buildings. I was dragged around to a few but really only liked the old Governor's Residence with its stately palm trees and columns. The town was poor, without much to occupy the population and we only visited it on infrequent occasions. One such time was when we visited some friends who had recently moved from Kingston to May Pen, which is about another twenty or so miles past Spanish Town.

We left Kingston early on a Saturday, meaning to drive through to May Pen before the heat of the day, spend a pleasant time with the family, and return in the evening. It was only when we were on our way that my mother thought to ask, "They do know we're coming, don't they?"

My father prevaricated before reluctantly admitting, "Not really... but they should be in. Tom's often said there's nothing to do in May Pen."

"Oh, Jay! You mean to say we could get there and find them out?"

"They'll be there."

We arrived shortly after ten in the morning and found they were out, with no note to indicate where they had gone or how long they might be. My father insisted on staying in the hope that they would arrive, but after half an hour, he relented and led us all in search of a pleasant picnic spot. After buying some snacks and sodas, we found a place by the Rio Minho River a few miles to the northeast and spread a blanket on the grass beneath the shade of some overgrown citrus trees. I set off to explore the riverbanks while my parents dozed or read magazines with some cold drinks to hand.

I wasn't sure what was found in this area, but I decided I wasn't interested in the common butterflies that could be found back in Kingston. I saw the usual array of sulphurs, whites, grass yellows, blues and skippers, but gave them no more than a cursory glance. I was looking for bigger game. I found the Zebra (*Heliconius charitonius*) in the shaded forest close to the water, their black and yellow stripes gleaming in the sun-dapples; and in the open glades I found orange long-winged Julias (*Dryas iulia*). I caught a few of each to keep my eye in, but only kept a single near-perfect specimen of each. Banana Butterflies (*Colobura dirce*) also frequented the deep shade and I caught sight of Leafwings (*Historis odius*) in the upper branches of mango trees.

Coming back out into the open grass and vine thickets near the river, I spotted high-flying swallowtails that I thought were either *Papilio andraemon* or female *Papilio thersites*. I looked hungrily at them, willing them to fly lower, but evidently their minds were stronger than mine for they ignored my mental commands. Both butterflies featured in my collection, but I lacked the female Thersites. I had almost caught a female at Jack's Hill, but it eluded me still.

I returned to the car, where my parents were packing up, having decided to motor back to Spanish Town. My collecting tin was almost empty, but in view of the non-cooperation of the swallowtails, there was little I could do about it. I helped gather up a few items and idly looked at the old gnarled citrus tree under which we had camped. I hoped there might be a ripe orange on it. Instead, I saw several large caterpillars and immediately dropped everything to investigate. The caterpillars were mottled--olive green with patches of black and cream. Then I started to see differences, some were a distinct olive green to grey over most of the body, with white splashes along the sides, whereas others were more irregularly coloured, looking rather like splashes of bird dung.

I put this down to different stages in the life cycle, but even some of the very largest were different. I knew two swallowtail species fed on citrus--*Papilio andraemon* and *Papilio thersites*, both of which I had seen flying near here. The chances were good that these caterpillars belonged to one or other (or both) species. If they truly were swallowtail caterpillars and not something else, that is. There was only one way to find out. I prodded at one with my finger.

At once, two fleshy orange fingers poked out from the hump at about the third segment and I caught a strong whiff of citrus oils. These fleshy fingers were the osmateria and were a protective device peculiar to swallowtails. I poked at another one and whitish horns protruded. Now I grew excited. I had two species of swallowtail caterpillars and if I could manage to rear them, I would have perfect specimens when they hatched out from their chrysalises. What is more, if some of them were Thersites caterpillars, it was probable I would at last have my female Thersites. I was sure I could find more citrus leaves in Kingston, so I would have a ready supply of larval food.

"Mum, Dad, have we got a jam jar I can use?"

"What do you want it for?"

"There are caterpillars on this tree. I want to rear them."

"I think there's one in the boot," my father said.

There was, and it still had its screw top. Unfortunately, it had accommodated something oily in the past and there was a strong smell of engine oil in it. I took it down to the river and cleaned it as best I could, scouring out the worst of the oil with river sand. I then dried it with my handkerchief and smelled it again. It still smelled of oil, but not as strongly. Perhaps if I...

"Dad, can I punch some air holes in the top?"

"No. I'll need that jar again, and if it leaks oil I won't be happy."

This was a setback, but not an insurmountable one. I loaded a number of fresh citrus leaves into the jar and added a dozen large caterpillars, six of each of the types. In theory, I should have six Thersites and three should be females. Even if luck was against me, surely I'd still get one. I added another four of each, though this made the jar very crowded. *It's only until I get home*, I told myself. I left the lid off for the moment, so the caterpillars could get plenty of fresh air. Any that wandered to the rim of the jar were poked back down, and soon my fingers were stained with the stinky oils from the osmateria.

We drove back to Spanish Town where we found a small restaurant and had lunch. I wanted to bring my jar of caterpillars in with me but I had to leave it in the car. I wedged it on the back seat and made sure the lid was only on loosely, and wound the windows down a little bit so they wouldn't overheat. When I returned from lunch though, I found that they had forced the lid off and gone wandering. Five caterpillars had escaped and though I searched the car thoroughly, I only found four of them. I thought perhaps the fifth had escaped the car through the open window. I made sure the others were secure.

My parents were loath to go home right away, but they had seen Spanish Town before, so wanted to look elsewhere.

"Where's it to be?" my father asked. "Hills or beaches?"

'Hills' got my immediate vote as it would be cooler and there were likely to be more butterflies. My mother voted for the beach, and so that's where we went. Beaches are all right, I suppose, but I prefer forest for butterfly hunting. Then my father said the closest good beach was in Hellshire. I perked up--I had always wanted to go there. Hellshire lies south of Spanish Town and is a broad peninsula with some nice beaches and coves. Apart from that is hot and dry, but it was a place that might harbour some interesting things.

"There might be butterflies up in those hills," I remarked as we drew close.

"We're going to the beach, though," my father replied.

"You could drop me off."

"I'm not leaving you alone out here in this wilderness."

"I wouldn't mind."

So we went down to the beach. My mother found a nice spot where she could put a blanket out on the white sand. The place was deserted and I wandered around disconsolately, seeing almost no butterflies along the sea strand. I looked up at the scrub-covered hills and saw a track leading up to a vague clearing about a mile away.

"Could I go up there, Dad?"

He stared in the direction I was pointing my net. "I don't like the idea of you wandering off alone."

"I do it all the time, Dad. Besides, I'd only be up there in that clearing. There's no one around and I could wave to you to show I'm safe. Please, Dad, there's no butterflies down here."

"All right, but don't talk to anyone and come straight back if you see people you don't like the look of."

I debated what to do with my caterpillars and decided to leave them in the car. It was in the shade, so the temperature should not rise high enough to harm them, even with the lid screwed down. I picked up my net and a bottle of Pepsi and headed for the hills.

The track up into the hills looked wide enough for a vehicle, but it was rutted and rough. I climbed easily, keeping a lookout for butterflies along the sides of the sparse vegetation. Everything was very dry and I felt my sweat prickling my forehead and dampening my shirt. Dust rose into the air as I scrambled up the hill road, coating my shoes and legs. The soil was reddish underneath the dry scrubby plants, and the whole area had a deserted and uninhabited feel about it, though I found an open area that showed evidence of fire, with fragments of charred twigs showing through the soil. I turned a corner and came to the open area I had seen from the beach--it was a graveyard.

The graves were old and overgrown, most no more than vague mounds with palings of weathered wood leaning tiredly at their heads, or lichen-covered stones with worn, unreadable inscriptions. They exuded an air of abandonment, a lonely feeling of having been forgotten by friends and family. Certainly, there was no evidence of recent activity. I wandered among them for a few minutes, carefully avoiding walking on any of the mounds.

There were butterflies here, but hardly more than down at the beach. I caught a white peacock (*Anartia jatrophae*) and saw a few tattered buckeyes (*Precis evarete*). Small daisy-like flowers attracted tiny blues, and a handful of grass yellows. A Queen (*Danaus gilippus*) led me off on a short chase, leaping graves and dodging thickets, but I lost it when it sailed off over the hillside.

I remembered my promise to my father and waved my net above my head in case he was looking from the beach. I could just make out the car, but I couldn't see my parents. I looked around me once more and then off at the scrub-covered hills. I had told my father I was only going to the clearing, but it couldn't hurt if I went just a little bit further. I could even follow the track rather than push through the thin scrub. I convinced myself that my father would expect this of me, and walked back to the cemetery entrance.

The track rapidly petered out above the graveyard, becoming no more than a faint path for a hundred yards and then nothing but the hint of a line through the scrub. I pushed onward, hoping to find something worth my effort. It came--in the form of a Cuban Crescent (*Phyciodes frisia*). These little butterflies with black and orange and cream splattered wings are found elsewhere, but for one reason or another I had never collected it. It moved ahead of me, settling every few paces and I crept up on it and snared it in my net. If I caught nothing else today, my day would still be worthwhile.

I reached thick vegetation and the last remnants of the track vanished. I saw how far I'd come from the old graveyard and decided I'd better turn back. I found a rock and sat down, wiping the sweat from my brow and opening my warm bottle of Pepsi. I drank thirstily, feeling the liquid and sugar lift my energy levels. I burped loud and long and started to rise when a movement a few yards away stopped me. A lizard sat side-on on the red earth beneath a tangled shrub and looked at me suspiciously from a beady eye.

But what a lizard. I had never seen anything like it outside of zoos. It was large, at least two feet in length, and looked ancient, more like a dinosaur than a living animal. A series of short spines adorned its back, and the skin of its throat hung in a broad fold, rather like the throat pouch of a tree Anole. I wondered what on earth it was ... and then whether I would be able to catch it. I picked up my net and it hissed at me. I had never been threatened by a lizard before. I stared back at it, wondering how fierce it could be. It was only a lizard, after all, even if it was the largest one I'd seen. I could pop my net over it and carry it back down to the beach in the folds. I slowly rose to my feet and as I moved, it turned and ran for the cover of the thicket, its legs scrabbling at the bare earth and its long tail whipping back and forth furiously.

I charged forward, but by the time I got to the thicket it had disappeared. For a few seconds, I could hear faint rustlings and then that died away too. I searched, poking the handle of my net into the undergrowth in the hope of disturbing it, but without any discernible result. I had a feeling that the lizard was an iguana, but I also thought the man at the Institute of Jamaica had said they were very rare. I had no evidence of my sighting and I didn't think he'd take the word of a twelve year old boy.

I sighed and turned away, heading back through the scrub to the dirt road, the distant blatt of a car horn spurring me on. I was panting and wet from sweat by the time I arrived back at the car, and full of my sighting.

"I saw a huge lizard...it was an iguana, I think...I tried to catch it but it got away...they're rare..."

"I thought you said you were only going to that clearing. You should have been back long before."

"Sorry, Dad. It's a graveyard, but there wasn't much there and I thought you wouldn't mind if I..."

"Just get in the car."

I got in. As we accelerated away from the beach, I picked up the jam jar with my precious caterpillars and stared at the container. The whole of the inside was lined with condensation and there was a puddle of amber-coloured liquid in the bottom. Even from the outside I could see three...no, four...caterpillars drowned in it. I opened it with shaking hands and spilled out caterpillars and hot, wet leaves onto the seat beside me. Several were motionless and a few others moved feebly. I smelled the glistening leaves and could detect the stink of engine oil. Evidently, I had not cleaned the jar well enough. The oil residue, together with the heat of the car, had acted to kill my precious caterpillars. I sorted out the dead from the living and found I had only five survivors. I nursed these in my handkerchief until we got home, where I transferred them to a clean jar and scrounged some citrus leaves from a neighbour. They refused to eat however, and within a day, were all dead. I mourned their loss bitterly.

By an odd chance, I found a single caterpillar in the car a day or two later. It was the one that had gone missing in Spanish Town. Although it had been subjected to the heat, it had missed the oil poisoning and survived, though very hungry. It devoured the citrus leaves I provided and eventually pupated. I was still hopeful that I might get the female Thersites I sought, but it was not to be. It was a Thersites all right, but a male, and even then useless for my collection as evidently something had gone wrong during development and it hatched crippled, with tiny folded and twisted wings that doomed it from birth. I put it out of its misery.

My trip to May Pen and the Hellshire Hills had been a bit of a disaster. I had a Cuban Crescent for my collection, but the only other thing that excited me was my sighting of the iguana. I told the man at the Institute of Jamaica, but I don't think he believed me. At least, he didn't seem interested, telling me I must have seen an ordinary skink. Well, I know what I saw, and why shouldn't a twelve-year-old boy see something rare if he's in the right place at the right time? The Hellshire Hills opened its dry and dusty cloak that day and afforded me a glimpse of a rarity, perhaps to make up for my other disappointments.

Hummingbirds & Swordtails

"A Mrs Urquhart phoned me today," my father said at dinner one night. "Your science teacher from school. She's invited you to visit her this Saturday. What's all that about?"

"She said we could look at her hummingbirds," I said cautiously, trying to judge his mood. "Me and Max Wright."

"Why would she invite you to her home for the day?"

I started to shrug but turned it into a stretch. My father did not like indecision. "We're the only two in our class who like butterflies and things. She asked if we'd like to come and see her garden and bird feeders and we said yes, as long as it's all right with you, Dad."

"I rang the school and they said she has their fullest confidence."

I hesitated. "So, er, can I go?"

"I don't see why not."

That Saturday, Mrs Urquhart picked us both up from school, where our parents had dropped us. I had left my butterfly net behind as our teacher had already told us that she allowed no collecting on her property. While the other Max and I waited, we swapped stories about recent captures and sightings. I told him about a strange white brimstone butterfly I had seen near Government House.

"It was just like the yellow ones we see, but a very pale yellow, almost white."

"I think the female *Anteos* are pale," Max said. "The males are the rich butter yellow."

"Is that all it is?" I said, disappointed. "I hoped it was a new species or...or a mutation."

"I'd still like to catch one. They don't seem very common."

Mrs Urquhart arrived in her old car, and we piled in. Instead of turning toward the Mona Estate however, she turned toward Half Way Tree. We were not going to her apartment in Mona, she explained, but to her home near Castleton. She only used the Mona apartment during the week to save herself a long drive every day. Her husband was up in Castleton and there was much more to see up there.

It was a fairly long drive but an interesting one. We passed through Half Way Tree and onto Constant Spring Road, heading north. Kingston was always a busy city and even out here in the suburbs there was plenty to see. It was Saturday morning, and the streets were full of people attending small markets on every other street corner, all gaily dressed and talking patois in loud voices. Over it all rode music, both from radios and live, from steel drums and guitars. The music rose and fell in snatches, wafting in through the open windows as the car sped past. It was fascinating.

From Constant Spring the road wound up Stony Hill and from there through the tiny townships of Coakley and Toms River and on to Castleton on the Wag Water River. This river winds its way down the other side of the mountains and empties itself into the sea in Annotto Bay. Today, though, we left the Wag Water and ascended a small dirt road that went up into the hills. We passed a small house about half way up the road and finished at an old rambling house set among the trees.

Dr William Urquhart waited on the wide veranda and we were introduced to him. He had cold drinks waiting for us and I accepted a Pepsi. Max Wright sipped on a Coke, and we sat and listened while Dr Urquhart, who was a retired professor, told us about his work. He was interested in the history of Jamaica, particularly from the time of Columbus to the taking over of the island by the British in 1655. He talked for a little while as we finished our drinks and then let us go with a smile.

"I expect you'll want to see the hummingbirds."

Mrs Urquhart took us round to the back veranda. Here the house overlooked a riot of flowering shrubs and small trees that merged imperceptibly with the surrounding forest. Affixed to the eaves of the house and the veranda posts were what I thought were garish plastic flowers and I wondered for a moment why she would have such ornaments when just beyond the chipped and weathered wooden railing were cascades of bougainvillea, hibiscus and trumpet vine. Then I saw movement near one and recognised it for what it was--a hummingbird feeder.

A male Vervain hummingbird hovered in front of a small red plastic flower. Its angled body was almost stationary as a blur of wings kept it in place, its tail tilted up in a jaunty manner. A small curved bill delicately probed the feeder, its tongue sipping at the nectar in the jar fixed to it. Mrs Urquhart pointed to some seats at the rear of the veranda and motioned us to quietly take our places.

"Don't make any sudden movements," she whispered. "They're used to Bill and me, and they don't mind quiet talking, but stay as still as you can."

We watched the male for a few minutes and then it was off in a blur of wings, streaking for the cover of the trees. A moment later, it or another male Vervain returned and flitted from feeder to feeder. Then a female Vervain joined it and they jostled for position in front of one feeder despite others being available.

"Are they a pair?" Max Wright whispered.

"Yes. We have three pairs nesting in our garden this year. I'll show you one of them later. Look..."

The Vervains scattered as another bird approached. This one was larger, with a green back and white belly, but it too hovered in front of a feeder, inserting a long red and black bill.

"A female Streamertail," Mrs Urquhart said. "Her mate should be around somewhere. Ah, here he comes."

An emerald green bird swooped toward the veranda, making a high-pitched whining hum as it flew. It settled on a branch a dozen feet away and stared at us and at the feeder, pointing its bright red bill this way and that. Despite its beauty, it was not its colour that made us smile; it was the two black feathers of its tail that hung beneath it, longer than the bird itself. Truly, this bird was aptly named 'Streamertail'. The male called--a loud 'teet teet' sound and the female backed away from the feeder and joined him on the branch.

"It's also called Scissortail and Doctorbird," Mrs Urquhart said.

"I can see why scissortail," Max Wright said, "But why Doctorbird?"

"Have you ever seen those old pictures of doctors from last century in their black frock coats?"

Max shook his head, eliciting a sharp 'tsee tsee' from the male Streamertail. I whispered, "I think so."

Mrs Urquhart smiled. "Their coats had long tails that hung down behind, rather like that male up there."

Max Wright laughed and the male Streamertail took flight. It hovered for a few moments, its wings making a thrumming sound and then streaked for the cover of the trees, its streamers trailing.

"Never mind, he'll be back later. How about we go and look round the garden?"

The Urquharts' garden was another wonder. My own garden back in Kingston boasted a pawpaw tree, some banana sprouts and an ackee tree, but I was dazzled by the number of fruit trees here. I saw bananas and the ackee of course, as well as others I was familiar with, like mango, breadfruit, pawpaw and citrus, but there were others I had never seen. Max Wright and I ran from one to the other, touching immature and ripe fruit, asking about each one. Mrs Urquhart kept pace with us, identifying each one and adding a fact or two if she had time.

"Malay apple... hog plum... Mammy apple... when they're ripe they taste a bit like mangoes. That's a naseberry...try one, there are some ripe ones, I think. No, don't eat the skin...and watch out for the seeds..."

The naseberry tasted like a very sweet pear, its flesh brown and with a gritty texture. It was very nice and I scattered the seeds so that more could grow.

"Passionfruit vines, you probably know," went on Mrs Urquhart. "Pawpaw, soursop, custard apple... ah, you might like this one too." She picked up a purplish fruit from the ground and checked it for insect or animal damage. She cut the skin with her thumbnail and pulled it apart. The flesh was purple and white and leaked a milky fluid. "Star apple. Don't eat the skin, it's a bit bitter."

The fruit was smooth and slightly gelatinous and delicious. I sucked the flesh from the large dark seeds and turned my half inside out to get the last of it, tossing the empty skin and seeds into the undergrowth.

She picked up a fallen soursop and said. "I'll prepare this one for lunch. Come on, you can watch the hummingbirds while I prepare it."

"What's through there?" I pointed at a small gate in her boundary fence. I could see concrete peeking through ferns and low shrubs.

"That was our next door neighbour," Mrs Urquhart explained. "The house burned down about ten years ago and they never rebuilt. You can go through and have a look after lunch, if you like. There's still a pond and some nice trees."

While lunch was being prepared, Max Wright and I sat on the veranda and watched the hummingbirds. By keeping very quiet and still, we enticed both Vervain and Streamertails down to the feeders. Then we saw another type, a hummingbird about the size of a female Streamertail, but of very different colouration. Where the Streamertail was emerald and white, this one sported black and bronze and purple, with flashes of green and blue as it hovered. Then with a whir, it was gone. We ran inside and told Mrs Urquhart about this wonderful bird.

"It was a Jamaican Mango."

"I've never seen one before," Max Wright said.

"I have," I added. "In the Hope Gardens, but never close up. It was beautiful."

"Well, they're not rare, but localised. We're lucky to have a pair here."

She served lunch on the veranda, but round the side, away from the hummingbird feeders. Dr Urquhart joined us and said grace. I felt a bit awkward, as this was not something we did at home, but he smiled at me afterward and asked me about the Mango Hummingbird, putting us at ease again.

We ate rice with flaked white fish and fried ackee fruit from the garden. It was delicious, the yellow ackee like a nutty cheese that contrasted with the salty fish and the plain white rice. Instead of bread, we had slices of baked breadfruit, smeared liberally with butter.

"I thought I'd keep it traditional Jamaican," Mrs Urquhart said with a smile. "Strictly, we should serve rum with it, but I thought your parents would not approve." Instead, she served iced tea with guava juice as a drink and soursop fool for desert.

The soursop fool was a thick creamy white slurry served in bowls and eaten with spoons. It was both sweet and sour at the same time, and before I knew it I had finished my bowl and was running my finger round the inside to wipe up the last smears. I looked up and saw the others looking at me and I blushed with embarrassment, wiping my fingers on my napkin.

Mrs Urquhart smiled. "I like to see a boy who enjoys his food."

We went out into the garden again and Mrs Urquhart took us into one corner where a stunted mango tree held branches low down to the ground, at a height where a boy might see. At first I did not recognise what I was looking at, and then I saw the pale silk of spider-web and green of dried moss and lichens. Astride a narrow branch, a tiny nest lay open for our inspection. Mrs Urquhart looked around and then beckoned us close for a quick look before motioning us away.

"It's a Streamertail nest," she said. "They haven't started to lay their eggs or I wouldn't have allowed you that close."

We withdrew a dozen paces further and watched until first the female returned, and then the male. They uttered high-pitched 'chinking' cries and fluttered from branch to branch, so Mrs Urquhart led us away.

The property next door had once been a great garden if its ruins were anything to go by. The concrete I had seen were low stone walls, now tumbled, and a terrace through which trees had pushed. One of these was *Lignum vitae*, and Mrs Urquhart led us to this national flower of Jamaica. Even years later, when my knowledge of trees grew substantially, the *Lignum vitae* remained one of my favourites. It is a small tree and slow-growing, with wood that is so dense that it will sink in water. Small oval compound leaves covered its crown with a glossy green mantle studded with pale blue star-shaped flowers.

"*Lignum vitae* means 'wood-of-life' and was named that because it was thought to have a whole lot of medicinal properties." Mrs Urquhart shook her head. "It's an anti-inflammatory, a mild anaesthetic and a laxative, but that's about all. For me, its main attraction is its beauty."

I had to agree with her. The pale blue flowers set among the glossy green foliage appealed to me--and to ants apparently. I had been resting my hand on a branch and swarms of little black ants rushed onto me. I stepped away and hurriedly brushed them off before they started stinging.

An ornamental pond had once lain next to the house and it was still here, though overgrown and covered with weed. Frogs haunted its green depths, but clear water still trickled from the outlet through a series of channels and a chain of tiny pools on the edge of the ruined terrace. Max Wright and I followed the tiny stream away from the pond and found to our delight that the pools harboured life. Swimming in the bathtub-sized ponds were little fish, mostly silvery-green but some with flashes of red and black. I got down on my hands and knees to examine them more closely and saw that the red and black ones had extraordinary tails. The two-inch long fish had the bottom part of their tail fin extended by nearly another inch. I called Mrs Urquhart over excitedly pointed out my find.

"It's a swordtail," she said.

"Are they wild fish?"

"Green swordtails are found in Mexico, but I think all these probably came from an aquarium. They're nice, aren't they?"

I leaned back and looked at the series of little pools, each with its shattered stone and concrete surrounds, trails of weed and its own population of exotic fish, and thought it more than nice. It was beautiful.

We wandered among the ruins of the house and garden a bit longer and we became aware of a tiny green bird following us. I thought it was a hummingbird at first but as it flitted from one branch to another, its wings making a buzzing sound, I saw that it was not. Larger than a Vervain Hummingbird but smaller than a Streamertail, this little round green bird was in almost constant motion. Then it stopped and looked at us quizzically, and I saw it had a white breast and a bright red throat. It 'chirruped' and snatched a caterpillar from the underside of a leaf before flitting off through the foliage.

"A Jamaican Tody," we were told.

"I've never seen one before."

"They're actually quite common, and they don't mind people, so I'm quite sure you'll see others if you keep your eyes open."

We returned to the Urquhart's house for afternoon tea and to watch the hummingbirds again. There were also butterflies around the flowers in the garden, particularly the hibiscus and trumpet vine, but they also had pink, white and red Pentas in flowerbeds. These had swallowtails on them-- Andraemon, Thersites and Pelaus. I saw a female Thersites so close I could almost reach out and touch it. I made an involuntary motion to catch it as if I held a net in my hands, but as a guest of the Urquhart's all I could do was gaze at it hungrily. While I watched I saw a hummingbird come to a spray of pink Pentas flowers and hover by it, sipping the nectar. The hummingbird was quite different from the ones we had seen that day and I went running to tell Mrs Urquhart.

"There's a new hummingbird on the flowers--it's brown and yellow. Come quickly."

Mrs Urquhart and Max Wright came running and found the new bird had only moved a few paces away. Mrs Urquhart leaned closer and studied it for a few moments before calling us closer.

"Look at how it feeds. What colour is its beak?"

I stared, dumbfounded. "It doesn't have one. There's just a... a tongue like a butterfly's."

"That's right. It's not a hummingbird, but a hummingbird hawkmoth. One of the Sphingid moths."

We watched it for several minutes before it flew off. I would dearly have loved to try and catch it but I respected my host's wishes. Now I knew they existed, I would find another one some other time.

Our visit came to an end. We bid farewell to Dr Urquhart and then his wife, our teacher, took us back down the long hill road to Priory School and our waiting parents. We never went there again, but Mrs Urquhart would often make some comment to us after class about something we had seen in her garden at Castleton--about hawkmoths and todies, about *Lignum vitae* and fruit trees, about hummingbirds and swordtails.

Hamsters

Following the debacle with my captive pond, it was a while before my parents would allow me to bring anything live into the house or to own another pet. Into this hiatus fell (literally) a small bird of some indeterminate species. I found it in the gutter on the way home from school one day and carried it with me, determined to look after it. My mother gave me a shoebox and a piece of towelling and I kept it in the airing cupboard while I thought about what I was going to feed it.

It was an unprepossessing creature--all bare belly and gaping beak with bulging blind eyes and a sparse covering of feather stubs. Ugly in fact, but it fascinated me. I read a couple of books and asked a few people, including Mrs Urquhart, my science teacher, and determined that a bird of this type-- whatever it was--was likely to eat seeds or insects. I prevailed upon my mother to buy me a packet of bird seed at the store and I prepared the nestling's first meal. I crushed some seed and mixed it with a little water to make a lumpy paste and offered it on the end of a toothpick. It ignored me and my offering, and squatted in its towelling nest.

I tried various things, like smearing the paste on its soft bill, or gently tapping it, or even making chirping noises, but nothing worked until I got up with a sigh and my shadow fell across its closed eyes. At once, it raised itself up, quivered its little stumpy wings, opened its bill and made wheezing noises. I grinned and introduced some seed paste to its gaping gullet, and then some more.

"You do realise it'll die?" my father said when he came home. "It probably got injured when it fell out of its nest."

I nodded, but continued administering seed paste to an eager nestling. After a bit, it would settle back and not respond to my movements or a hand passed over its eyes. A little later, it moved, wriggling backward and pointing its bottom in the air. I wondered what was happening until a huge packet of bird poo was ejected beyond the bowl of the makeshift nest. It would do this every few hours and seldom soiled its 'nest'. I learned that the mother bird would remove these poo packets, but as I was only the substitute, I was still learning these niceties.

The next morning I went out on an edible insect hunt and developed a healthy respect for the abilities of foraging birds. After an hour's search of shrubs and soil, I had a single small green caterpillar, a very hairy one, some wood lice, and a tiny worm. I rejected the hairy caterpillar, as I knew some moths have hairy larvae as protection and these may have been irritating hairs. The woodlice I also released as being too indigestible, but fed the green caterpillar and tiny worm to the nestling. It swallowed them without comment.

This continued for a few weeks, in the course of which the baby bird grew, opened its eyes, and clothed itself in feathers. It would now squeak and bob up and down, its bill gaping, whenever I came near the shoebox, demanding to be fed. My mother bought another packet of seed and I got better at finding caterpillars and worms, to which I added small grasshoppers after I had killed them and removed their legs and wings.

My next task was to teach it to fly. I wondered how mother birds accomplished this task and imagined all sorts of unlikely scenarios. In the end, I cupped its little body in my hands and took it into the back yard where I carefully sat it on the clothesline. It swayed and looked around suspiciously, but showed no inclination to take to the air. I took the line in my hands and gently started rotating it. The young bird glared at me and adjusted its footing frantically, before flapping its tiny wings in an effort to keep its balance. I thought this was a grand exercise, so kept it up for a few minutes before taking the bird back inside.

The next day, I repeated the exercise, but on the third day it responded by flapping wildly and tumbling to the ground. I picked it up and put it back on its unstable perch. It promptly threw itself off again in a desperate attempt to escape me. Gradually, over the space of a day or so, it managed to glide and flap most of the way across the back yard before landing inelegantly on the lawn. A day later it reached a shrub and hung upside-down from a branch until I rescued it. The next day it sailed over the fence into a neighbour's tree. I retrieved it with some difficulty and found it a nice big juicy grasshopper as a reward. The next time I took it outside, it flew from my hand and away across the road to a clump of trees. I ran after it and could hear birds chattering in the branches, but could not spot my little one. I waited for it, hoping it would return for food if not companionship, but I never saw it again.

My parents were impressed with my animal caring activities and offered to buy me a pet. I went to the pet shop with them with no great expectations. I did not particularly like dogs, and a cat would remind me too much of the one we'd left behind in Germany. I now had some experience with a bird, but having just had my love rejected by one, was not ready to offer my heart to another feathered bundle. I considered a white mouse, but utterly rejected the idea of more fish. A snake was a possibility, but I'd have to see what was available before arguing my case. When we arrived at the pet shop, there were the usual puppies and kittens, assorted aquarium fish, flights of cage birds, mice and turtles--and a hamster.

One cage held a solitary rodent with lovely white and orangey-coloured fur. It sat up on its haunches and looked at me with little pink nose quivering and I was captivated. Money changed hands and I was in possession of a female golden hamster, a plastic and wire cage, a bag of wood shavings, a small bag of dry food, a wire wheel and food and water bowls.

I named her 'Honey' for her colouring but, as I found out, it could equally have been for her disposition. She had the sweetest nature, and unlike some other hamsters I have known, never bit me. I handled her a lot, right from the start, and that may have had something to do with it. I'd carry her around in my shirt pocket and she'd put her paws on the lip and peer out myopically or try burrowing through the bottom. I found that if I put her on the floor she would disappear under my bed, into the cupboards, or under the door, seeking a refuge where she could hide from imagined dangers.

She'd run around on my bed happily enough and seldom tried to climb down the cover to the floor. If I took her from her cage in the daytime, she'd head under the covers and go to sleep, marking her progress with an interrupted trail of dark brown droppings.

Golden hamsters are classified as crepuscular, which just means they become active at dusk and dawn. If I left Honey alone, she would sleep all day, curled up in an informal nest of wood shavings and food in one corner of her cage, peering out blearily if disturbed. When evening came, however, she'd be up and about, scurrying all over her cage, rearranging her bedding, inspecting every scrap of stored food she had, or exercising on her wheel.

Everyone knows what a rodent wheel is, so I need not go into lengthy descriptions. Suffice it to say that it was of chromed iron, squeaked, and rapidly rusted under the influence of hamster urine. You mustn't get the idea that hamsters are dirty animals, for they are in fact very clean. Honey used one corner of her cage as a toilet and would run over there every time she felt the need. It was a small cage, however, and she could not avoid treading in wet sawdust or newspaper and tracking it onto her wheel if I delayed changing her litter.

By the time I went to bed each evening, Honey was wide awake and running for dear life on her wheel, her little legs a blur, head and tail curved upward. Sometimes she would stop abruptly and the momentum of the spinning wheel would carry her back and over for a turn or two. With each turn, the wheel squeaked, and though it was repetitive and annoying, I grew used to it. I would sit at my desk pinning the butterflies I had caught that day and Honey would run beside me.

Hamsters eat mostly dry food, and the pellets I got from the pet shop were of a mixture formulated for rodents. To this basic diet I added a variety of seeds and cereals and she thrived. Early on in our relationship, I introduced her to various human foods like cheese and greens and peanut butter. She ate them readily enough, but she'd also store the rest in her food cache for midday snacks and as often as not, forget them. I'd then find a stinking mass a few days later when cleaning up her cage. Also, her droppings became soft and started to smell--a bit like ripe marmite--so I put her back onto a dry diet.

Hamsters are opportunistic feeders and have a pair of large cheek pouches in which to carry anything they find back to their nest. When I first saw a bulge on the side of her face I panicked, thinking she had developed an abscess or growth, but then a few moments later, after a trip to her nest, it had vanished. I watched her carefully and saw what happened. I'd give her a dozen dried peas and she'd quickly stuff them into her pouches until they bulged, whereupon she'd waddle back to her sleeping quarters and use her little pink front paws to push the peas out. They'd be perfectly dry and she'd bury them in the wood shavings for later use.

I was curious about how big her pouches were and gave her larger and larger amounts until she could literally hold no more, her pouches looking like some obscene growth on each side of her head. Occasionally, I gave her dry pasta and she'd treat it in the same way, dutifully carrying it back for later consumption. Then I gave her a piece of uncooked spaghetti, several times her own length. She immediately stuffed it in one cheek pouch and then stopped and stared at the length that was still outside. After a moment's hesitation, she took it out, changed her grip, and tried pushing it into the other pouch. When that didn't work, she tried the first one again. After a few more tries she suddenly grasped what the problem was and quickly gnawed the long piece of pasta into pouch-sized pieces, stuffed them all in and contentedly added them to her burgeoning store.

After I'd had Honey for a few months, my friend Chris Peacock asked his parents if he could have a hamster too. They said he could and he bought a male which he called Leo, presumably because he had a lion's colouration. I saw Leo whenever I went over to his house to play, but I wasn't terribly impressed. The male hamster was lean and quick and inclined to offer a nip if he thought he was being handled too much. Accordingly, Leo remained in his cage a lot more than my Honey.

A few months later, the Peacock family went on holiday and they asked if I would look after Leo while they were away. I happily agreed, but they added that on no account was I to allow them to be together. I agreed to that too, but I remember thinking it was rather unfair they weren't allowed to play together.

Their cages sat side by side on my desk and I now had two hamsters to distract me. Every evening, I'd clean out their toilet corners, add fresh wood shavings, check that their water was fresh and that their store of food was well supplied, and then I'd let them out for a run on my bed--Honey first, and then Leo. I noticed that Leo seemed inordinately interested in the places where Honey had run, scurrying back and forth as if in pursuit of a phantom hamster. I felt very sorry for him and saw how he often climbed the wire of his cage closest to Honey's. I got to wondering why Chris' parents did not want the two hamsters to be together. Was it because they thought they might fight? I didn't think Leo looked like he wanted to fight.

I put them together one evening and for one heart-stopping moment I thought the Peacocks' fears were justified. Leo ran across to Honey, there was some squeaking and chittering, and then he leapt on her back, scrabbling with his hind legs to stay in place. I started forward, knowing I had to separate them before Honey got hurt. I was going to get bitten if I plucked Leo off, but... Honey was not acting as if she was distressed. I watched anxiously, but a few minutes later Leo hopped off Honey and they both started cleaning themselves. I hurriedly put them back in their cages, thankful my hamster was unhurt.

A couple of days later, Leo returned to his family and life returned to normal. For a few days anyway; then Honey started getting fat and she got very busy in her nest, throwing out all the old material and bringing in new, taking out every piece of food and reburying it. Another week, and there were suddenly three pink slugs in the nest with Honey. I went running for my mother to come and see. She confirmed the fact--Honey was a mother.

My father looked hard at me. "Did you put the hamsters together when you were looking after Leo?"

I admitted it. "They looked so lonely in their cages and I didn't think they'd fight."

"They didn't fight; they mated."

Is that what it was? I wondered whether I could ask some questions, but decided against it. I didn't even know what question I wanted to ask.

"Well, they've certainly proved they weren't fighting," my father went on. "You'll have to tell the Peacocks you disobeyed them."

"Do I have to? No harm's been done, has it? I mean, Honey's the one with the babies, not Leo."

"And Leo is the father. Of course you have to tell them."

Reluctantly, I did as I was told. My father took me round and I owned up to my actions and mumbled an apology. Mr and Mrs Peacock gave me a short lecture on respecting other peoples' property and let me go. I slunk off, too embarrassed to look them in the eye.

Honey and her three babies were another matter. They were endlessly fascinating and I was always tearing down the wall of the nest so I could look at them. Honey was very patient and just tucked them away beneath her if she thought I was too insistent. They grew apace and soon had faint coverings of downy hair and their eyes opened. I faced the task of naming them.

My mother was fond of Beatrix Potter and thought they looked a bit like little pigs lining up to get a drink. She suggested I look to the tale of Pigling Bland for inspiration. I read the story and looked at the three fat little babies sucking away and named them Suck-Suck, Yock-Yock, and Chin-Chin. The first two turned out to be females and the last one was a male, so that was perfect too.

A week or two later, my match-making actions were vindicated, though there is a possibility they might have precipitated Leo's disappearance. One day, he escaped and was never seen again. Chris was distraught, but I was in a position to give him little Chin-Chin as a replacement. What's more, Chin-Chin was the natural son of Leo, so there was a continuity that could not be denied. Mrs Peacock voiced a suspicion that Leo only left in a vain search for his mate, but that could not be proven and she agreed Chin-Chin was an obvious solution, so no more was said about my indiscretion.

I kept Suck-Suck and Yock-Yock, and together with their mother Honey they formed an amiable trio, though there was some dispute over who could use the wheel. They remained with me until I left Jamaica, at which point I found homes for them all with my friends.

Yellow Fever

Vacation time was an opportunity to do as I liked without the constraints of school. The only problem was, my father worked, so he could not be running me out to prime butterfly sites or on adventures into the hills or along the north coast. This meant I was left to my own resources and sometimes I came up a bit short. I could always shoulder my net and head to Hope Gardens or search bits of wasteland within cycling distance, but sometimes I got lonely and sought out others of my own age. Steve Riley and Max Wright were the only butterfly enthusiasts I knew, but I had other friends.

Chris Peacock was the same age as me and sometimes we would go fishing on the wharves of old Kingston Town. This was a full day's exercise as we had to be dropped off at the wharves early in the morning by my father and picked up after work. Our mothers would pack us sandwiches and bottles of soda, and one father or other would slip us sixpence for bait. We'd arrive in the fresh cool air of morning and stake out a place in the shade at the end of a wharf where the rolling swell hissed against the pilings and the fronds of weed swayed back and forth. The water was deep and green and sometimes, lying on my stomach on the weathered planking with my head over the edge, I thought I could see movement deep below, at the limits of visibility. Each time I saw it I thought, *this is the day I catch a big one.*

We were armed with handlines and an assortment of hooks and sinkers in a little tin, and the first thing we'd do was check our lines for any abrasions or snarls, cutting and snipping as necessary, tying on new lengths and fitting new hooks. Then one of us would go looking for a bait-man. Many Jamaicans liked to fish, but the ones fishing from the wharves were usually older and would supplement their income by harvesting tiny mussels from the pilings and selling them as bait. We could buy a baked bean can full of shelled mussels for sixpence, and this would usually last the two of us most of the day. Back at our site we would bait up and throw our lines in the water.

There was an excitement to feeling the sinker drag the baited hook out of sight into the green depths. The line was balanced on a fingertip, running down into the water and allowing tiny vibrations to be carried up to us, with an occasional sharp tug as a fish rushed in to snatch at a morsel of mussel, unwilling to commit to a larger mouthful and the hook. We would sit on the edge, dangling our feet, and read the indecision of the fish so far below us. Tiny tugs told us they were interested, and then would come a space of a few minutes when nothing happened, our line standing still in the water. Up would come the line, and the bare hook would gleam as it came through the surface. A fresh mussel, and down it would go, ready to tempt the unseen fish again.

Another series of nibbles and tugs and the line would suddenly go taut as a fish swallowed bait and hook. With a shout of glee, we'd haul the hapless victim up onto the wharf and dispatch it with a blow from a lump of wood. The hook would be eased out of the lip or gill and we'd stand grinning at our prize, which commonly measured no more than a few inches in length. A few times though, we caught something worth catching.

I remember a time when the line slipped into the groove between the second and third segment of my finger and paid out so fast it drew blood. While I was dancing around, yelling with pain, Chris hauled my catch in. It was a fairly large eel and it proceeded to wrap itself around the line, not allowing us to get close enough to kill it. An old Jamaican came to our rescue and we gave him the eel as a reward. The first time we had caught something, we had proudly carried our catch home, only to have it laughed at, so after that we gave our fish away, or if they were too small to even consider eating, threw them back or used them as bait.

Another time we caught a tiny puffer-fish. The hook fell out as we hauled it up and the little thing flopped for a moment or two before sucking air in and expanding into a small prickly ball about the size of my fist. This failed to intimidate us and it deflated with resigned squeak. We laughed and threw it back, watching as it swam rapidly back into the depths.

My father would collect us after work and we'd pile into the car, sun-reddened and stinking of mussels and fish. The experience would be enough for us for another week or two, and we'd be looking for other things to occupy us.

Chris has an interesting piece of wasteland behind his house, often with a tied up donkey in residence. We'd fill its bucket with water and bring it handfuls of grass, but we were not game enough to feed it by hand. It had a vicious temper and would bite or kick if we got too close. Further down the plot of land were some tall trees and one which grew in the bottom of a gully had a trunk that came near to one side. It was an old tree, pitted and gnarled and a branch had been ripped off in a storm, allowing the heartwood to rot. Inside the gaping hole hung large waxy combs with a drizzle of bees moving in and out. A dull hum rose from the wild hive. We stood and watched in fascination until mischief entered the hearts of two young boys.

I picked up a rock. "What do you think?" I asked, tossing the rock from hand to hand.

Chris grinned and picked up one of his own. "We don't want to get too close. Bees sting."

We moved back a few paces, and then a few more. "Ready?" We threw, and the rocks clattered against the tree trunk. The hum of the bees rose in pitch momentarily and subsided. We picked up more rocks and moved closer. These rocks missed also and we tried again, almost from the lip of the gully. This time we scored direct hits. The hum of the hive became a roar and bees erupted from the hole seeking the source of the disturbance.

"Cripes!" Chris yelled, and took to his heels. I followed suit and soon overtook him, faster than a speeding Peacock, leaping small bushes in a single bound. It did not save me though, and I took three stings to the back of my neck and another on my arm. Chris fared worse, receiving a good dozen stings before we got clear. Chastened, we swapped stories of pain, laughing at each other's fear in the face of danger.

Chris and I skirted danger again a week or two later when we happened upon an old house that was undergoing repairs. It was pretty well gutted and as there was no one on site, we scrambled in through a window and started exploring. There was very little inside the house but high-ceilinged empty rooms and we went upstairs, where we found that one whole side of the house had been removed, leaving sheets of board stretching out in front of us.

"Wow, what a view," Chris said. He pushed past me and walked out onto the boards. I followed, but was shocked into immobility when Chris screamed and fell, plummeting through the roof. The boards were no more than thin sheets of plaster over narrow ceiling beams and Chris had fallen through. Then he shouted and I snapped out of my freeze.

"Help!"

I moved forward and saw that he was hanging from one of the beams; his feet suspended at least ten feet from a pile of rubbish below him.

"Hold on," I cried, and started forward. The next moment, the plaster board gave way beneath me and I fell, but luckily or unluckily, partly astride a beam. I cried out in pain and struggled into a sitting position, staring across a dozen feet to where my friend still hung. "Hang on." I gingerly edged forward, but Chris could hang on no longer, falling to the pile of rubbish below. I turned awkwardly and started back along the beams until I made the safety of the house where I limped downstairs and went to find Chris.

He was sitting on the rubbish pile, wiping away a few tears of pain and fright, and I commiserated with him, assuring him I had tried to reach him but...well, I was wounded too. I dropped my shorts and showed him my scraped and raw thigh, already darkening with a bruise. He seemed impressed as all he had was a splinter in one hand.

Chris introduced me to two of his friends who lived near him but went to a different school--the Williams brothers, Ben and Joe. The Williams family lived on a large piece of land with an old, rather ramshackle house and some livestock in the form of a few beef cattle in a pen out the back and numerous chickens that ran free. Chris and I would sometimes go round there in the holidays for marathon Monopoly games. On those occasions we would usually stay for lunch, most often peanut butter sandwiches and cordial, but once a tuna and macaroni casserole. It was my first taste of tuna and it became a lifelong delight.

One day, after a very long session of team monopoly which Ben and I had lost through his ill-advised sale of all our properties for all the money, we wandered out into the front yard where the cook was about to prepare dinner. She had a chicken under one arm, a large zinc tub, an axe and a chopping block. I stared, knowing what must surely happen but not quite believing it.

The cook laid the chicken on the block, holding tight to its legs, and with a swift blow cut off its head. The head just looked rather surprised, but the decapitated chicken, when released, ran for it. The zinc tub was thrown over it and for what seemed an age; we could hear thumps and bangs from under it. These quietened, and the bedraggled and bloodied bird was hauled around the back for plucking. I felt slightly sick, so excused myself and rode home on my bicycle.

As I rode home I noticed a high-walled property down a side road and went back to investigate. It was a lonely road, without houses, and the grass and trees were brown and stunted. The wall was in bad repair, but along one side had wide iron gates, firmly padlocked. Peering through, I could see a tangle of dry vegetation, some uneven gravel paths and some tall flat stones leaning at tired angles. I couldn't think what it was, but as I was late already, I didn't investigate further. Instead, I asked Joe Williams when I was next round there.

Joe was the older brother, about a year or two older than me, and he enjoyed lording it over the rest of us. He smiled when I told him about the old stone wall, the iron gates and gravel paths.

"Oh yeah, I know what it is."

"What?"

"Come on and I'll show you."

Intrigued, we followed him down the road, along the side road to the iron gates, where we peered through the bars into the tangled vegetation and long grass.

"So what is it?" Chris asked.

"I think I know," Ben whispered.

"You keep quiet," Joe said. "Let's go in." He led us away from the gate and round the side where a section of wall had crumbled into a pile of rubble. It would be a scramble, but we could enter the enclosure this way.

"I don't want to go in," Ben said.

"Fine, you be a baby and stay out here. What about you two?" Joe looked at Chris and me. "Or are you babies too?"

I looked over the crumbled wall and wondered why Ben didn't want to go. I couldn't see anything to worry about, but I didn't like the way Joe was looking at us.

"There isn't a crocodile wandering about, is there?" I asked. "You know, like the one that's let loose in that used car yard in town?"

Joe laughed. "No, the only living things in there are bugs and lizards. There are some butterflies too," he added, looking at me.

I shrugged and started up the pile of stones. Chris followed, and with a last dig at his younger brother, Joe came after us. I jumped down the last few feet into the long grass; thankful Jamaica had no poisonous snakes, and looked around. The air was still and hot, and the only noise was the sound of insects stridulating in the undergrowth.

"So what is this place?" I asked Joe. "Someone's garden?"

"I'll show you." He led the way through the undergrowth, swinging branches out of the way and chopping his hand through strands of spider web until we came to a relatively open avenue of gravel. We crunched down this a few yards and then Joe stopped and pointed. "There."

A low stone building lay half-submerged in the grass, its façade weathered and stained. I could see no doors or windows, just a flat roof. I went closer and rubbed my hands along its rough contours. Chris walked around one corner and squatted down.

"There's some writing here, but it's very faint."

I went to look, squatting down beside him and tracing letters and numbers etched into the stone.

"W... I... L... L... I... something... M... A... N... something... something..."

"It reads 'William Ansley,'" Joe said. "Born 1734, died 1756, of the yellow jack."

"It's a grave?"

"Yeah. Just a few feet from your hands are the mouldering remains of a young man. Scared?" He laughed as Chris stood up quickly. "This is a yellow fever cemetery, long abandoned to the lizards and the ghosts."

I stood up and looked around. It was very peaceful and I didn't feel threatened by the memory of long-dead people. I figured as long as we didn't disturb them, they wouldn't disturb us. "Where are these butterflies you said were here?"

"Somewhere around." He waved vaguely at the undergrowth. "You're not worried that a corpse might come out? There are some crypts with broken covers, you know. People round here say they see strange lights in here at night and hear things too..." Joe laughed as Chris started edging away, back to the gravel path.

"Cut it out, Joe," I said. "It's all right, Chris, nothing's going to hurt you."

"That's all you know. At night, this place is..."

"That's right, at night. It's broad daylight now. Come on, Chris; let's leave Joe to his games. I want to find those butterflies--or is that another one of your tales?" I walked off down the gravel path and after a brief hesitation, Chris followed me.

"There aren't really ghosts here, are there?"

"No, and certainly not in the daytime." *I hope.* We came across another avenue and turned onto it as it led to a more open space. We found more crypts and a scattering of graves with headstones. We read a few more and they confirmed this was a yellow fever cemetery. Almost everyone here had died of the disease, and most in the 1700s and early 1800s. We also found evidence that someone had come here a lot later. One of the plots had a date in the early 1900s and the family name was the same as an older one next to it. An old man laid to rest in a grave near his long-dead relatives. There was a scraggly hibiscus bush planted by his grave, and as we stood looking at the headstone, a large white butterfly flew up from the bush.

It circled and alighted once more and I crept closer. I didn't have my net with me, but I wanted to check my identification. I was almost certain it was *Anteos maerula*, the Angled Sulphur. The male is bright lemon yellow, and I had some in my collection. The female, however, is a paler, cream colour and I thought this might be one. I did not have one in my collection, and though I could not catch it, I wanted to confirm the sighting. If it was, I might be able to return later with my net. When I was within a few feet, though, it opened its wings to take flight and I saw that not only were the wings pure white, but there was a short but broad band of orange-yellow on its forewings. It was *Anteos* all right, but *Anteos clorinde*, and wasn't normally found in Jamaica. It might have flown down from Cuba, and as it took flight and sailed above the trees, it might well have been flying back there.

I came to the yellow fever cemetery again, with my net, but I never saw the *Anteos clorinde*. What's more, the curators at the Institute of Jamaica did not believe I'd seen it. A little later, I was reading a book on Greek myths and death customs and I read that sometimes the ghost of a person will appear as a white butterfly. I didn't really believe that, but I thought it an interesting coincidence that I should see a large white Angled Sulphur that shouldn't have even been there on my first visit to the Yellow Fever Cemetery.

Moths

Butterflies are the flashy extroverts of the order Lepidoptera, and moths their drab, introverted cousins. With few exceptions, butterflies are abroad on sunny days, fluttering their often brightly coloured wings for all to see, while moths are creatures of the night, spending the days camouflaged on tree trunks or fence posts. Consequently, small boys tend to collect butterflies rather than moths, and it was the same with me. The bulk of my collection were butterflies, but I was not averse to adding the odd moth if I came across one. I have related how I stumbled upon a large hawkmoth on the way to school one day, almost caught a *Manduca* hawkmoth in the Blue Mountains, and had found a large Black Witch flying near Mavis Bank, but on occasion I actively pursued moths.

Funnily enough, I have had as long an association with moths as I have with butterflies. When I lived in Düsseldorf, Germany, we had buddleia bushes by our garage and I would sit entranced as a six-year-old, the summer sun beating up from the red gravel driveway, watching the red admirals, small tortoiseshells, painted ladies and peacocks sucking up nectar from those gorgeously scented purple flowers with their thin proboscises. I sometimes caught them in my hands and admired them before letting them go, with never a thought in my head to collect them. When I went to boarding school in England at the end of that hot summer, I was introduced to the wonders of silk moths.

One of the lanes in the town of Gerrards Cross in Buckinghamshire was lined with mulberry trees, and chomping away on their leaves were fat caterpillars. One of my teachers told me what they were, so I collected a few, plus an armful of leaves, and kept them in a shoebox in my desk at school. Each day I'd remove the scraps of leaves and piles of knobbly green droppings and replace it with fresh new leaves. The caterpillars grew enormously and turned into pupae, spinning a pale yellow cocoon of silk. I watched in fascination as the caterpillar rocked its head back and forth, a thin thread of fluid issuing from its mouth which instantly solidified into a silken thread.

I found a book in the library that described the making of silk, where the cocoons were dunked in hot water to release the individual threads which were then wound onto spools for later spinning. I tried it, dunking a cocoon in warm water. A thread floated free and I lifted it on a pencil, gently pulling and rotating the pencil and soon I had a fine yellow strand of silk unravelling from the floating cocoon. I didn't unwind all the silk from a cocoon because I felt sorry for the little creature, so after winding some silk off each one, I dried them off and put them back in their box. They hatched a few weeks later, apparently none the worse for their immersive ordeal and I took them outside and released them. They sat on the grass, fluttering their wings and refusing to fly, so I left them to it, hoping they would go off and repopulate the mulberry trees when they were good and ready. They were gone when I went outside later, but I read that adult silkworm moths cannot fly, so maybe some lucky bird had a feast.

There were other interesting moths in England, and I used to hunt them in the undergrowth on school sports days. The only sport I enjoyed was cricket--I was an all-rounder--and while waiting for my turn to bat, I'd fossick in the long grass and examine the rough bark of the trees around the field. My favourite moths were the 'Underwings'. They'd sit motionless on the bark, relying on their drably mottled forewings to hide them from the keen eyes of birds and small boys, and if their attempts at hiding didn't work, they'd jerk their forewings forward, revealing brightly coloured hind wings--or underwings. This flash of colour--usually red, but sometimes yellow--was often enough to startle a bird, but it also served to attract a small boy. Then the moth would have to put up with several minutes of handling before being allowed to whirr off in search of another refuge.

The long grass and shrubbery hid a number of small, rather ordinary looking moths whose main claim to fame--in my eyes--was their exotic common names. I'd find 'Pugs' and 'Plumes', narrow rolled-wing 'Grass Veneers', 'Waves', 'Carpets' and 'Footmen', 'Arches', 'Emeralds' and 'Rustics', as well as many more I didn't recognise. Sometimes I would see a flash of colour in the grassy borders and for a moment would suspect a butterfly, until I saw the distinctive flight of the insect. These were the day-flying moths--the 'Burnets' and 'Tigers', as well as the 'Crimson Speckled' and the 'Cinnabar'. Burnets had black wings with red spots, Tigers had black and white forewings with yellow hind wings, the Cinnabar was red and black all over and the Crimson Speckled had white wings liberally dusted with tiny red and black spots.

When I first saw these eye-catching moths flying in the grass, feeding from flowers, I wondered why they weren't immediately snapped up by birds. I caught a Cinnabar moth in my hands and found out. I was a little rough and the moth 'leaked', the exudates smelling rather strongly of something I couldn't quite identify. I looked at the yellow stain on my fingers and sniffed it, then (and I really don't advise this) touched the tip of my tongue to the fluid. What can I say? I was a young boy filled with more curiosity than sense.

A bitter taste filled my mouth and I spat, trying to rid myself of the vile contamination. For a few moments I thought I was going to be sick, and then I managed to control my rebellious stomach. Obviously the birds must experience something similar when they caught one of these moths. The trouble was the moths were common yet there weren't sick birds littering the countryside. I was missing a part of the puzzle. I found out much later (they didn't teach such things at my school) that striking patterns of red, black, yellow and white on a moth or butterfly (and other creatures) are aposematic or warning colours. A young, inexperienced bird or boy will sample one of these insects, spit it out, and leave anything similar alone. I know I never tasted another one!

All this has taken me a long way from Jamaica, but I wanted to show that I had had a long association with moths before I ever arrived in that sundrenched isle. The wonderful butterflies of Jamaica had captured my interest, and except for a handful of specimens, had kept my collection free of their nocturnal cousins. This situation was about to be rectified.

This particular day, I decided to cycle to a piece of wasteland to catch butterflies, and took the road that led past a newly-erected shopping centre in Half Way Tree. It was a Sunday morning and the parking lot was deserted, so I cycled through it, describing great loops across the painted lines and riding up on the footpath close to the shop windows and their banks of fluorescent lights, now extinguished. I saw a number of shapes on the ground and on the walls and slowed to take a look. The shapes were moths--but not any moths I had seen before.

They were pale, in shades of grey and fawn with streaks of brown in differing shades and were five or six inches across. I was excited, and set about collecting as many as I could see until my collecting tin was full. I wanted more, so I quickly rode home and picked up another collecting tin and returned to the shopping centre. Alas, in the half hour I was gone, other small boys had wandered through and made a game of squashing as many as they could find. I scoured the pavements and walls as high as my net could reach, but I only found another two.

I set out my specimens and a week or two later, when I could safely take the paper strips off the wings, I took two of the best specimens to the Institute of Jamaica for identification. They were *Thysania zenobia*, owl moths of the family Noctuidae, found in South America, the Caribbean and the southern USA. Interestingly, they are migratory and must have been passing through on their way north or south, for I never saw them again, though you can be sure I looked.

I did find other moths under the lights in the shopping centre, as it became one of my favourite haunts of a Sunday morning. The shops were open late on a Saturday and the lights would be on all night for security purposes, so if there were any moths flying by Half Way Tree, there was a good chance they'd stop there. I wasn't always alone on these trips, as people would wander by but they generally left me alone.

About a month after I found *Thysania*, I happened upon a scattering of hawkmoths under the lights. These are often large, heavy-bodied moths with elongate wings that fly fast and are often hard to disturb when they have settled. The first one I saw was a *Protambulyx strigilis*, with tawny forewings and yellow hind wings. It has a four inch wingspan (10 cm) and was uncommon, so I quickly killed it and transferred it to my tin. I then moved on to a lovely *Agrius cingulatus*, which has pink on its hind wings and pink stripes on its body. It was on the footpath and I was just reaching down for it when a woman spoke behind me, making me jump.

"Don' yu touch 'im, young sir. Dose bot be real evil."

I turned and looked at the speaker, a large Jamaican woman in a floral print dress and a large, wide-brimmed hat.

"It's only a hawkmoth," I said.

"It be a bot," she reiterated. "An evil bot. It bite yu an' yu swell up an' die."

I frowned and looked back at the inoffensive hawkmoth on the footpath. "It can't bite," I said. "It doesn't have jaws, only a proboscis to suck with."

"It bite I tells yu...or sting," she added. "Yu no touch."

I squatted beside the moth and poked it with my finger. True to form, the moth only shifted slightly, displaying a hint of the pink on its underwings. "See? It's harmless."

"Don' touch." She turned and called out to two men walking by on the nearby road. "Come 'elp me. Dis boy 'e sure gonna die. 'E touch devil bot." The men ran over, demanding to know what was happening. The woman gabbled quickly, lapsing into a Creole dialect I couldn't understand, pointing at me and the moth.

One man regarded me solemnly. "Dis fine lady righ'. Yu die fo' sure if yu touch dat devil bot. Yu body it swell up an' yu cry out in ah-gony."

The other man disagreed. "Yu stoopid mon. Dat be no devil bot. Devil bot much much big. Dis pick'ninny bot. 'E no 'arm dis boy."

"Who yu cahll stoopid? Dis devil bot..."

"Das righ'," added the woman. "Frien' o' my sister 'as devil oat fly in 'ouse, she scream an' fall down. Dose t'ings much evil."

"Yuse be both stoopid. I be ejy-kayted an' I tells yuse..."

The argument looked like it might develop into a fight, so I picked up the offending 'devil' moth, swiftly killed it, and slipped away before they involved me.

On a later date I saw another wonderful sight at that shopping centre. I had the place to myself and I was going over the pavements and walls for a second time, wondering where all the moths were hiding, when what I thought was a black swallowtail butterfly flew by. I chased it, and even as I did so, I knew it was not a butterfly. It was almost certainly a moth, but a moth such as I had never seen before. Its wings were black and had tails like a swallowtail, but when it alighted for a moment on a bush, I saw yellow-green stripes on its forewings and patches of iridescent blue on its hind wings. I wanted it--I thirsted for it--I lusted after it--and flailed valiantly with my net. It effortlessly evaded my clutches and soared over a building and out of sight. Later, on one of my frequent trips to the Institute of Jamaica, I found one just like it in one of the cabinets. It was a day-flying moth called *Urania sloanus*, but when I brought my sighting to the attention of a custodian, he smirked knowingly and told me I must have been mistaken. He said the moth had been extinct for fifty years at least. I thought about this and tried to compare my memory with the cabinet specimen of an extinct moth. Could I have been mistaken? Well yes, of course. These were men of science and I was only a twelve year old boy who chased butterflies for fun.

Perhaps it really was a swallowtail after all--but if it was, I didn't know which one. None of Jamaica's swallowtails look like *Urania*. Or possibly it was another species of *Urania* blown over from Mexico. In the end, I had to forget about it. I hadn't caught it, so I couldn't prove what it was. I returned to that shopping centre many times, but I never saw that day-flying moth again.

I did see other day-flying moths though. My parents sometimes took the hill road over the spine of the island from Kingston to Annotto Bay, and in the hills we would stop at Castleton Botanic Gardens. I don't remember many people ever being there, so we could enjoy the solitude of a beautiful, if slightly run-down, tropical garden. I remember once we went with friends of my mother. While the adults sat on picnic blankets and talked, I would explore the undergrowth with two little kids for company. Philip was a year or two younger and liked to follow me around while I caught butterflies. He had a sister called Rowan, younger still, and she would often tag along too. Philip had a brother, Jonathan, but funnily enough I have no recollection of him.

We played along the river--the Wag Water--which flowed over large boulders, gurgling shallowly over rocks and gravel--turning over stones to search for water insects, or trying to catch the brightly hued dragonflies that hawked for insects over the water or sat with outspread wings on the sun-baked boulders. It was hard catching these predators as they possessed large, wrap-around compound eyes and could see us coming. Many times my net would sweep over a rock only for the dragonfly to zip, with whirring wings, out of the very throat of my net, and escape. I caught a few, but tended not to add them to my collection, just admiring them for a few minutes before releasing them.

The long grass on the far side of the river bordered jungle, and we would scramble from rock to rock and splash through warm shallows to sample the hidden delights of these wild places. It was on this visit with Philip that I found a few day-flying moths. As we hauled ourselves out onto the far bank, I could see little flashes of colour winging away from us. Naturally, I pursued, and with a sweep of the net caught what I thought was a new species of butterfly. It was only after I had pinched its thorax and tipped its limp body out onto the palm of my hand, that I recognised it for a moth.

Butterflies and moths belong to the same insect order--Lepidoptera, but there are some telling differences. Generally, butterflies have slim bodies, antennae with knobs on the end, have bright colours, fly in the daytime, and when at rest, hold their wings above them. Moths, on the other hand, have fatter bodies, feathered antennae, drab colours--often camouflaged--fly at night, and sit with their wings flat. There are exceptions to all these 'rules' and it is always exciting when you happen upon one of them.

The body in my hand was one of these exceptions. It had a fat body, feathered antennae and, though dead, its wings were splayed out on each side--telling me it was a moth. However, it was active in bright sunlight and was coloured, with narrow front wings a lovely deep blue-black and hind wings red with a black border. Despite these butterfly characteristics, I was sure it was a moth, though I could not identify it.

As usual, the Institute of Jamaica came to my rescue, and identified it as *Empyreuma anassa*. Alas, it did not have a common name, so I had to concoct one of my own for future reference. I called it the 'Blue and Red Moth'-- hardly an imaginative name but a serviceable one.

I found it again in another part of the island. I have related my exploits on Strawberry Hill and how we drove further into the Blue Mountains to Newcastle and the Hardwar Gap--well, on another occasion we drove specifically to Newcastle to stay the night at a small hotel in the hills. It was a secluded chalet-type house with a wide veranda and set about with shrubbery and wilderness.

The nights were positively chilly, and although I patrolled the chalet veranda lights in the evening, I found very few moths worth adding to my collection. The days were not much better as mist clung to the hilltops until the morning sun burnt it away. I would be up with the dawn, not wanting to waste a moment of my stay. I'd walk the deserted paths around the chalet, treading softly over the lawn and chilling my feet in the dew-soaked grass. Everything would be still, sounds damped by the mist, distant objects invisible, closer ones made mysterious by the softening effect of the fog. Pimento and other spices were grown in the area and the odours clung to vegetation and permeated the still, moist air. To add to the feeling of loneliness, the mournful cries of the Mountain Witch would issue from the mist-shrouded hillsides and I'd shiver, looking back momentarily to the safety of the chalet, even knowing that the haunting calls came from a rather beautiful dove with purple wing feathers and a silvery crest.

Nothing much stirred while the mist lasted, but as it evaporated under the tropic sun and a gentle breeze ripped it into tatters, the first life would stir into its daily activity. Birds flew from their roosts to forage in the grass, or chatter and squabble in the trees, the first butterflies perched in sun-dapples, warming up before taking flight, and occasional flashes of aposematic colour alerted me to the presence of day-flying moths.

The 'Blue and Red Moth' made its appearance again, and despite having it in my collection already, I could not resist its charms, and added one or two more. There seemed to be a slight difference in the width of the black borders of the hind wing in these ones. That may just have been a gender difference, or it may have been a separate subspecies. I would have to ask at the Institute of Jamaica.

As the sun rose higher, burning away the mist, the scents of the spice orchards intensified, filling the air, and butterflies became more common. Flying among them I saw some I had not seen before and raced after them, swinging my net wildly through the long grass. I crouched beside my net, sifting out the plant debris, brushing aside the outraged spiders caught up in the folds, and revealed an insect with clear wings. For a moment, my heart leapt as I thought it was a Clearwing Butterfly--*Greta diaphane.* Then I saw that it had feathered antennae and a broad body--it was a moth, but a new one for me. I added it to my collecting tin and hunted for more, turning up another three. One of them had a different pattern of black on the clear wings, so again I was looking at a gender or species difference.

Back at the Institute, I found that butterflies and moths display considerable variation in the number, size and colour intensity of spots, streaks and borders on their wings, so the differences in the 'Blue and Red Moth' were likely just natural variation, whereas the difference in the Clearwings indicated different species. One of them was *Nyridela xanthocera,* and the other three were *Phoenicoprocta jamaicensis.* The names were almost longer than the moths themselves, so I quickly made up common names for them--the Barred Clearwing and the Jamaican Clearwing--so I could tell them apart when next I encountered them. Alas, it was a wasted effort, as I never saw them again while out hunting.

I came to moth hunting late in my sojourn in the Caribbean and undoubtedly if I'd had been more aware of the limited time at my disposal, I could have made some useful additions to my collection. However, as a young boy without much concern for the future, I assumed I would have plenty of time and put it off. It would be thirty years and half a world away before I once again had the opportunity to collect tropical moths, and that time I made the most of it.

Cockpit Country

M y father, as I have said, was manager of a Kingston insurance company, but occasionally he would step out of the office and visit clients in the field. He had investigators who could look into claims, so he had no real need to, but I think he enjoyed the opportunity to see the countryside. On one occasion, fairly late in our stay, we travelled through to Mandeville in the Parish of Manchester, on a short holiday, and while we were there, he said he wanted to drop some papers off to be signed by a client in the town of Vauxhall. It would take the better part of half a day, and he gave my mother and me the option of remaining in Mandeville, or coming with him. My mother said she'd stay, but I asked where Vauxhall was. My father took out a map and showed me.

I studied the folded paper carefully. "It's on the edge of the Cockpit Country," I observed.

"That's right. You still want to come?"

"Can I bring my net?"

"Yes, but I'm not promising we'll have much time for catching butterflies."

"Jay, is it safe?" my mother asked. "You hear such dreadful things of the Maroons and the Cockpit."

My father smiled. "There's a lot of exaggeration and besides, we're only going to the edge of it. We'll be safe as houses."

We headed west on the A2 highway toward Spur Tree, Santa Cruz and Tombstone. That was another thing I loved about Jamaica--all the lovely place names. These ones made me think of the Wild West and for a while I imagined myself riding shotgun on a stagecoach beset by bandits and Indians. Then something occurred to me.

"Dad, what did Mum mean about the Maroons? Who are they and why are they dangerous?"

My father considered his answer, no doubt wondering whether a quick answer might suffice. "What do you know about the history of Jamaica?"

"It was discovered by Christopher Columbus."

My father nodded. "In 1494. Then what happened?"

I thought about my history lessons. "The Spanish ruled the country. That's why we have Spanish Town and names like Santa Cruz and Ocho Rios."

"Then who took over."

"The British."

"That's right. Oliver Cromwell sent soldiers to take it from Spain. Under both the Spanish and British, the colonists grew things like bananas and sugar cane as crops, but they needed something from Africa as well."

"Breadfruit and ackee."

"No, those came later. What they needed to work the fields were slaves."

"Oh."

"Well, as you can imagine, conditions were bad, so some of the slaves escaped and hid in the hills near the Blue Mountains and in the Cockpit Country."

"And they're the Maroons?"

"They were known as runaways, people who live on mountaintops, and later called Maroons after the Spanish word for them--'*cimarrón*'. They signed a treaty with the British in the 1730s, allowing them self-government, and remained at peace until war broke out some fifty years later. The Maroons at Accompong in the Cockpit Country remained peaceful, but the British destroyed all the other settlements. There is still some resentment against the British, but they're safe enough as long as you don't do anything silly."

I thought about this for a while. "They wouldn't think catching butterflies was silly, would they?"

My father roared with laughter. "Quite possibly. However, we're only going to Vauxhall which is right on the border of the Cockpit, so we're unlikely to see any Maroons."

I thought some more. "Why is it called Cockpit?"

"It's the name given to a particular landform. The whole area is made of limestone and tropical rainfall has eroded fissures and holes until there is a jumble of rounded hills and sinkholes. It can be quite dangerous to wander through--not because of the people, as your mother thinks, but because you might easily fall over a cliff."

"By why the name Cockpit?"

"Back in the old days, people used to make roosters--cocks--fight in small rings or arenas called cock pits. These arenas had a flat floor and high sides where the people watch. Someone got the idea that the hills and sinkholes looked like that so... Cockpit Country."

"Could we go and see it, Dad? Please? I mean, if we're going right to the edge anyway."

"It's not a good idea to go in there without someone who knows the area, someone who's a local."

"But we'd stay on the track and not wander off, so we'd be safe."

My father hesitated. "There are a few dangerous people there. We're British, and some people resent Jamaica being British. I don't want to get into a situation where you'd be threatened."

I said no more, knowing I had no hope of changing his mind. Instead, I sat back and enjoyed the ride to Tombstone, where we turned north on a very second-class road that led to the town of Maggotty and Vauxhall just beyond it.

"Why Maggotty, Dad?"

"The founder named it after his birthplace in England, but that's all I know."

The small town lay on a bend of the Black River and was the usual collection of ramshackle houses and dirt roads, bordered by expanses of cane fields that spread up to the mountains of the Cockpit. We drove through quickly, and on to Vauxhall. This town was even smaller, and was really no more than a collection of houses spreading up the side of a small forested hill. The only roads into the village were of gullied earth and not suitable for a vehicle. My father parked at the side of the main road under the shade of a mango tree and got out.

"Stay in the car, Max. I shouldn't be more than half an hour."

"Can I get out and stretch my legs?"

He nodded. "Stay within sight of the car, and if you're worried, for whatever reason, get back in and lock the doors." My father picked up his briefcase and set off up the wide dirt track that led up the hill.

I got out with my net and explored the side of the road, glancing back toward the car every few minutes to check I was still close enough to run to it in an emergency. There was nobody about and I felt bolder, scouring the trees and shrubs along the road for butterflies. The Cockpit Country was one of the haunts of *Papilio homerus* and I hoped to find one here. It looked unlikely territory, but you never knew.

There were many butterflies about, but mostly small ones. I saw grass yellows (*Eurema lisa* and *Eurema daira*), a few unidentifiable hairstreaks high up out of reach, and a few skippers that I ignored because they looked like ones I already had. Two or three sulphurs (*Phoebis sennae*) flew across the road in front of me, but I left them alone too. I had set my sights on larger butterflies today and regarded the little ones as so much chaff.

I saw I was two or three hundred yards from the car, so I turned and walked back, netting a few of the grass yellows as I went, just to check there wasn't anything new. There wasn't. As I drew level with the car, I saw a movement in the old leaves at the base of the mango tree and spotted a flash of orange and rich brown. I swept with my net and was rewarded with a Leafwing (*Historis odius*) in excellent condition. I felt very pleased with myself, knowing that the trip was a success even if I didn't catch a Homerus swallowtail. I saw my father returning, so stayed by the car. Another man was walking alongside him--a Jamaican--so I stood with a polite smile on my face, waiting to see what was happening.

"Charles, this is my son Max. Max, say hello to Mr. Peterson."

"Good morning, sir."

"Hello Max. Ah see you has a butterfly net. You like collecting bots?"

I grinned. At last I'd met someone who didn't think collecting butterflies was strange. "Yes, sir. Do you collect them too?"

Charles Peterson laughed. "No, but ah has a cousin in Mo' Bay who does."

"Mr. Peterson has very kindly agreed to escort us up to Accompong, Max."

I got quite excited. Accompong was the Maroon village and there was very good butterflying up there if old reports were to be believed. If this Mr. Peterson could get us there safely, I might really have a good chance to get my Homerus. I jumped in the back seat of the car and Mr. Peterson got in beside my father. He turned back the way we had come, and drove through Maggotty, turning up a dirt road toward the mountains.

The road was windy, narrow, and rutted, so my father crept the car along. Every now and then he pulled as far over onto the verge as he could to allow another vehicle past--a grossly overloaded truck, or a small bus--or to overtake a group of pedestrians who were disinclined to move out of the way. They stared at us but without the accompanying smiles that is usual on country roads. Eventually, we reached a crossroads where the state of the road became so bad, my father felt he could not drive any farther.

"Don' worry," Mr. Peterson said. "We'll walk from here. It's only a mile or so."

We set off up the hill track. I tried to stay in front so that any butterflies we came across would be undisturbed by the adults, but after I recovered an *Adelpha abyla* from my net, I found they had moved past and I had to run to overtake them again. After I repeated this with a *Colobura dirce* and a *Dryas iulia*, I gave up, tagging along behind and leaping into the undergrowth after flashes of winged colour. Every now and then, my father would turn and exhort me not to dawdle and I'd dutifully break into a run until the next butterfly happened along.

It was hard work on a hot day, and my father and Mr. Peterson stopped to rest in the shade. I asked if I could go on fifty yards to a patch of *Lantana* flowers I could see and my father gave his permission.

"Don' wander off da track," Mr. Peterson added. "Dere's potholes roun' here."

The *Lantana* bush nearly made me miss the most exciting butterfly I'd seen all day. There were plenty of sulphurs, whites and blues on the flowers, and a few larger butterflies that kept me busy sweeping and adding my growing catch to my collecting tin. I stood with my net clamped between my knees, slipping a Dagger Tail into its paper packet, when I saw a small flicker of movement in the greenery above me. I finished putting my prize away and turned my attention to the foliage. Nothing moved, but I looked carefully at each branch, looking for a shape or a colour that was just slightly out of place...and saw it...a cream and gold and green wing against the translucent green of a large leaf backlit by the sun. I measured the distance with my eye and jumped, swinging my net in a short arc, and the butterfly disappeared into the folds. I took it out carefully and goggled at its beauty. It was a Malachite, *Siproeta stelenes*, and the green patches on its wings glowed in the sunlight. My hands trembled as I put it in its packet, and I started searching the leaves for others.

I saw one just as it took off. It flicked its wings and flitted along the edge of the vegetation until it came to a gap and landed on a leaf in the sun a few paces from the road. I ran up the road after it but slowed as I got near, and stepped carefully off the road after it, keeping my eyes glued to its gorgeous wings as it spread them to entice me onward. I was nearly within reach when my foot came down on nothing and I stumbled, clutching at the shrubs for support. I came down hard, but the shrubs held and I saw a steep slope yawning beneath me as I scrambled back onto the safety of the road. I had nearly fallen into one of the cockpits.

The Malachite was long gone, of course, so I hurriedly brushed myself off and acted nonchalant as my father and Mr. Peterson approached. I said nothing about my near miss, and just fell in behind them as they passed. We continued up the road for a while, with me searching the vegetation as I went. I saw another Malachite and missed it, and then my heart skipped a beat as a *Papilio pelaus* flew by and I thought for an instant it was a Homerus. I let it pass unmolested, and was rewarded a moment later by my second Malachite.

We reached a house beside the road, and another, and from the second a small boy ran out and up the road before us.

"He carry word of our coming," Mr. Peterson observed.

"Does it matter?" my father asked.

Mr. Peterson shrugged. "Dey will know one way or t'other. We shall see."

More houses lined the road and people came out to watch us pass. Some called out a greeting to Mr. Peterson, but most stood silently. One called out something and I could hear anger in his voice, if not the words. I walked closer to my father. We walked on up the dirt road, past the houses, to where the road curved back on itself and a tiny track ran through an open patch of grass to the forest.

"Accompong up dere," Mr. Peterson said.

He stepped off the road and as he did so, a group of about twenty young men walked out of the forest and stood looking at us from a distance of about fifty yards. Several of them openly carried machetes. We stopped and Mr. Peterson looked worried.

"Stay here. I go talk dem."

He advanced on the young men, his hands in plain view. I stayed close to my father and watched. Mr. Peterson talked and the young men talked back, volubly, with much waving of machetes. I looked past the men, to the forest edge, and saw a vision in black and yellow, cruising along at a height of about six or seven feet. It was a Homerus swallowtail and without thinking, I started forward.

My father's hand grasped my collar and pulled me back. "Where the hell do you think you're going?"

"It's a Homerus, Dad. Look." I pointed with my net.

"I see it, but that's all that's going to happen until we get the go-ahead from Mr. Peterson. And put that net down, they might think it's threatening."

I lowered my net, though none of the men seemed to take the threat of a twelve year old boy and a butterfly net very seriously. Mr. Peterson walked back to us.

"Dey say we cannot go Accompong. De young men want no white men dere. Sorry, we mus' turn back."

My father scowled, but nodded. "Very well. It's a pity, but you tried your best, Charles. Thank you."

We retraced our steps, and as we stepped back onto the road, the young men melted back into the forest. The Homerus still flew along its borders and I looked back over my shoulder longingly. Twice now, I had seen the butterfly, and for the second time missed the opportunity of catching it.

The houses were deserted when we passed them again, but the sides of the road still swarmed with butterflies. I caught several on our long walk back down to our car, knowing this might be my last chance to catch butterflies in the Cockpit Country. I took another Malachite, another Leafwing, A Zebra (*Heliconius charitonius*) and two *Mestra dorcas*. I was reasonably happy with my haul.

The drive back to Vauxhall was uneventful and we dropped Mr. Peterson off at the bottom of the hill with our thanks. He was apologetic that we had not reached Accompong, and told us that if we wanted to try again, he would seek permission from the elders of the village beforehand.

"I don't think we'll worry your mother with a description of our trip," my father said as we drove back to Mandeville.

I nodded. "We've been gone a long time. Where do we say we've been?"

"Well, you've been catching butterflies, haven't you? If she asks, we just say you found a good spot to hunt your small game and I waited. It's not so far off the truth."

"I'll have to put the place on my labels."

"She's hardly likely to read those. Are we agreed?"

"Yes, dad."

We drove on, and I looked back out of my open window at the mountains and the cane fields, hoping I'd have another chance to sample the butterfly riches of the hills and maybe even catch a Homerus swallowtail in the fascinating landforms of the Cockpit Country.

Duppies & Black Widows

J ust before I turned thirteen, a new family moved in across the road from
us. They were the Warrens, fresh out from England, and they had two
daughters--Bridget, eleven, and Jane, eight. Both were friendly and eager
to learn about Jamaica and the exciting things found even within the confines
of Carvalho Drive. I took them in hand, and showed them my hamster, my
Meccano set, my stamps, and my butterfly collection. They were moderately
interested in Honey, but I could tell I had made no converts to Lepidoptery,
so turned to other things. Bridget had a quiet nature and often hung back,
watching me or Steve Riley when he joined us, until she was sure of herself.
Jane, on the other hand, was outgoing and boisterous, and was in the
forefront of overturning rocks or clambering up trees.

Naturally, Mr. and Mrs. Warren wanted to meet me, and have a word
with my parents, before allowing their daughters into the company of a wild
boy. I had dinner with the family once or twice, and while there was never
any hint that Bridget might consider me a boyfriend (and certainly the
thought never crossed my mind), we got on well enough, and the Warrens
welcomed me into their home. We all went to the cinema a few times on a
Saturday morning when one or other set of parents would drop us off at the
theatre and pick us up later, or take us for ice-cream sundaes at the
American-style drugstore with its air-conditioned iciness and glasses of
crushed-ice water with every ice-cream served.

The Saturday matinees were not all fun and sweets though. All manner of
boys and girls went to them and the intermission was a time of cacophonous
chaos. I was given a sheath knife for my birthday and proudly wore it on my
belt the following Saturday. I quickly found myself the focus of much
unwanted attention. Bigger boys gathered and demanded to see this knife.

Having no option, I handed it over, and for many minutes agonised over whether it would be returned to me. A couple of my other friends were there, but they sort of merged with the furnishings, not wanting to attract the attention of the big boys, but Bridget stood by me. Eventually the film started again and the knife was dropped point down into the floor at my feet. Needless to say, I never took it out with me again.

Bridget was introspective and liked to read books, but Jane had a large collection of dolls and often played with them in the garden. She encouraged me to join in and I did, both of us quite happy to let our imaginations run free through the medium of little plastic figurines. It didn't worry me in the slightest that I was playing with dolls, but it did concern my father, so after the first time, I never let on that I'd been doing so. It was only an intermittent pastime though, and most of the time we were running about, climbing trees or throwing stones, or hunting for lizards.

The Warrens had very little in the way of a garden, but they had a little ornamental bush near their back door, and one day I noticed it was covered with small green, yellow, orange and red fruit--tiny shiny conical fruit. I stopped and looked and Jane told me, "Mummy says we mustn't eat those."

"Why not?" I picked a nice red one and sniffed it, and then gently touched it to my tongue and lips. Instantly, I realised 'why not' when my lips started tingling and, within minutes I could feel a burning heat spread through my mouth. My lips swelled and tears were forced from my eyes.

Jane ran inside and fetched her mother who took me in hand and treated me with lots of soap and water on my face, had me rinse my mouth out repeatedly, and applied an ice pack to my lips. Only as the burning died away did she scold me, and I listened contritely to her explanations that hot peppers could be dangerous.

Bridget was a reader, like me, and she had many books in the bedroom she shared with her sister. Often, in the evenings, we would sprawl over bed or floor, lost in one or other of her books. I usually dug into the encyclopaedias her parents had bought, and I was content to just read consecutive entries, no matter their content. Jane seldom joined us in our bibliophilic pastimes, but bounced around chattering and playing instead. She had one book she liked though, and insisted on showing it to me. It was a sex education book with drawings of boys and girls at various ages, showing the development of various body parts. I looked through it politely, but it held no special interest for me, so I was soon reading the encyclopaedias again.

After a couple of months, the sisters were allowed out after dark, as long as they stayed with me and close to home. As we often ate dinner at slightly different times, we needed a signal to let each other know we had finished and were available to play. We decided a whistle was appropriate, and more often than not, I'd be out there in the gathering dark, blasting out a 'wheet-whee-oo' to call the sisters out. Occasionally, I'd hear it and I'd hurriedly finish my meal and with a nod from my parents, dive for the door. I can't remember ever failing to answer the summons, but sometimes the muscles of my face would be sore as I sat outside, whistling in vain. If I was lucky, Bridget would race out to tell me they couldn't come out that evening, but if not, I'd eventually have to find something else to do.

Imagine a twelve year old boy and two young girls abroad in the cool darkness, looking for something fun to do. None of us were scared of the dark, but loved to hide in the shadows and watch people walk by. Most Jamaicans walked quickly, keeping to areas lit by streetlamps and avoided even looking at the darkness. Many had a belief in ghosts, or 'duppies' as they are called there, and credited them with a very real existence. Some people believed the duppy might in fact be a malevolent spirit rather than a ghost, but either way, Jamaicans are scared of them. I have seen adults run from the suggestion that a duppy was around.

This belief provided us with some wonderful opportunities. We took to hanging around the corner of Carvalho Drive and Hope Road, where a couple of old mango trees threw deep shadows close to the dirt footpath. We stood in the deep leaves near the trunk and when someone came walking, we would utter low moans and rustle the dead leaves. The man or woman would usually just quicken their pace, but sometimes one would stop and stare fearfully into the shadows.

"Who dat? W'at yu do, mon?"

We'd usually spoil the atmosphere by giggling at this point and run off pursued by angry cries. Other times we stood our ground and made semi-intelligible groans and the man would retreat, sometimes precipitately. Once, we stepped into view under the trees and a woman caught sight of our white faces. She screamed loudly and bolted, while we doubled over with laughter. I think it was possible that our small size and white faces convinced her we were dead, as children--even white children--would not be out after dark for fear of those very duppies that terrified her. This gave us the idea for our next refinement.

"We should look more like ghosts," Jane said.

"What do ghosts look like?" I asked, quite reasonably I thought, as none of us had ever seen one.

"Well...they wear white sheets, don't they?"

"That's just in comic books."

I asked my parents about ghosts that night and found to my surprise that both of them had had paranormal experiences. My mother had seen a ghost wolf in India when she was a child. I asked her about it and she told me she had been ten at the time and her older sister Phyl had been very sick. As they lay in adjoining beds in the early hours of the morning, this huge wolf had come in and sat at the foot of her sister's bed, fading into nothingness in the dawn light. I shivered, thinking this was deliciously creepy, but it did not answer my question about what ghosts looked like.

My father told me he had seen a crying girl run across the road in front of him when he was cycling home after work one day when he was sixteen. The girl had disappeared on the edge of the impenetrably thick woods beside the road and even he found it hard to push his way through it when he went after her.

"What did she look like, Dad?"

"Just like a normal girl, though she was wearing old-fashioned clothes. That's why I hopped off my bike and went looking for her. I thought she might have been hurt or something. It was only when I found I could hardly get through the tangled undergrowth that I realised she must have just evaporated."

"Were you frightened?"

"Interested, more than frightened." He went on to tell me about other experiences he'd had. None of them involved an actual apparition, so I just listened politely, my mind going over the problem of making us look more like a ghost to Jamaicans.

I asked our gardener next day. The cook had told me once about duppies but I wondered if his experience was the same.

"Wha' for yu wan' know, young sah?"

"My father told me ghost stories last night and I wondered what Jamaican ghosts looked like."

"Dey is all sorts. Yu got ones use' be peepul, dey still look like peepul, but dey 'tink of the grave..." He tapped his nose. "Udder duppy him look like calf or horse but wit' t'ree legs and eye of fire. Carry yu straigh' t'hell. Yu don' wan' mix wit' dem, young sah."

I thanked him and left, thinking that perhaps Jane's sheet was the best idea. I sneaked one out of the airing cupboard, knowing I'd have to return it before my mother found out. That night I draped the sheet over me and hid behind one of the old mango trees. When a woman came along, Bridget and Jane made high-pitched moaning noises and the woman stared into the shadows.

"Who's dere?" she called. "Is dat chillun?"

I stepped out from behind the tree draped in the sheet, a vaguely human white form, and made a 'whooo-ooo' noise. The woman dropped her shopping bag, uttered a loud scream, and fled. We fled too, knowing we'd gone too far. The woman, or her relatives, would be back to reclaim her bag, and if they found us we would suffer for it, either at their hands, or at the hands of our parents. We hurried home and I hid the sheet for later replacement and we made ourselves innocently visible to our parents so we could say we had been there all the time. A little later we heard a commotion at the end of the street but ignored it, and nothing happened, though the next day our cook told my mother a story in hushed tones of a dreadful duppy seen near our house. My mother looked at me but said nothing.

Bridget refused to play 'duppies' again, so we had to find something else to do in the darkness. I borrowed my father's torch and we went hunting crickets. These little insects chirped away in the long grass at the base of the concrete block walls that lined the road-front of the properties. I did not want them for my collection, though I did have a few other insects besides butterflies and moths, so we'd hold them in our hands for a few minutes before letting them go. This activity soon palled, but I discovered something else a lot more interesting.

One night when I was hunting alone, a cricket tried escaping up the block wall, and as I pursued it, it crawled into a hollow where the concrete had eroded. I shone the torch in and poked at it with a grass stem, but it just crawled deeper. Then I saw a movement behind it, and suddenly a black spider gripped the cricket and sank its fangs into the struggling insect's body. I watched in fascination and saw a glint of red on the black spider's shiny abdomen. I recognised it immediately as a Black Widow spider, *Lactrodectus mactans*. I don't like spiders in general, but this one was spectacular and I controlled my fear.

I had seen black widows before, preserved in bottles at the Institute of Jamaica, and even in our veranda, but had never seen one in action. A large female lived in an upper corner of our veranda and my parents were content to leave it there. It never came out of its corner, but caught small insects in its flimsy net, so they saw no reason to disturb it. I took my guidance from them and viewed the spiders as a natural part of my surroundings. I stood on a chair and looked at the black widow in our veranda close up, noting its shiny black colour and the vivid red hourglass on the underside of its bulbous abdomen. It sat in its web and did nothing, but the one in the wall hungrily took the cricket that crawled into its space. It gave me an idea.

The next evening, I showed Bridget and Jane the large spider in its hole and told them to watch as I introduced another cricket. Bridget stepped back with a shudder while Jane squealed with a mixture of revulsion and delight. Both of them watched the cricket's last struggles with interest though. A little bit of exploring found other holes in the concrete blocks, each with its own spider in residence. Most were black widow spiders, but a few were a sort of brownish grey and their hourglass decorations were a faded orange rather than a vivid red. I thought that perhaps these might be male spiders, but I wasn't sure.

The next day after school, we searched through the encyclopaedias and found a reference to black widow spiders and a close relative, the brown widow. The females are always much larger than the males, so it looked as if the large faded spiders were a separate species. We also found out they were dangerous, capable of giving a person a nasty bite, so if we were going to play with them, we knew we would have to be careful. After thoughtful consideration, we decided it best not to tell our parents.

We were out that evening, catching crickets in the long grass and feeding our hapless victims to spiders up and down the wall. The fate of their siblings did not deter others from singing, so we continued our actions right up until the girls were called inside. I stayed on a little longer, staring at the lucky recipients of the feast and at the unlucky morsels of food. It made me a bit queasy, particularly as I empathised more with the insect than with the spider. Curious, I explored my feelings and caught a small moth, pushing it into a web and watching its struggles as the black widow efficiently bound its wings and legs before administering the fatal bite. I shuddered, imagining I could see an accusatory stare in the faceted eyes of the moth and resolved never to push another moth into a spider web.

I talked it over with the Warren sisters the next day, and they were quite happy to cease feeding the black widows. The fate of the crickets had disturbed them too, particularly as we had had a direct hand in their deaths. We looked at the spiders in their holes many times in the ensuing days, but never for long, and we never fed them again. The spiders did not seem to suffer from our decision, as we often saw crickets and other insects wrapped up in the flimsy webs, but our consciences were eased by our decision.

We played other games on the darkened streets that did not involve duppies or spiders, often ranging far up Carvalho Drive to a patch of wasteland where our own imaginations got the better of us and we fled from dark shapes and strange noises. After a few months, Bridget lost interest in our nightly excursions, and as Jane would not venture out without her sister, I was thrown back on my own resources.

Reflecting on Rotting Fruit

My father sprung a surprise on me in late April of 1961. As you will have gathered from my stories, my father was an exacting man who expected a lot from his only son, and did not hide his disappointment at my lack of manly virtues. Running around the countryside with a butterfly net in my hand was not his idea of a proper pastime for me. He sometimes went out of his way to take me butterflying--as in my visits to Green Wall, Jack's Hill, Strawberry Hill--but after more than two years in Jamaica I think he was resigned to the fact that I was a lost cause. So it was with some surprise that he came to me with the offer of a trip to a prime butterfly site.

"I have to visit the branch office in Port Morant and see a client in Bath. It'll be for a couple of days. Do you want to come?"

"Where's Port Morant?"

"East of Kingston along the coast."

"And Bath?"

"Inland in the John Crow Mountains. Do you want to come?"

"Can I bring my net?"

He sighed. "I wouldn't expect anything else."

I researched the area thoroughly, asking the curators at the Institute of Jamaica for information on the butterfly fauna of the region. The Homerus swallowtail was a possibility in the John Crow Mountains, and that butterfly alone would have been enough to draw me there, but there were others to be found in the forested region around the town of Bath--Leafwings, Tailed Leafwings, Thersites swallowtails, Malachites, Banana Butterflies and Daggerwings to name a few. I would be happy to add any of these to my collection.

Bath is a small town in a very mountainous region only about forty miles from Kingston, but as the roads are narrow and wind through precipitous gorges, it is not a journey to be hurried. The town is famous for its hot mineral springs (hence the name) which are reputed to have healing properties. My father was of the opinion that the so-called 'cures' were dubious at best, but many people believed in them. The client he was going to see in Bath owned a small bath-house and often made claims on his insurance policy, which was why my father, as manager, was off to see for himself.

My mother packed us a small suitcase for our overnight trip and waved goodbye, promising to look after my hamster, Honey. I was excited, and fidgeted, checking my net, collecting tins and paper packets, worrying that I'd left something important behind. So much so that my father tersely told me to sit still or he'd turn the car around and take me home. I sat still--or at least as much as a thirteen year old boy can.

The road led through downtown Kingston and then east along the coast road. I remembered going to Harbour View, where the turn off to the Palisadoes Airport and Port Royal lay, then through the tiny towns of Bull Bay, Eleven Mile and Grants Pen, to Poor Man's Corner where my father had had his hand stitched up, to Yallahs and beyond. We came to Green Wall, and I looked for the place where I'd caught the perfect Banana Butterfly before leaving it to be devoured by ants. I missed it, as one mountain stream cascading off the steep verdant hillsides looked very like another--and it had been nearly two years. The road led on through Belvedere, Church Corner, Morant Bay, and at last to Port Morant. I stared about me avidly, always looking for good butterfly hunting spots. There were many possibilities, and I considered asking my father to stop, but decided against it. *Maybe on the way home,* I thought.

"What do you want to do while I'm at the office?" my father asked.

"How long will you be?"

"No more than an hour or so. You can sit and read magazines if you like."

I grimaced at the thought of extreme boredom. "Could I go to a park or something?"

"I don't know that Port Morant has a park."

"There was a patch of bush near the road as we came in."

"Max, I can't just drop you anywhere. I have your safety to think of."

"Nothing's going to happen, dad..." I saw the determination in his face and hurried on to my fall-back position. "Maybe there's a field or bush near the office. Then I could run to you if I needed to."

There was. The insurance office in this little town was part of the local agent's house, and it was situated on the road north out of town. Houses were scattered along one side of the road, and long grass and trees spread out on the other. My father got out of the car and cast his gaze over the wasteland for several minutes before nodding reluctantly.

"Stay within sight of the road and houses, don't approach anyone, run to that house there..." He pointed to one of them. "...if you need to, and come when I call you--three blasts on the car horn."

I waited until he crossed the road and disappeared into the designated house before turning to survey my temporary kingdom, orb and sceptre in hand...well, collecting tin and net. The countryside fell away slightly, angling down toward the distant shore and consisted mainly of unkempt grass with scattered trees. The vegetation was a little on the dry side, so that would probably limit the selection of butterflies available, but it would do to while away an hour or two.

I forged through the long grass bordering the road and onto barer soil beyond it. My passage disturbed several grass yellows and I caught a few of them to get my eye in. I didn't keep any of them, just checked their identity and let them go. Flying over the shorter turf, I found a scattering of small blues and a handful of skippers zipped away in little brown and orange blurs. I left them alone too, searching for bigger game.

It wasn't long in coming, though the butterflies themselves were common enough--*Mestra dorcas*, the White Peacock, a Buckeye or two, an Angled Sulphur and a Cleophile. Again I caught them, examined them, and released them. I would keep a specimen in excellent condition, but I had all these in my collection already. Then I saw another Cleophile and ran after it as something didn't seem quite right about it. It saw me coming and soared, trying to escape over a thicket of thorns. I leapt; net extended, and snared it, though I snagged my net on the thorns as I did so. I bunched my captive in the folds of the material while I extricated the thorns without damaging my precious net. Then I turned my attention to my prize.

It looked like a Cleophile, though a bit larger than normal. The front wings had more white on them and the black border to the hindwings was less definite. I hesitated, wondering whether it was different enough to keep, or whether I should just let it go. The state of its wings decided me, for the edges were tattered and the overall colouration was faded. I removed it carefully and let it fly away, though I remained staring after it for a minute or so. Something nagged at my mind, but I couldn't think what it was. I had an awful feeling I shouldn't have released it--that I would regret my decision. I found out later the mistake I had made. On comparing specimens at the Institute of Jamaica back in Kingston, I realised that I had released the only Danaid Eggfly (*Hypolimnas misippus*) I had ever caught. At the time, I put my feeling of unease behind me and continued to search the wasteland for other species.

I heard the car horn sound three times and started back toward the road. I was almost there, starting to run as my father blew the horn again, managing to convey impatience through the mechanical sound, when I made my best catch of the day (excepting my then unsuspected Eggfly). Something black flew by and I extended my net automatically as I ran, and was rewarded by a large butterfly struggling in the fabric. I killed it and left it in the net, bursting through the long grass to find my father about to lean through the window and sound the horn again.

"I'm here, dad," I cried and climbed into the front seat, throwing my net into the back. In my haste, I forgot about my quick capture until we were almost in Bath. It turned out to be a Jamaican Polydamas, a tail-less swallowtail and a welcome addition to my collection.

The trip to Bath township was slow, the road being narrow, in poor condition, and winding through narrow gorges, clinging to precipitous hillsides. My father drove with care, negotiating the steep inclines and hairpin bends with skill. From time to time he would glance up at the steep hillsides and mutter something about unstable soils and how we would be lucky to escape alive. Being a naive teenager, I thought the prospect of an avalanche exciting rather than scary, and yelled with excitement every time a rock tumbled down the hillside or I spotted a fresh scar in the verdant plant life. Happily, we got through to Bath a little after noon unscathed. My father drove us to the client's house, a rather rundown bathhouse with a guesthouse and rooms to rent. We would be staying overnight and heading back the following morning.

I had no time to lose if I was to sample the butterfly life of Bath, so I left my father to change his clothes and interview his client, and headed out with my net. The countryside around Bath was mountainous, and densely vegetated, so I was confined to the roads and tracks leading off into the green wilderness. A surprising number of people were around, considering the sparse sprinkling of dwellings, but I thought that they must be there to sample the supposedly healing waters. As long as they left me alone, I was quite happy to leave them alone.

I found a track that headed up a hill at a gentle gradient and followed it. It led me away from the township and was generously dotted with open areas where the sun shone through the canopy, fostering the growth of weed species. I have often found that weed species grow fast and produce flowers in abundance, which can be useful for attracting butterflies. *Lantana* grew here, and its heads of tiny red and yellow blossoms drew in several species including ones that I wanted. I saw--and quickly caught--fine specimens of Pelaus and male Thersites swallowtails, a handful of skippers and assorted Pierids and Blues. I wandered up and down the trail for an hour, sampling the butterfly life, but the ones I really hoped to find, like the Malachite, Tailed Leafwing and Daggerwing, eluded me. I walked back down to the road to look for another track.

I tried one or two others some distance from housing, but they quickly petered out, so I moved in closer to the township. I found a lane, but just as I was about to set off I saw an old Jamaican man sitting on the front porch of a ramshackle bungalow, smoking a pipe. Nothing particularly strange in that except that beside him, propped against the wall, was a butterfly net. I took a few steps closer and stared, wondering if it could be something else, like a shrimping net. I had never come across a Jamaican interested in butterflies--or 'bots' as they called them. I just had to know, so I walked over to the fence and called out.

"Er, excuse me...er, sir. Is that a...a butterfly net?"

The old man regarded me solemnly for a few moments before taking the pipe from his mouth. "Yes it be, young mon, like yous."

"Do you collect butterflies?"

He nodded. "Yes. Yu want for see my collection?"

I hesitated, remembering dire tales of what happened to young boys and girls who ventured into the houses of strangers. The man obviously saw my hesitation and stood up slowly before stepping down from the porch and crossing the twenty or so paces to the fence.

"We should be introduced, young mon. My name be Childers--Samuel Childers of Bath."

"Er, Max Overton of...of Half Way Tree. That's in Kingston."

Samuel smiled. "I know where Half Way Tree be. What yu doin' in Bath? It be a long way to come on yu own to look for bots."

"I came with my father. He's a manager for an insurance company. He's with a client. We're staying at...at a bathhouse. I don't know the name of it." I pointed up the road.

"Winston, no doubt. He be a friend of mine. So, young Max, would yu like to see my bots, now dat we be introduced?"

I very much wanted to see his collection, and strictly he was no longer a stranger. I frowned, wondering whether I should get my father's permission first. However, he would not want to be disturbed if he was with a client and besides, Samuel was a friend of this Winston, who was undoubtedly my father's client.

"Yes please, Mr. Childers." I said.

"Yu call me Samuel."

Samuel led the way across to his little house and opened the door, preceding me into the cool, dim interior. The furnishings were old and worn, but everything was neat and spotless, and I looked around for a Mrs Childers. The house felt empty though, so I said nothing, just looked around at a range of ornaments and pictures. The old man saw me glance at a framed photograph on a side table and satisfied my unasked question.

"Dat be my wife, Marjorie. She pass on to her reward twenty year ago."

I continued to say nothing, not sure of how I should respond.

"Dis way. I have my bots in back." He moved through into darkness and I followed, a trifle nervously, but he snapped on a light and I saw that the back room looked more like a laboratory than a bedroom. I saw a microscope on a bench, some glassware and an assortment of unidentifiable equipment--and a set of shelves stacked with large wooden butterfly cases. Samuel took one down and laid it gently on the bench, undoing the clasp and pushing the lid back. Inside were rows of immaculately mounted butterflies, all Pierids as far as I could see, ranks of yellows and whites of every species I had and many more besides. The display cases in the Institute of Jamaica barely contained more specimens. Box after box was opened, Samuel delighting in being able to show off his collection.

"Nobody round here be interested in bots," he said with a smile. "It be a pleasure to meet a young mon who 'preciates them."

"Do you have the Homerus swallowtail?" I asked.

Samuel smiled. "Of course. Yu want for see?" He opened another box and showed me six gorgeous velvet-winged apparitions in black and yellow. They were perfect, without a mark on them. "I caught dem all here in Bath."

He showed me other swallowtails, in similar condition, and then opened box after box of nymphs. I recognised most of them, but one medium sized butterfly with wings some three inches across, attracted my attention. At first glance it looked a lot like the Jamaican Admiral, but the butterflies (a whole row along the top of the case) had only orange on the front wing instead of the Admiral's pale blue stripe. There were Admirals in a line underneath--or so I thought--until Samuel told me they were the females of *Doxocopa laure*, and the line above were the males.

"I thought those were *Adelpha abyla*," I said.

"Ah, yu know de science names. Very good."

"Only some of them." I was bemused by the mixture of Jamaican patois and scientific expertise. I pointed at the strange butterfly. "What was this one again? Doxy...?"

"*Doxocopa laure*." He spelled it out for me. "Or if yu prefer, de Jamaican Reflecting Butterfly."

"Why 'Reflecting'?"

Samuel held the box at an angle in a shaft of sunlight and moved it back and forth slightly. I gasped. A pale blue iridescence played over the surface of the wings.

"Dat be why," Samuel said.

"Are they local?" I asked. "I'd very much like to catch one...or two."

"Yes, I caught dese in Bath, but yu won't be catching dem coming to flowers. Like the *Historis, Colobura* and *Marpesia* butterflies, dey prefer fermenting fruits--and it be a bit early for fallen mangoes."

He saw my disappointed look and smiled again. "Maybe dere be something I can do. Dey like the midday sun, so tomorrow we look for dem together. I knows a likely spot."

"We're leaving tomorrow."

"Dat be a pity. Perhaps yu father would delay departure until de afternoon?"

"I could ask him," I said doubtfully.

"Well, if yu can, be here at eleven o'clock and we see what we can find."

I broached the subject with my father that evening. We had eaten our meal and were sitting out on the narrow veranda of the guesthouse, he with a beer and me with a Pepsi, listening to the frogs and crickets.

"What time are we leaving tomorrow?"

"Around ten o'clock."

"Could we leave later? There's a butterfly that only flies at midday and..." I had been about to add Samuel's authority to my plea, but decided my father probably wouldn't appreciate second-hand advice from a stranger-- particularly one who collected butterflies.

My father shook his head. "I'm not delaying just for a butterfly."

So that was that--except it wasn't. It rained during the night and I heard the downpour on the tin roof. I remember thinking, as I lay in my bed, that heavy rain would spoil my butterfly hunting the next day, and then remembered I wouldn't be hunting anyway.

The next day dawned bright and sunny and I was up early, determined to see if I could find a few butterflies before we left. I had hardly started when my father called me back.

"A slight change of plan, Max. The rain brought down a landslip and blocked the road. They'll have it cleared in a few hours so we'll be leaving this afternoon." He saw my struggle to contain my elation and smiled. "You can look for that butterfly of yours after all. Just be back by two o'clock."

I arrived at Samuel Childer's house at eleven o'clock, net in hand and eager for the chase. He took his time filling his pipe with tobacco and putting on his shoes and I fidgeted, hopping from one foot to another.

"Peace, young Max, we get dere soon enough."

Samuel led the way out of his gate and down the road half a mile or so to a forest path and we started to climb until we were well above the level of the road. We came to an open space bordered by tall shrubs including a few mango trees. Although there was no fruit on the trees, I thought I could smell the sweet odour of rotting fruit. I said so.

"Dat be 'cos I come out late last night and spread de bait."

"Bait?"

Samuel grinned. "I tol' yu Reflectings only come to rotting fruit, so I bring dem some." He led me over to a small pile of decomposing fruit. I could recognise mango, banana and paw-paw, and there were hints of other types amid the yellow-brown sludge.

"Where did you get it all?" I asked.

"I keep some in my freezer for bot bait. I 'cide to use some when yu tell me yu want for see Reflectings."

"And you think they'll come here? To this rotting fruit?" Flies were already swarming over the pile and the odour was clearly drifting toward the forest in the very slight breeze.

"Could be. We jus' have to wait and see." Samuel sat with his back to a mango tree and lit his pipe, puffing happily. I stood closer to the fruit, searching the open space around it eagerly until he called me away.

"Yu come back, young Max. Yu scare dem away yu stan' too close."

We watched and waited, and the minutes ticked by. Something stirred in the forest, a glimpse of brown and orange, and a Leafwing flitted across the open space, circled the bait and landed. Its proboscis unfurled and it probed the sweet fermenting fluid leaking from the fruit. I quivered, and half rose to my feet, but Samuel restrained me.

"It be only a *Historis*. Wait a bit, young Max, maybe Reflectings come to de rotting fruit."

The Leafwing stayed and was soon joined by another. A Banana Butterfly came to feast but shied away when one of the Leafwings opened its wings, but still the Reflectings stayed away.

"What time is it?"

"Half one."

My heart sank. It would take me twenty minutes at least to get back to the guesthouse. I had only ten minutes in which to get my Reflecting Butterfly. I scanned the clearing, looking for any sign of my prize.

"It's not coming, is it?"

"Be patient, young Max. It come when it be ready."

"But my father said I had to be back by two."

"Ah, den yu have a 'cision to make. We leave now an' be back in time, or we wait an' be late."

Being late meant risking my father's displeasure and possibly his belt. How much did the Reflecting Butterfly mean to me? Was it worth the pain that would likely follow? Or rather, I thought, the chance of a capture. There was no certainty that *Doxocopa* would put in an appearance. I weighed up my choices and decided to stay another half hour.

Two o'clock came and went. Some Pierids joined the Leafwings--a small cloud of pale yellow and white--and the Banana Butterfly recovered its courage and returned. At last, half an hour after I was due back, I sighed and got to my feet.

"It's no good, Mr. Childers, I'll have to go."

"Wait, young Max. See dere," Samuel whispered, pointing to the forest. "He come, jus' like I say he would."

I looked, and saw a butterfly winging its way toward us. I could not make out the colour or pattern, but I put my trust in Samuel's expertise. The hour of my victory was at hand.

The butterfly circled and landed atop the pile of fruit and I leapt forward, net swinging horizontally.

"Wait!" Samuel yelled.

Effortlessly, the Reflecting leapt skyward, evading my net by inches and took off for the forest edge with a small boy in hot pursuit. I lost it when it soared up into the canopy and after several agonising minutes I walked back to Samuel, head hanging dejectedly.

"De point of de rotting fruit be de bot he get drunk an' he no fly. Yu should have waited a bit, young Max. It be gone now an' won' be back. No great matter. Yu come again sometime an' do better. Yu learn how catch Reflecting."

He led me back down the path to the road, where I thanked him for his trouble and for showing me his butterfly collection, before hurrying away to the guesthouse. My father was on the veranda reading a paper and looked up as I arrived.

"There you are. They've just this minute told me the road is clear, so we can leave. Did you catch your butterfly?"

I shook my head. "I saw it, but I couldn't catch it."

We drove back down the winding road and it wasn't until we came out onto the coastal plain around Port Morant that I ceased my scan of the passing vegetation, hoping for one more glimpse of the iridescent blue sheen on the wings of a Jamaican Reflecting Butterfly.

I saw it a week later in the cabinets of the Institute of Jamaica, but I never saw a live specimen again. Nor did I ever have a chance to offer up rotting fruit in the hope of capturing it for, unknown to me, my days in Jamaica were numbered.

Rafting the Rio Grande

In May 1961 we went to San San Bay again, and stayed in the same lovely villas just above the sea strand. I welcomed the opportunity to hunt for the *Dynamine* with red undersides I had seen on my previous visit here. If I'd known this was to be my last visit, I might have paid more attention to my surroundings, and made the most of my time there. I should have climbed the hill behind the bay to see if I could find another Tailed Leafwing; investigated the little stream that burbled under the road; or gone further afield to sample the butterfly fauna of the area, but I thought my days and opportunities stretched out endlessly in front of me, so I did not bother.

We were only in San San for three days, so as soon as we arrived and my parents had started down to the tiny white sand beach for a swim, I excused myself and dashed away with my net. The place I'd seen the 'red *Dynamine*' was a mile or so up the main road toward the Blue Hole, and it took me nearly an hour to get there, being distracted by other butterflies on the way. I caught myself a Pelaus swallowtail, and nearly caught an ordinary Leafwing before arriving at the shady stretch of road with the verdant verge where I'd caught *Dynamine egaea* last time.

The verge had changed in the intervening time, becoming coarser and drier, the weed plants taller and more straggly. There were fewer flowers and definitely fewer butterflies, but I searched diligently all the same. After a bit, I saw that pale green metallic flash that was the male *Dynamine*, and chased it down. Shortly after, the black and metallic blue of the female caught my eye. I collected two of each before putting them out of my mind and concentrating on the ones that shouldn't exist. I had no luck, and after an hour or two I reluctantly headed home.

I collected around the villas the rest of that day. I was starting to think that I had been mistaken about the butterflies I had seen before, so I concentrated on enjoying myself with the other things to hand. One of the gardeners brought me a large stick insect, fully twice the length of my hand and I put it on a small shrub where I could examine it at my leisure. It was long and green with spikes on its thorax and abdomen, and it moved in a jerky fashion, swaying to and fro before rocking forward and starting another step. Then it would stop and remain motionless, and though I could see its shape well enough, I could imagine the difficulty a bird or other predator might have.

It clung tenaciously when I pulled it off its branch and looked completely out of place on my forearm. Its feet prickled my skin and I was just about to pick it off and put it back on the shrub when it shook its wings out and launched itself into the air with a rustling whirr. I was so surprised I just stood and stared as it flew ponderously across the lawn and into the branches of a tall tree. I ran after it and could see it hanging upside-down, trying to imitate a twig once more. I could reach it with my net, but I decided not to--I would leave this remarkable insect in peace.

That night, at dinner, my father had something to tell us.

"We're going to raft the Rio Grande tomorrow."

My mother said nothing, so I asked nervously, "Er, do we have to wear life jackets?"

"Bet you wish you'd learned how to swim properly now." He shrugged. "You don't need them. It's a smooth trip down about ten miles of the lower river on bamboo rafts. Great scenery and we can picnic on the way. You'll love it."

"Butterflies?" I asked.

"You and your damn butterflies. Don't you ever think of anything else?" He shrugged again. "Bring your net if you like."

Next morning, we drove up to Grant's Level, near Berrydale in the hills behind Port Antonio. The broad gravel bank on the side of the river was littered with long narrow bamboo rafts that looked altogether too flimsy to support us. The river didn't look dangerous, but I still felt nervous--perhaps I should have learned to swim properly. I walked up to one of the rafts and started pacing out its length. It was about twenty-five yards long and only a little over two wide, made of uneven bamboo poles that curved slightly in the middle so that the ends were raised. Towards the back, a raised section bore a bamboo seat raised still further.

My father was talking to one of the men and I could see money and car keys changing hands. We loaded our belongings onto the raft--a picnic basket with food and drinks, a blanket or two to ease the discomfort of the bench seat, suntan lotion, hats and insect repellent. Then our car was driven off by one of the Jamaicans.

"He'll drive it down to St Margaret's Bay where the rafting ends," my father explained.

We loaded our luggage onto the raft which had been manhandled into the water and when we boarded, the raft sank a few inches so that the river washed over the bottom boards. I looked around me to check on my things.

"My net!" I cried. "Where is it?" It was not on the raft or the river bank.

"You must have left it in the car. Well, it's too late now; you'll have to make do without."

The raftsmen pushed off from the bank and poled us out into the current where the bamboo craft swayed and bobbed until they had it pointing downstream. Then it drifted off smoothly enough, moving slowly through the sluggishly moving water. The raftsmen did not propel us with their long poles, content to just guide us and let the river have its way with us.

The first part of the journey was through relatively open country, and then forest closed in on first one side and then both, until we drifted between walls of green in which palms and bamboo stood out. Once in a while, banana plantations swept down almost to the water's edge and workers in them called out and waved as we crept past.

I was still annoyed at myself for forgetting my net, and my agony was compounded by the butterflies I saw. The river acted as an opening in the forest canopy and many species flew along the boundary or crossed the river in front of or behind us. Whites and yellows were the most plentiful and I could identify *Phoebus, Kricogonia* and *Anteos* without any trouble. Nymphalids were common too--*Adelpha, Historis* and *Colobura*--and a handful of swallowtails, mostly *Papilio andraemon* and *Papilio pelaus*. I knew I could not have caught them even if I'd had my net, but it would have given me hope for the lunch break.

In the meantime, the river carried us through short stretches where the bamboo arched over us and we drifted in deep shade, our attentions caught by the movement of fish beneath the placid surface, or birds in the treetops or on the banks, disturbed by our slow intrusion. A blue egret stood hunchbacked and on one leg in the shallows, seemingly bemused by the shoals of tiny fish swimming around its foot. Black swifts darted through the air above the river, feasting on myriad tiny insects that swarmed above the waters.

Movement in the wall of green revealed hints of red and once, when we drifted close enough to touch leaves, I saw a little Jamaican Tody regarding us from a branch, his bright red throat feathers standing out against the green. Hummingbirds were there too, in the more open patches where flowering vines brought nectar feeders together. I saw the less common Eastern Streamertail with its red bill, and the western Black-billed Streamertail, so I knew we must be right on the boundary of their overlapping territories. Other birds remained unseen, making their presence known by their calls and I could only guess at these, though I recognised the harsh 'ah-ah-eeek' of the yellow-billed parrot and the flowing burble of doves and pigeons.

The river was not always smooth as it rushed down over stretches of pebbled bed, though the water was never more than a foot or so deep, rippled and white-foamed as it raced over the rocks. The raftsmen would pole us through, concentrating on keeping us safe while I whooped and hollered with excitement. We were never in any danger, I know, as these rapids were pretty tame, but we could all feel the shudders as the bamboo craft bucked and bounced over the rounded pebbles. A pool would follow and our passage slowed once more.

In places, the rocks of the banks came right down to the water's edge and the raftsmen would pole us along within touching distance of sheer rock or vertical carpets of moss and fern. Once, when we were manoeuvring close between a large rock and a cliff face, a lizard hurled itself off the rock, perhaps in an attempt to reach the security of the shore. It landed on the raft a foot or so from the startled raftsman who screamed and jumped back, nearly falling overboard in his panic. Many Jamaicans regard lizards as dangerous creatures--venomous even--and go out of their way to avoid them. After a few frantic minutes, this particular six-inch *Anolis* lizard leapt overboard and swam to shore with the raftsman uttering imprecations behind it and my father roaring with laughter.

We stopped for lunch on a sand and gravel bank, and to my dismay, it was in the middle of the river, rather than on one side where I could have gone exploring. I ate my chicken leg and fruit, drank a soda, and went wandering while my parents stretched their legs near the raft. One end of the gravel bank came close to the shore, separated by a channel a few yards across where the water rushed swiftly over the stones. On the far side of the channel, the vegetation presented a solid wall of greenery except for an open slash as if a giant machete had carved its way through the plants. Vines connected both sides of the slash, some of them in flower, and small sprays of blooms attracted hummingbirds and butterflies. I wished again I had my net with me, for some of the sprays might have been within reach of a net if I braved the uncertain footing of the narrow rapids.

As I watched, *Papilio homerus* came sailing along the river's edge some ten feet above its surface, paused at the slash to investigate the sprays of flowers, hovering in front of one no more than six feet up, before leisurely making its way up the open slash away from the river. I groaned at another lost opportunity. This was the third time I had seen the Homerus swallowtail, and the third time I had been unable to even attempt a capture. I vowed that the next time I saw it; nothing would stop me catching it.

We set off again, and the rest of our short voyage was similar to the start. The river broadened and became slower and the vegetation receded from the banks. More houses were evident, and it was clear that we were entering civilisation once more. We went under the bridge that carries the main coastal road and followed the shore to the beaching point for the rafts at the entrance to St Margaret's Bay where we disembarked and went to find our car. All was satisfactory, so we drove back to San San Bay through Port Antonio.

My parents took themselves off for another swim in the sea, so I took my net and went for another look for my 'red *Dynamine*'. I knew we were heading home the next day, so this might be my last chance in a while. The walk along the main road to the shaded verge was uneventful, and the actual site as devoid of butterflies as it had been the day before. I wandered disconsolately until I noticed another road paralleling the main road a bit further inland. It was only a dirt road and I could only catch glimpses of it through the trees, but I thought it might be worth a look.

I wrapped the folds of my net around the pole to prevent it catching on twigs or thorns and stepped off the verge into the dense undergrowth, uttering a series of mild swear words as I became entangled. I made it through eventually and found myself on an old overgrown track. I followed it in one direction, and it curved out into open farmland. This was not the sort of habitat I thought my 'red *Dynamine*' favoured, so I turned around and went back, following the road in the other direction. This way ended in a gate onto the main road after a few hundred yards--equally useless.

I found *Dynamine egaea* at last, both males and females, but every one I caught was untainted by the red I thought I had seen on my last trip to San San Bay. It was extremely disconcerting as I started to wonder if I'd imagined it. Certainly the scientist at the Institute of Jamaica hadn't thought much of my sighting, so perhaps... I decided I would continue catching *Dynamine* in this area for another two lengths of the road--slowly moving up one side and back down the other, and if I hadn't seen the red underside ones, I'd give up and go home.

I walked the two lengths without success and decided to do two more. I really didn't want to give up. An hour later I was thoroughly dejected, having completed those extra two lengths and one more. I had caught and released a dozen *Dynamine egaea* and was starting to wish I'd kept some of them. At least I would have something to show for my efforts. I caught a green male and killed it, slipping it into my tin, and then a black, white and blue female as I started back down to the gate.

Another female followed, and then an atypical female with only a metallic blue streak on its black wings. Instead of its wings being held above it, my net had caught it in the downstroke and I could only see the upper surface. I was excited, as a variation of a known species was almost as wonderful as finding a new species. I killed it and took it from the folds. Its wings flipped back into the normal position as it did so and I shouted with triumph. There was red on the underside--it was my 'red *Dynamine*'. I stared at the patterning, at the red wash on the underside of the forewing and the figures made by the circular lines on the hindwing. As I looked, I realised what the name of my new find was--no longer 'red *Dynamine*' but '88' as the roundels on the underside were positioned in such a way as to show the figures of two eights.

I tucked my '88' butterfly away with shaking hands and set about the search for another with renewed vigour. It took me another hour, but I found one and slipped it gratefully into my collecting tin. I grinned insanely, feeling my heart bursting with triumph.

I looked around and saw the length of the shadows and knew that I had stayed out far later than I should have. I ran to the gate and out onto the road, racing back toward San San. The fireflies were starting to come out when I got back and I was in trouble. My father refrained from beating me, which had happened before, but I found myself soundly chastised. All I could do was apologise and tell him about my new butterfly. He wasn't interested and sent me to my room without dinner. My mother brought me a plate later, but it was in my room, during my enforced period of quiet that I found out I had perhaps caught two new species that afternoon, not one.

I mounted my '88' butterfly and though the figures were hidden on the underside, admired the black and blue-streaked upper surface. I thought I would mount the other specimen underside-up to show the '88' markings, but when I looked closely, I saw that the roundels spelled out an '89' (or a '98') rather than an '88'. Surely I couldn't have made that big a mistake. I thought for a few minutes and then unpinned the first butterfly and examined its underside. Sure enough, here was the '88' I remembered. The '89' was something different, perhaps a different gender, or even a different species. The red on the underside of the '89' was darker and more definite, but that was the only difference apart from the 'numbers' on the hind wings.

I found out years later that the '88' and '89' butterflies are natives of Central America and are not found in the islands of the Caribbean. How they got to San San Bay in Jamaica is a mystery, and I can only assume they were blown over in a storm and somehow survived. I never did get to show them off to the scientists at the Institute of Jamaica as events overtook me, but years later, I wrote to a butterfly expert in America asking about my capture and sending him a photograph of my '88' and '89'. He did not believe I caught them there, saying I must have caught them on the Central American mainland, but what can I say? I have never been to Central America and I'm sure I remember catching them that day after rafting the Rio Grande.

The only alternative is that this is a 'false memory', but if that is the case, where did the two little butterflies in my collection come from?

Jamaica Farewell

A ll things come to an end, even though I hardly realised it at the time. Unknown to me, my parents' marriage had fallen apart as my father became enamoured of one of my mother's friends. The first I knew of anything amiss was late June 1961 when my mother called me to the dining room table and sat me down.

"Do you remember me talking about my sister Phyllis? Your Auntie Phyl?"

I shook my head. She probably had, but I'd never met the woman so hadn't paid any attention.

"She lives in New Zealand with your Uncle Ren, and your cousins Martin, Ricky and Morna."

I tried to look interested, wondering what all this was about.

"She has invited us to stay, so we are going to visit her."

I thought about this. "Where's New Zealand?"

She told me, but after a few moments my mind wandered. I knew I'd have to look the place up in my geography books, and I wondered what butterflies it had. "When are we going?" I asked when she stopped talking.

"In a week or two. Your father has booked seats on an aeroplane for you and me."

"Isn't he coming?"

My mother looked away. "No. He has to finish up his work here." She left it unsaid, but I formed the idea that he would be joining us later.

"How long are we going for?"

"I don't know. We'll take everything with us though."

I thought about this, but considered it just another adventure rather than an ending. "All right. Can I go and play now?"

She let me go and I ran off. You would think that faced with my imminent departure from this island where I had enjoyed myself so much, I would be bubbling with excitement or sorrowful, but I was neither. I accepted what my mother had said and just continued with a normal life. My departure from boarding school in England was played out all over again. I left it to the last moment before telling my friends I was leaving; I made no special effort to fill gaps in my butterfly collection; I did not go to see places I loved for the last time. I just picked up my little travel bag and hopped in the taxi for the trip to the Palisadoes Airport.

I had packed some comic books, my father's copy of 'Greeks and Trojans' which he had given me, a notebook and pencils, and a jar of hawkmoth pupae. A week before I left, I had happened on a plant stripped of its leaves by a dozen large spike-tailed Sphinx moth caterpillars. I did not know what species they were so I collected them and put them in my old fish tank with some earth in the bottom. They dutifully pupated in the earth, so on the day we left I dug them up and transferred them to a jam jar and stowed them in my travel bag.

I had already given Honey, my hamster, and her double-barrelled offspring, to my friends, so I waved goodbye to the Warren sisters from over the road and settled back in the taxi. I had flown before many times, in old propeller-driven 'Elizabethans' and 'Viscounts', and enjoyed the experience, so I thought this trip would be more of the same. When we got to the airport and started lining up at the departure gate, I was enormously excited to see we were travelling in one of the new Boeing 707 jets I had watched take off on a previous visit to the airport.

I was very impressed with the acceleration on take-off and was glued to the window as we climbed to ten thousand feet only to immediately drop down again to Montego Bay. The airport there is a short one and a few weeks before a jet had overrun the runway and ended up in the bay. I was interested to see if it would happen again, having little concept of the outcome should it do so. It didn't, and a little later we took off again, climbing steeply as we raced northward. The pain of leaving Jamaica had not set in yet as I was too excited about seeing new things.

We landed in New York at Idlewild Airport and took a long taxi ride into the city. Again, I was glued to the window, and spared not a thought for my mother who must have been going through agonies, having to organise us on an international journey without my father there to manage things. When we arrived at the hotel, I first tried the television, not having seen one since leaving England, and then I wanted to go out and explore. My mother was totally against the idea.

"No, Max. The streets are dangerous. We're only here for a day, so let's stay in the hotel."

"Aw, Mum, I want to be able to say I've been to New York, not just be stuck inside a hotel room."

We compromised, and I was allowed to step outside onto the sidewalk and look up at the towering skyscrapers and watch the busy traffic for a few minutes before being ushered back inside. The ground floor of the hotel had several little boutique shops including a drugstore, where I browsed the comic section and bought a little plastic egg containing 'silly putty'. This was great fun for a small kid as it is silicone polymer that can bounce, will flow slowly if left alone, can be drawn out into long strands if pulled slowly or snap if hit or pulled suddenly. If it is pressed against a picture in a comic book, it will form a coloured image on its surface by taking up a layer of the ink. I spent hours playing with it in our hotel room and hardly noticed when we left.

The next leg of our journey was across the continental United States to San Francisco. It was late afternoon when we got there and we had a good view of the city and the Golden Gate Bridge as we circled before landing. We did not stay long in California, never even leaving the airport, before heading out in the dusk over the Pacific. I don't remember much of that segment as we were served a meal and I slept intermittently, staring out in my wakeful moments at a star-sprinkled night sky as we crept above the featureless cloud surface or the black face of the ocean.

I woke as we touched down in Honolulu, Hawaii, in the middle of the night. We disembarked, and I was able to wander outside on the tarmac. I remember standing by a wire fence looking out toward city lights, feeling the warm air on my face and smelling different scents. After a half hour or so, my mother called me back into the terminal and we started the process of leaving the United States.

The next leg south-westward over the Pacific carried us to Fiji. The day dawned and in the mid-morning a stewardess took me and another boy forward to the cockpit where we could see the captain and co-pilot sitting in front of rows of switches, dials and lights. They chatted to us and made us very welcome, so I asked the pilot for his autograph, which he willingly gave. Another autograph I got on that flight was of an American boxer travelling down to Australia for a bout. I can't remember who he was, but he was very pleasant.

Our trip from Jamaica had been trouble free and my mother, though no doubt thoroughly traumatised by her separation and sudden responsibilities, managed very well until we got to Fiji. There we learned that our seats on the connecting flight to New Zealand had not been booked and we found ourselves stranded in Nadi. We moved to a hotel while my mother made telephone calls to my father, to the airlines, and her sister. The upshot was that we could get seats on a flight leaving in about 36 hours.

Our flights from New York to Fiji had taken us across many time zones and I think I suffered from jet lag by the time we arrived there. I started feeling sick and my head started swimming every time I shut my eyes. That first night in the hotel was horrible--I woke up from a nightmare that continued into my waking life. I dreamed that jets were taking off and landing on me, and as they did, my fingers grew alternately as thin as needles and then as thick as sausages. I woke in a sweat, crying out for my mother, and though awake, my fingers still felt the same and I was afraid to go back to sleep. The nightmare occurred again the next night, but diminished, and it gradually faded after that, though it has returned over the years when I am stressed or very tired.

I was not impressed with Fiji--perhaps because I had just come from a jewel in the Caribbean. I thought the countryside was dry and brown and thoroughly uninteresting with very few butterflies. I was not allowed out of the hotel grounds as my mother was very afraid now we would run out of money. I had an American dollar of my own and got talking with a member of the bar staff. He was a tall Fijian in a skirt or sulu, and engaged me in friendly conversation. He showed me Fijian coins and I swapped a few of the lower denomination ones for my dollar.

Back in my room I checked my bag and examined my little jar of Jamaican soil and Sphinx moth pupae. They were still alive and twitched their abdomens when I prodded them, but I felt sorry for them. If their sleep was as disturbed as mine, they were having a dreadful time. I knew what I had to do, so I carried them outside and scraped a shallow hole under a Hibiscus bush. I laid the pupae in the hole and carefully covered them with loose soil, hoping that my actions would ensure their survival. I cringe when I consider what effect my unthinking actions might have had on the ecology of the island.

Our flight took off on time and my mother relaxed slightly, knowing that the next stop was Wellington, New Zealand, where her sister and brother-in-law would meet us. I was now quite eager for our long journey to end, to meet my cousins, and to see what New Zealand had to offer a thirteen year old. However, our journey had not yet come to an end. A southerly gale was blowing up from Antarctica when we started our descent into Wellington, and after circling for an hour, the pilot announced that we would have to land at another airport. We veered off and went north, eventually touching down at Hawera--an air force base in the region of Taranaki.

There was no passenger terminal here, so the jet parked out on the runway and we were allowed out to stretch our legs. I wandered out to the grass on the edge of the aerodrome and looked out at a cold green landscape with more than a hint of moisture in the air. I was missing Jamaica, but I was still eager to get out into the real New Zealand.

The afternoon passed slowly, and at last we got the word that the storm had abated slightly and the pilot was prepared to carry us to our original destination. We took off into the dusk and were soon being buffeted by winds as we approached Wellington for the second time. Wellington airport runs north and south across a narrow peninsula linking the main city with a low mountain suburb. The harbour is at the northern end and turbulent Cook Strait at the southern extremity of a rather short runway, so there is not much margin for error.

The rain was bucketing down and the wind bounced off the surrounding hills to produce lovely crosswinds as we made our approach. I could dimly see the lights of the city through the rain and people cried out around me as the wind caught the plane and hurled us shuddering to one side or other before the pilot corrected our course. I was far too excited to be worried about our safety. We touched down and braked, roaring toward the end of the runway and a watery fate before the deceleration eased and passengers cheered the pilot.

My aunt and uncle were there to meet us once we cleared Customs and there was a long ride through rain-gleaming streets and darkened highways before we started climbing the hill at the top of Stokes Valley. The house was the last one on the road with only night-hidden bush-covered hillsides beyond. The next hour was a bewildering round of introductions, non-stop talking and eating as my uncle Ren produced a delicious lamb curry for dinner. I learned my cousin Martin was sixteen, Ricky was eleven, and Morna was eight. The house was small and my mother would be sleeping in Morna's room, while Martin, Ricky and I would be sharing a caravan parked at the top of the road. We were out of sight of the house and its lights and the caravan shuddered in the wintery wind gusts. I looked out at the black hillside, heard the patter of raindrops on the roof and smelled the odours of a new country. I smiled. I knew I was going to like New Zealand.

Postscript

My childhood travels came to an end with my arrival in New Zealand, and it would be many years before I left the shores of the 'Land of the Long White Cloud'. I brought with me a love of Lepidoptery and looked forward to enlarging my collection with what I hoped was a large range of new species. Alas, I was to be disappointed. New Zealand is an oceanic group of islands, some fifteen hundred kilometres from Australia and a thousand kilometres from the other islands of the Southwest Pacific Ocean. Being this remote, few butterflies have made their way over the waves to this refuge.

There are a few familiar species--the Cabbage White, the Monarch, and the Painted Lady--all ubiquitous and migratory species. There is a nettle feeder too, the Red Admiral, but New Zealand's species is different from the northern hemisphere one. Australia has lent New Zealand its Yellow Admiral and occasionally one or two others are blown over in storms. There are a few little blue butterflies, and one or two small coppers, but the only others are a few nymphs and satyrs of strictly limited distribution. I collected the common ones quickly enough and then came to a halt. Unless I could go to out of the way places, my butterfly hunting was at an end. Moths might have provided an outlet but most were small and drab, and the larger ones uncommon. There is one hawkmoth and an Australian Emperor moth, plus a handful of Puriri and Ghost moths. The day-flying Cinnabar moth is there too, in the farming districts.

After some very frustrating weeks and months, I gave up. Other pursuits intruded, and I was required to attend to my high school studies at St Patrick's College, Silverstream. I retained a love of biology however; even if I couldn't indulge a love of butterflies, and in due course I attended Victoria University of Wellington where I majored in Botany and Zoology, going on to complete a Master's degree with Honours in Botany. Thoughts of butterflying faded further as I entered the work force.

I taught biology and chemistry at high school level for two years, and then a brief stint at Ecology Division of the Department of Scientific and Industrial Research, where I helped with a possum survey. I learned how this delightful Australian marsupial had been released in New Zealand to start up a fur trade, but had gone on to assume pest proportions, devastating the native forests. We live trapped them, measuring their vital statistics before tagging them and letting them go. They had to be drugged before we could handle them and on occasion their hearts stopped. I learned how to do possum heart massage. I also did my own research on the allelopathic potential of New Zealand native plants at Ecology Division before moving on to work as a tissue culturist for a private firm in Hawke's Bay, churning out high health carnations, orchids and nerines. Serious tissue culture work followed at the Ministry of Works and Development in Palmerston North, researching the potential for shelter-belt and erosion control trees. Palmerston North has a university--Massey University--and I soon found myself back there engaged in PhD work on--Oh joy! Butterflies.

As I have indicated, New Zealand has two Admirals--its own native Red Admiral, *Bassaris gonerilla*, and the introduced Australian Yellow Admiral, *Bassaris itea*. They are closely related, and are both nettle feeders--or rather, their caterpillars are. However, the Yellow Admiral larvae feed, by preference, on the introduced, soft-stemmed *Urtica urens*, whereas the Red Admiral feeds on the fiercely-stinging native nettle tree, *Urtica ferox*. I started my studies, and found a patch of another nettle, *Urtica dioica*, which has woody stems. Both Admirals fed on this species.

In the course of my work, I found many larvae vigorously chowing down on a patch of *Urtica dioica*, and brought them back to my laboratory to raise. Among the numerous Reds and Yellows that in time emerged from their chrysalids, I found a female specimen that was neither--and both. It had features that belonged to both and the main colour bar on its forewings was neither red nor yellow, but orange. I showed my supervisor and we agreed it was a hybrid. Only one had ever been taken before, so it was a rarity. I hoped to find another amongst the hatching butterflies as I wanted to test if it was fertile, but it died suddenly only three days later. I added it to my collection and considered the implications of my discovery.

If the native Red Admiral and the Australian Yellow Admiral could hybridise, it meant that they were genetically related and may even have stemmed from a common ancestor in the not too distant past. How closely related they were depended on whether the hybrid was fertile--which I could not test as my only individual had died. I would have to find more, but first I needed to ascertain the reproductive behaviour of both species. Then I might be able to induce them to interbreed in the laboratory.

I constructed large cages, filled them with pots of nettles and sponges soaked in nectar and settled down to watch. Over a period of time, using dozens of pairs of Admirals, I found that mating activity took place at different times of day, but with a slight overlap. The next step was to offer Yellow females to Red males and vice versa. Eggs duly appeared on the potted nettles. These hatched into caterpillars, pupated and emerged--and I had seven hybrids.

Unfortunately, they were all male, so I could not test their fertility to each other, but I could backcross them to Red and Yellow females. It turned out that Yellow females were more accepting of the hybrids and I obtained five adults from these crosses, all showing colours and patterns midway between the parents. I only obtained one individual from a Red female, hybrid male cross, and it had features of both parents too.

You may wonder why I had so few adult butterflies to work with--surely it was possible to breed more? Well, my studies came to a messy end just as I was starting to get some really fascinating results. Butterflies are prone to a number of parasites, parasitoids, fungal and bacterial diseases, and one morning I came in to find several dead caterpillars sitting in a puddle of stinking black fluid. Within days, the disease swept through my laboratory, infecting every surface. I strove mightily to disinfect everything, but nothing worked and very soon I found I could not raise caterpillars in any part of the Biology Building. I had no option but to shelve my research until I could find a solution.

I was not to find one, and the next year I moved to Australia. This 'Great Southern Land' had always intrigued me, but for twenty-eight years I had lived in New Zealand without once thinking of crossing the 'ditch' (The

Tasman Sea) and experiencing a new country. Once I had decided to move, there was only one option--Townsville in Far North Queensland. Based on my childhood experiences in Jamaica, the place I moved to had to be in the tropics and had to have a university, severely limiting my choice. I arrived in December 1990 and found employment at the university the following May.

A condition of my employment was that I enrol as a PhD student, so once again I found myself doing butterfly research. Unlike New Zealand, Australia is a wonderful place for butterflies and moths. After some seventy species of butterfly in Jamaica and about twenty in New Zealand, I found four hundred species, and even a hundred species just in the city of Townsville. It was paradise regained!

My research involved butterfly communities within and around a tropical city, investigating the species composition in natural areas--open woodland, mangroves, riparian forest and vine thickets--and comparing these to artificial plant communities in well-watered gardens and parks. I was in heaven for four years, wandering through my forty-six sites, noting down every butterfly I came across and adding many to my collection. I also wandered up and down Queensland and northern New South Wales, ferreting out other species. I filled several display cases with my butterfly specimens and gorged on the abundant tropical moth species too--from the huge Atlas moths with a twelve inch wingspan to the tiny Emeralds and everything in between, including hawkmoths and day-flying moths. There are too many interesting and spectacular butterflies and moths in Australia to describe, so let me just say that my years in Queensland fulfilled all my childhood dreams.

But all things pass. My marriage came to an end and I met an American author, little knowing that my life was about to change completely.

I had written a few poems as a boy in Jamaica, a science fiction story at high school, my Master's thesis, a handful of internal reports on allelopathy and tissue culture, until I resurrected my butterfly habit in Australia. A local monthly paper did an article on me and I followed up with a series of articles on different butterflies. I also wrote an article for a British journal on Butterfly Conservation, and completed a paper on teaching science, but it was the American author who turned my life around.

We met, we married in 1999, and she suggested I try my hand at writing a novel. I drew on a love of history (harking back to Greeks and Trojans) and wrote the introductory chapter to a novel of Alexander the Great. My wife edited it and ripped it to pieces--there was more red ink than black on those first pages! I learned my lessons though, rewrote the chapter and a few more, the number of corrections dropping as I gained experience. Eighteen months later, *Lion of Scythia* was published as an e-book and later in print.

I went on to complete what became a trilogy and then co-wrote a trilogy with my wife on Australian mysteries. We travelled to Illinois in the USA where, three years later, my wife suddenly died. I picked up the pieces of my life and returned to Australia, where a few years later I remarried, this time to an accomplished photographer and cover artist. I went on to write a number of other novels and I have others fermenting away in my mind, clamouring to be let out. Where possible, I remember my roots in Lepidoptery and incorporate a butterfly into the tale.

I continue my interest in butterflies, but I no longer collect their brightly coloured little corpses. Instead, I observe and sometimes photograph the living creatures and enjoy that as much as I ever did the actual collection. Above all, though, I write. It is a passion, and I enjoy the telling of the tale, fashioning a story from the germ of an idea, researching the details and listening in rapt fascination as the characters in my stories come alive and show me what life was like in past times, boasting of their exploits and hinting of dark secrets swirling beneath the surface of their fictional minds.

I still have my butterfly collection, though I no longer add to it except when a butterfly drowns in the swimming pool or is taken by one of the large Golden Orb spiders that infest my garden. Sometimes I sit and look at old specimens, some of them half a century old, and remember things I thought I had forgotten. It was one such viewing that sparked an idea in my head--the idea to write down my Jamaican stories. I have been able to meld the two great loves of my life, butterflies and writing, and offer up these glimpses of my early life.

My youngest son, John, and his wife Heather, have a daughter of their own--Payten. My eldest son, Duncan, and his wife Kayla, have two children, Noah and Ella. I can now offer these children, as well as my beloved grandson Alex, son of my stepson Cory, a link with the past, and can hope that my stories may inspire them to pursue the loves of their young lives. We each of us follow our dreams and I can honestly say that I have followed mine. The first stirrings of Lepidoptery and Writing came to me in Jamaica and now I have brought them together in my adopted country of Australia. I intend to keep both interests alive for as long as I can.

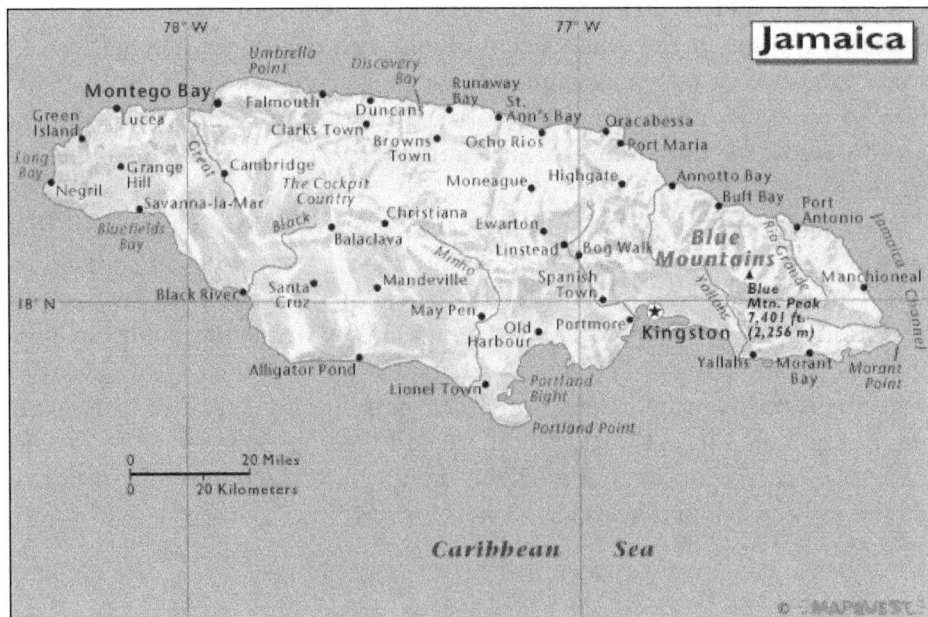

Jamaican Butterflies from my Personal Collection

1959 - 1961

Danaus plexippus (Monarch)

Danaus eresimus (Soldier)

Danaus gilippus (Queen)

Papilio andraemon (Andraemon)

Graphium marcellinus (Blue Kite, Jamaican Kite)

Papilio pelaus (Pelaus)

Calisto zangis (Eyed Brown)

Anartia jatrophae (White Peacock)

Precis evarete (Buckeye)

Phyciodes proclea (Crescent)

Mestra dorcas (Mestra)

Lucinia cadma (Lucinia)

Eurema proterpia (Tailed orange)

Eurema messalina (Little White)

Krigonia lyside (Spotted White)

Historis acheronta Cadmus (Tailed Leafwing)

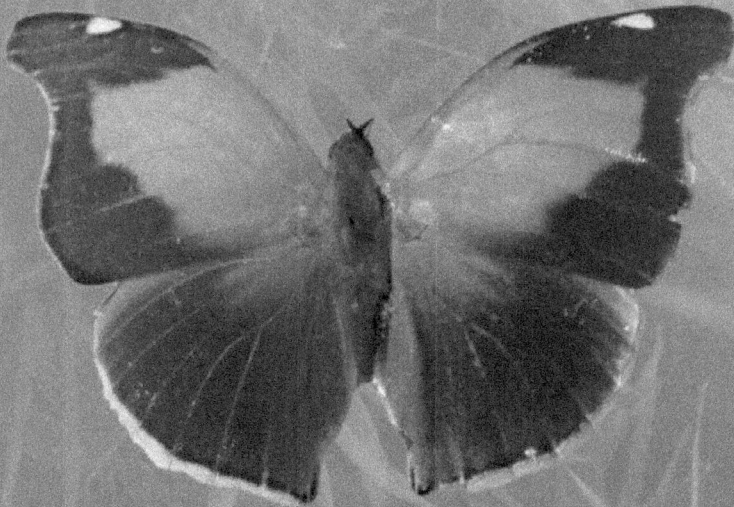

Historis odius (Leafwing)

Colobura dirce (Banana butterfly)

Adelpha abyla (Jamaican Admiral)

Marpesia chiron (Daggerwing, Daggertail)

Dynamine egaea — male (Green)

Dynamine egaea — female (Black & White Blue)

Diaethria clymena (88)

Diaethria phlogea (89)

Unidentified moth – Arctiidae

Thysania zenobia (Owl moth)

Unidentified moth – Noctuidae?

Siproetes stelene (Malachite)

Anaea troglodyta (Goatweed butterfly)

Dione vanillae (Silverspot)

Dione vanillae — underside (Silverspot)

Dryas iulia (Julia)

Heliconius charitonius (Zebra)

Phoebis sennae Male
(Cloudless Sulphur)

Phoebis sennae Female
(Cloudless Sulphur)

Anteos maerula
(Brimstone, Angled Sulphur)

Phoebis agarithe
(Orange Sulphur)

Phoebis argante
(Spotted Sulphur)

Chlorostrymon maesites
(Hairstreak)

Strymon columella
(Hewitson's Hairstreak)

Pyrrhocalles jamaicensis
(Schaus's Skipper)

Urbanus proteus
(Tailed Skipper)

Ephyriades brunnea
(Dusky Wing Skipper)

Nyctelius nyctelius
(Cane Skipper)

You can find ALL our books up on our website at:

http://www.writers-exchange.com

All Max's Books:

http://www.writers-exchange.com/max-overton/

About the Author

Max Overton has travelled extensively and lived in many places around the world-- including Malaysia, India, Germany, England, Jamaica, New Zealand, USA and Australia. Trained in the biological sciences in New Zealand and Australia, he has worked within the scientific field for many years, but now concentrates on writing. While predominantly a writer of historical fiction (Scarab: Books 1 - 6 of the Amarnan Kings; the Scythian Trilogy; the Demon Series; Ascension), he also writes in other genres (A Cry of Shadows, the Glass Trilogy, Haunted Trail, Sequestered) and draws on true life (Adventures of a Small Game Hunter in Jamaica, We Came From Königsberg). Max also maintains an interest in butterflies, photography, the paranormal and other aspects of Fortean Studies.

Most of his other published books are available at Writers Exchange Ebooks, http://www.writers-exchange.com/Max-Overton.html and all his books may be viewed on his website: http://www.maxovertonauthor.com/

Max's book covers are all designed and created by Julie Napier, and other examples of her art and photography may be viewed at www.julienapier.com

If you want to read more about other books by this author, they are listed on the following pages...

A Cry of Shadows
(Paranormal Murder Mystery)

Australian Professor Ian Delaney is single-minded in his determination to prove his theory that one can discover the moment that the life force leaves the body. After succumbing to the temptation to kill a girl under scientifically controlled conditions, he takes an offer of work in St Louis, hoping to leave the undiscovered crime behind him.

In America, Wayne Richardson seeks revenge by killing his ex-girlfriend, believing it will give him the upper hand, a means to seize control following their breakup. Wayne quickly discovers that he enjoys killing and begins to seek out young women who resemble his dead ex-girlfriend.

Ian and Wayne meet, and when Ian recognizes the symptoms of violent delusion he employs Wayne to help him further his research. Despite the police closing in, the two killers manage to evade identification as the death toll rises.

John Barnes, the detective in charge of the case, is frantic, willing to try anything to catch his killer. With time running out, he looks desperately for answers. Will John get them before it's too late?

Publisher: http://www.writers-exchange.com/A-Cry-of-Shadows/

Ascension Series, A Novel of Nazi Germany
(Historical: Holocaust)

Book 1: Ascension

A small boy discovers that being a Jew in Germany can be a dangerous thing. Fear prompts Konrad Wengler to put his faith aside and he tries desperately to forget his heritage.

He fights in the Great War and is wounded, becomes a policeman in his tiny Bavarian town, where he falls under the spell of the fledgling Nazi Party. He joins the Party in patriotic fervour and becomes a Lieutenant of Police and Schutzstaffel (SS).

In the course of his duties as policeman, he offends a powerful Nazi official, who starts an SS investigation of this troublesome police Lieutenant. When war breaks out, he joins the Police Battalions and is sent to Poland where he has to witness the atrocities being committed upon his fellow Jews.

The SS investigators have discovered Konrad's origins and follow him into Poland. He is arrested and sent to Mauthausen Concentration Camp. Suddenly, Konrad must face what it means to be a Jew and fight for survival. He has friends on the outside, a wife and a lawyer, but will they be enough to counter the might of the Nazi machine?

Publisher: http://www.writers-exchange.com/Ascension/

Book 2 Maelstrom

Konrad Wengler has survived his brush with the death camps of Nazi Germany, and has been reinstated as a police officer in his home town despite being a Jew. He throws himself back into his work, seeking to uncover the evidence that will remove a corrupt Nazi party official, but underestimates his enemy. The Gestapo have their own agenda, and despite orders from above to eliminate this troublesome Jewish policeman, they hide him in the Totenkopf (Death's Head) Division of the Waffen-SS.

Now Konrad must fight to survive in the snowy wastes of Russia as the tide of war turns against Germany. He experiences tank battles, ghetto clearances, partisans, and death camps (this time as a guard), as well as the fierce battles where his Division is badly outnumbered and on the defence.

Through it all, he must try to live by his conscience and resist taking part in the atrocities happening all around him. He still thinks of himself as a policeman, but his desire to bring the corrupt official to justice now seems far removed from his present reality. Konrad must first survive if he is to find the necessary evidence.

Publisher: http://www.writers-exchange.com/Maelstrom/

Fall of the House of Ramesses, A Novel of Ancient Egypt

Book 1: Merenptah

Egypt was at the height of its powers in the days of Ramesses the Great and the young king confidently predicted that his House would last for a Thousand Years. Sixty years later he was still on the throne and one by one his heirs had died and the survivors had become old men. When he at last died, he left a stagnant kingdom and his throne to an old man - Merenptah. What followed laid the groundwork for a nation ripped apart by civil war.

The northern tribes rebelled and joined forces with the Sea Peoples, invading from the north; while in the south the king's eldest son, angered at being passed over in favour of the younger son, plotted to rid himself of his father and brother. An ageing king takes to the field to fight for the House of Ramesses.

Publisher: http://www.writers-exchange.com/Merenptah/

Book 2: Seti

Merenptah is dead after only nine years on the throne and his son Seti is king in his place. He rules from the northern city of Men-nefer, while his elder brother Messuwy, convinced the throne is his by right, plots rebellion in the south.

The kingdoms are tipped into bloody civil war, with brother fighting against brother for the throne of a united Egypt. On one side is Messuwy, now crowned as King Amenmesse and his ruthless General Sethi; on the other, young King Seti and his wife Tausret. But other men are weighing up the chances of wresting the throne from both brothers and becoming king in their place. The House of Ramesses crumbles under the onslaught.

Publisher: http://www.writers-exchange.com/Seti/

Book 3: Tausret

The House of Ramesses falters as Tausret relinquishes the throne upon the death of her husband, King Seti. Amenmesse's young son Siptah will become king until her infant son is old enough to rule. Tausret, as Regent, and the king's uncle, Chancellor Bay, hold tight to the reins of power, and vie for complete control of the kingdoms. Assassination changes the balance of power and Chancellor Bay attempts a coup...

Tausret's troubles mount as she also faces a challenge from Setnakhte, an aging son of the Great Ramesses who believes Seti was the last legitimate king. If Setnakhte gets his way, he will destroy the House of Ramesses and set up his own dynasty of kings.

Publisher: http://www.writers-exchange.com/Tausret/

Glass Trilogy
(Paranormal Thriller)

GLASS HOUSE, Book 1: The mysteries of Australia may just hold the answers mankind has been searching for millennium to find. When Doctor James Hay, a university scientist who studies the paranormal mysteries in Australia, finds an obelisk of carved volcanic rock on sacred Aboriginal land in northern Queensland, he knows it may hold the answers he has been seeking. And when a respected elder of the Aboriginal people instructs him to take up the gauntlet and follow his heart, James, Spencer, an old friend and an award-winning writer, Samantha Louis, along with her cameraman and two of James' Aboriginal students, start their quest for the truth.

Glass House will take you deep into the mysteries that surround the continent of Australia, from its barren deserts to the depths of its rainforest and even deeper into its mysterious mountains. Along the way, the secrets of mankind and the ultimate answer to 'what happens now?' just might be answered. Love, greed, murder, and mystery abound in this action-packed paranormal/thriller.

Publisher: http://www.writers-exchange.com/Glass-House/

A GLASS DARKLY, Book 2: A dead volcano called Glass Mountain in Northern California seems harmless - or is it?

This is the fascinating setting of this mesmerising epic, the second book of the Glass Trilogy. Andromeda Jones, a physicist, knows her missing sister Samantha is somehow tied up with the new job she has been offered. Federal forces are aware that something is amiss, so Andromeda agrees to go on a dangerous mission and soon finds herself entangled in a web of professional jealousy, political betrayal and greed.

She helps construct Vox Dei, a machine that ostensibly is built to eliminate wars. But what is its true nature? Who is pulling the strings?

The experiment gets out of control, dark powers are unleashed and the danger to mankind unfolds relentlessly. Strange, evil shadows are using the Vox Dei and Samantha to try to get through to our world, knowing the time is near when Earth's final destiny will be decided.

Publisher: http://www.writers-exchange.com/A-Glass-Darkly/

LOOKING GLASS, Book 3: Samantha and James Hay have been advised that their missing daughter Gaia and Yowie nursemaid Cindy have been located in ancient Australia. Dr. Xanatuo, an alien scientist who, along with a lost tribe of Neanderthals and other beings who are working to help mankind, has discovered a way to send them back in time to be reunited with Gaia. Ernie, the old Aboriginal tracker and Garagh, leader of the Neanderthals, along with friends Ratana and Nathan, all characters from the first two books of the trilogy, will accompany them.

This team of intrepid adventurers have another mission for the journey along with aiding the Hayes' quest, which is paramount to changing a terrible wrong which exists in the present time. Lauded as the 'Australian Jurassic Park' *Looking Glass* is a mixture of Aboriginal mythology, present day UFO activity and pure science. It guarantees to please any reader who enjoys well researched, action packed and mind blowing events.

Publisher: http://www.writers-exchange.com/Looking-Glass/

Haunted Trail A Tale of Wickedness & Moral Turpitude
(Western: Paranormal)

Ned Abernathy is a hot-tempered young cowboy in the small town of Hammond's Bluff in the Dakota Territories in 1876. In a drunken argument with his best friend Billy over a girl, he guns him down. He flees, and wanders the plains, forests and hills of the Dakota Territories, certain that every man's hand is against him.

Horse rustlers, marauding Indians, killers, gold prospectors and French trappers cross his path and lead to complications, as do persistent apparitions of what Ned believes is the ghost of his friend Billy, come to accuse him of murder. He finds love and loses it, he finds gold in the Black Hills and must defend his new-found wealth against greedy men. Finally, he comes to terms with who he is and what he has done. Ned confronts the ghosts of his past and returns to Hammond's Bluff, where a shocking surprise awaits him at the end of the haunted trail.

Publisher: http://www.writers-exchange.com/Haunted-Trail/

Hyksos Series, A Novel of Ancient Egypt

The power of the kings of the Middle Kingdom have been failing for some time, having lost control of the Nile Delta to a series of Canaanite kings who ruled from the northern city of Avaris.

Into this mix came the Kings of Amurri, Lebanon and Syria bent on subduing the whole of Egypt. These kings were known as the Hyksos, and they dealt a devastating blow to the peoples of the Nile Delta and Valley.

Book 1: Avaris

When Arimawat and his son Harrubaal fled from Urubek, the king of Hattush, to the court of the King of Avaris, King Sheshi welcomed the refugees. One of Arimawat's first tasks for King Shesi is to sail south to the Land of Kush and fetch Princess Tati, who will become Sheshi's queen. Arimawat and Harrubaal perform creditably, but their actions have far-reaching consequences.

On the return journey, Harrubaal falls in love with Kemi, the daughter of the Southern Egyptian king. As a reward for Harrubaal's work, Sheshi secures the hand of the princess for the young Canaanite prince. Unfortunately for the peace of the realm, Sheshi lusts after Princess Kemi too, and his actions threaten the stability of his kingdom...
Publisher: http://www.writers-exchange.com/Avaris

Book 2: Conquest

The Hyksos invade the Delta using the new weapons of bronze and chariots, things of which the Egyptians have no knowledge. They rout the Delta forces, and in the south, the unconquered kings ready their armies to defend their lands. Meanwhile in Avaris, Merybaal, the son of Harrubaal and Kemi, strives to defend his family in a city conquered by the Hyksos.

Elements of the Delta army that refuse to surrender continue the fight for their homeland, and new kings proclaim themselves as the inheritors of the failed kings of Avaris. One of these is Amenre, grandson of Merybaal, but he is forced into hiding as the Hyksos sweep all before them, bringing their terror to the kingdom of the Nile valley. Driven south in disarray, the survivors of the Egyptian army seek leaders who can resist the enemy...
Publisher: http://www.writers-exchange.com/conquest/

Book 3: Two Cities

The Hyksos drive south into the Nile Valley, sweeping all resistance aside. Bebi and Sobekhotep, grandsons of Harrubaal, assume command of the loyal Egyptian army and strive to stem the flood of Hyksos conquest. But even the cities of the south are divided against themselves.

Abdju, an old capital city of Egypt reasserts itself, putting forward a line of kings of its own, and soon the city is at war with Waset, the southern capital of the Nile Valley, as the two cities fight for supremacy in the face of the advancing northern enemy. Caught up in the turmoil of warring nations, the ordinary people of Egypt must fight for their own survival as well as that of their kingdom.
Publisher: http://www.writers-exchange.com/Two-Cities/

And Many More

Kadesh, A Novel of Ancient Egypt

Holding the key to strategic military advantage, Kadesh is a jewel city that distant lands covet. Ramesses II of Egypt and Muwatalli II of Hatti believe they're chosen by the gods to claim ascendancy to Kadesh. When the two meet in the largest chariot battle ever fought, not just the fate of empires will be decided but also the lives of citizens helplessly caught up in the greedy ambition of kings.

Publisher: http://www.writers-exchange.com/Kadesh/

Scythian Trilogy
(Historical)

LION OF SCYTHIA, Book 1: Alexander the Great has conquered the Persian Empire and is marching eastward to India. In his wake he leaves small groups of soldiers to govern great tracts of land and diverse peoples. Nikometros is a young cavalry captain left behind in the lands of the fierce nomadic Scythian horsemen. Captured after an ambush, he must fight for his life and the lives of his surviving men. He seeks an opportunity to escape but owes a debt of loyalty to the chief, and a developing love for the young priestess.

Publisher: http://www.writers-exchange.com/Lion-of-Scythia/

THE GOLDEN KING, Book 2: The chief of the tribe is dead, killed by his son's treachery; and the priestess, the lover of the young cavalry officer, Nikometros, is carried off into the mountains. Nikometros and his friends set off in pursuit.

Death rides with them and by the time they return, the tribes are at war. Nikometros is faced with the choice of attempting to become chief himself or leaving the people he has come to love and respect, returning to his duty as an army officer in the Empire of Alexander.

Winner of the 2005 EPIC Ebook Awards.

Publisher: http://www.writers-exchange.com/The-Golden-King/

FUNERAL IN BABYLON, Book 3:

Alexander the Great has returned from India and set up his court in Babylon. Nikometros and a band of loyal Scythians journey deep into the heart of Persia to join the Royal court. Nikometros finds himself embroiled in the intrigues and wars of kings, generals, and merchant adventurers as he strives to provide a safe haven for his lover and friends. The fate of an Empire hangs in the balance, and Death walks beside Nikometros as events precipitate a Funeral in Babylon.

Winner of the 2006 EPIC Ebook Awards.

Publisher: http://www.writers-exchange.com/Funeral-in-Babylon/

Sequestered
By Max Overton and Jim Darley
(Action/Thriller)

Storing carbon dioxide underground as a means of removing a greenhouse gas responsible for global warming has made James Matternicht a fabulously wealthy man. For 15 years, the Carbon Capture and Sequestration Facility at Rushing River in Oregon's hinterland has been operating without a problem--or so it seems.

Annaliese Winton is a reporter, and when mysterious documents arrive on her desk that purport to show the Facility is leaking, she investigates. Together with a government geologist, Matt Morrison, she uncovers a morass of corruption and deceit that now threatens the safety of her community and the whole northwest coast of America.

Liquid carbon dioxide, stored at the critical point under great pressure, is a tremendously dangerous substance, and millions of tonnes of it are sequestered in the rock strata below Rushing River. All it takes is a crack in the overlying rock and the whole pressurized mass could erupt with disastrous consequences. And that crack has always been there...

Recipient of the Life Award (Literature for the Environment): "There are only two kinds of people: conservationists and suicides. To qualify for this Award, your book needs to value the wonderful world of nature, to recognize that we are merely one species out of millions, and that we have a responsibility to cherish and maintain our small planet."

Awarded from http://bobswriting.com/life.html

Publisher: http://www.writers-exchange.com/Sequestered.html

TULPA
(Paranormal Thriller)

From the rainforests of tropical Australia to the cane fields and communities of the North Queensland coastal strip comes a tale of the horror than can be unleashed by playing with unknown forces.

It starts with a fairy story to amuse small children, but when four bored teenagers and a young university student in a North Queensland town become interested in an ancient Tibetan technique for creating a life form; all hell breaks loose...literally. A seemingly harmless experiment unleashes terror and death and soon the teenagers are fighting to contain a menace that grows exponentially. The police are helpless to end the horror, and it is left to the teenagers to find a way of destroying the menace, aided by two old big game hunters, a student of the paranormal and a few small children. But how do you destroy beings that can escape into an alternate reality when threatened? Publisher: http://www.writers-exchange.com/TULPA/

Strong is the Ma'at of Re Series, A Novel of Ancient Egypt
{Historical: Ancient Egypt}

Book 1: The King
If there was one thing that filled Ramesses III with pride, it was that he was descended from Ramesses the Great. Elevated to the throne following a coup led by his father Setnakhte during the troubled days of Queen Tausret, Ramesses III set about creating an Egypt that reflected the glory days of Ramesses the Great. He took on his predecessor's throne name, he named his sons after the sons of Ramesses, he pushed them toward similar duties, and he thirsted after conquests like that of his hero grandfather.

Ramesses III assumed the throne name of Usermaatre, translated as 'Strong is the Ma'at of Re' and endeavoured to live up to it. He fought foreign foes, as had Ramesses the Great; he built temples throughout the Two Lands, as had Ramesses the Great, and he looked forward to a long, illustrious life on the throne of Egypt, as had Ramesses the Great.

But it was not to be. Ramesses III faced troubles at home; troubles that threatened the stability of Egypt and his own throne. The struggles for power between his wives, his sons, and even the priests of Amun, together with a treasury drained of its wealth; all forced Ramesses III to question his success.

226

Publisher: http://www.writers-exchange.com/The-King/

Book 2: The Heirs

Tiye, the first wife of Ramesses III, has grown so used to being the mother of the Heir she can no longer bear to see that prized title pass to the son of a rival wife. Her eldest sons have died and the one left wants to step down and devote his life to the priesthood. Then the son of the king's sister/wife, also named Ramesses, will become Crown Prince and all Tiye's ambitions will lie in ruins.

Ramesses III struggles to enrich Egypt by seeking the wealth of the Land of Punt. He dispatches an expedition to the fabled southern land but years pass before the expedition returns. In the meantime, Tiye has a new hope: A last son she dotes on. Plague sweeps through Egypt, killing princes and princesses alike and lessening her options, and now Tiye must undergo the added indignity of having her daughter married off to the hated Crown Prince.

All Tiye's hopes are pinned on this last son of hers, but Ramesses III refuses to consider him as a potential successor, despite the Crown Prince's failing health. Unless Tiye can change the king's mind through charm or coercion, her sons will forever be excluded from the throne of Egypt.
Publisher: http://www.writers-exchange.com/The-Heirs/

Book 3: Taweret

The reign of Ramesses III is failing and even the gods seem to be turning their eyes away from Egypt. When the sun hides its face, crops suffer, throwing the country into famine. Tomb workers go on strike. To avert further disaster, Crown Prince Ramesses acts on his father's behalf.

The rivalry between Ramesses III's wives--commoner Tiye and sister/wife Queen Tyti--also comes to a head. Tiye resents not being made queen and can't abide that her sons have been passed over. She plots to put her own spoiled son Pentaweret on the throne.

The eventual strength of the Ma'at of Re hangs in the balance. Will the rule of Egypt be decided by fate, gods...or treason?
Publisher: http://www.writers-exchange.com/The-One-of-Taweret/

The Amarnan Kings Series, A Novel of Ancient Egypt

SCARAB - AKHENATEN, Book 1:

A chance discovery in Syria reveals answers to the mystery of the ancient Egyptian sun-king, the heretic Akhenaten and his beautiful wife Nefertiti. Inscriptions in the tomb of his sister Beketaten, otherwise known as Scarab, tell a story of life and death, intrigue and warfare, in and around the golden court of the kings of the glorious 18th dynasty.

The narrative of a young girl growing up at the centre of momentous events - the abolition of the gods, foreign invasion and the fall of a once-great family - reveals who Tutankhamen's parents really were, what happened to Nefertiti, and other events lost to history in the great destruction that followed the fall of the Aten heresy.

Max Overton follows his award-winning trilogy of ancient Greece (Lion of Scythia, The Golden King, Funeral in Babylon) with the first book in another series set in Egypt of the 14th century B.C.E. Meticulously researched, the book unfolds a tapestry of these royal figures lost in the mists of antiquity.

Publisher: http://www.writers-exchange.com/Scarab/

SCARAB- SMENKHKARE, Book 2:

Scarab - Smenkhkare follows on from the first book in this series as King Akhenaten, distraught at the rebellion and exile of his beloved wife Nefertiti, withdraws from public life, content to leave the affairs of Egypt in the hands of his younger half-brother Smenkhkare. When Smenkhkare disappears on a hunting expedition, his sister Beketaten, known as Scarab, is forced to flee for her life.

Finding refuge among her mother's people, the Khabiru, Scarab has resigned herself to a life in exile, when she hears that her brother Smenkhkare is still alive. He is raising an army in Nubia to overthrow Ay and reclaim his throne. Scarab hurries south to join him as he confronts Ay and General Horemheb outside the gates of Thebes.

Max Overton's series on the Amarnan kings sheds new light on the end of the 18th dynasty of pharaohs. Details of these troubled times have been lost as later kings expunged all records of the Heretic king Akhenaten and his successors. Max Overton has researched the era thoroughly, piecing together a mosaic of the reigns of the five kings, threaded through by the memories of princess Beketaten - Scarab.

Publisher: http://www.writers-exchange.com/Scarab2/

SCARAB - TUTANKHAMEN, Book 3:

Scarab and her brother Smenkhkare are in exile in Nubia, but are gathering an army to wrest control of Egypt from the boy king Tutankhamen and his controlling uncle, Ay. Meanwhile, the kingdoms are beset by internal troubles and the Amorites are pressing hard against the northern borders. Generals Horemheb and Paramessu must fight a war on two fronts while deciding where their loyalties lie--with the former king Smenkhkare or with the new young king in Thebes.

Smenkhkare and Scarab march on Thebes with their native army to meet the legions of Tutankhamen on the plains outside the city gates. The fate of Egypt and the 18th dynasty hang in the balance as two brothers battle for supremacy and the throne of the Two Kingdoms.

Finalist in 2013's Eppie Awards.
Publisher: http://www.writers-exchange.com/Scarab3/

And Many More

We Came From Konigsberg
(Historical: Holocaust)

January 1945, and the Soviet Army is poised for the final push through East Prussia and Poland to Berlin. Elisabet Daeker and her five young sons are in Königsberg, East Prussia, and have heard the stories of Russian atrocities. They seek to escape to the perceived safety of Germany.

This is the story of their struggle to survive, of the hardships endured at the hands of Nazi hardliners, of Soviet troops bent on rape, pillage and murder, and of Allied cruelty in the Occupied Zones of post-war Germany. 'We Came From Königsberg' is based on a true story gleaned from the memories of family members sixty years after the events, from photographs and documents, and from published works of non-fiction describing the times and events that are described in the narrative.

Elisabet Daeker's sons, and subsequent daughters, all have families of their own, and have carved out meaningful lives for themselves in far-flung parts of the world. One thing they all claim, though, is - we came from Königsberg.

Winner of the 2014 EPIC Ebook Awards.

Publisher: http://www.writers-exchange.com/We-Came-From-Konigsberg/
A

You can find ALL our books up on our website at:
http://www.writers-exchange.com

All Max's Books:
http://www.writers-exchange.com/max-overton/